MW00770202

Never Doubt Thomas

Never Doubt Thomas

The Catholic Aquinas as
Evangelical and Protestant

Francis J. Beckwith

BAYLOR UNIVERSITY PRESS

Unless otherwise stated, Scripture quotations are from the New Revised Standard Version Bible, copyright 1989, Division of Christian Education of the National Council of the Churches of Christ in the United States of America. Used by permission. All rights reserved.

Cover Design by Savanah N. Landerholm
Book Design by Baylor University Press, *Typesetting* by Scribe Inc.

Earlier versions of parts of this book were published as portions of other pieces that appeared elsewhere, but have been revised, and in some cases significantly, for inclusion in this volume:

"Natural Law, Catholicism, and the Protestant Critique: Why We Are Really Not That Far Apart." *Christian Bioethics: Non–Ecumenical Studies in Medical Morality* (2019). Used by permission.

"Doting Thomists: Evangelicals, Thomas Aquinas, and Justification." *Evangelical Quarterly* 85, no. 3 (July 2013): 211–27. Used by permission.

"Like It Was Written on My Soul from Me to You: Assessing Jerry Walls' Critique of the Catholic Account of Purgatory." *The Heythrop Journal* (2013). https://doi.org/10.1111/heyj.12072. Used by permission.

The Library of Congress has cataloged this book under ISBN
978-1-4813-0724-6.

Printed in the United States of America on acid-free paper with a minimum of 30 percent recycled content.

To Fr. Timothy Vaverek,
the unofficial Catholic chaplain to the faculty of
the world's largest Baptist university.

Contents

Acknowledgments

This book is the result of many years of thinking about and wrestling with the work of St. Thomas Aquinas. But such reflection, if one hopes to do it well, is nearly impossible without the assistance and support of family, friends, and colleagues. First and foremost, I would like to thank my wife, Frankie, who selflessly in the summer of 2018 took charge of our housing move while I was putting the finishing touches on this manuscript. Without her love and support, it is difficult to imagine that I would have met my deadline. Speaking of deadlines, I owe a debt of gratitude to Carey Newman, director of Baylor University Press, who has the patience of a saint (though I'm not sure what saint that is).

With the exception of its final chapter, my research and writing for this book began in February 2015 in Rome, Italy, where I served as a visiting fellow at the Pontifical University of Santa Croce, thanks to the gracious assistance of Luis Telez and Fr. John Wauck, Opus Dei. With the help of Fr. Thomas Joseph White, O.P., Fr. Bernhard Blankenhorn, O.P., and Sr. Catherine Joseph Droste, O.P., I was also able to secure library privileges at the Pontifical University of St. Thomas Aquinas (the Angelicum). My only regret is that I could not find a way to get the Jesuits involved.

Baylor University, where I serve on the faculty of its philosophy department, granted me a generous research leave for the Spring 2015 semester. I am grateful for the support of my department chair, Michael Beaty, as well as my dean, Lee Nordt, and the members of the College of Arts & Sciences Research Leave Committee who thought my project worthy of pursuit.

From the time I left Rome through the writing of this book I had the privilege to teach three courses on Aquinas, one at the University of Colorado and two at Baylor. The first I team-taught in fall 2016 with the esteemed Aquinas scholar Robert Pasnau, while I was serving as a visiting professor at Colorado's Center for Western Civilization, Thought & Policy. When Bob first invited me to teach the course with him, I enthusiastically said yes, but with this caveat: "Just because I consider myself a Thomist does not mean that I am an Aquinas scholar." He replied, "But you have skin in the game." I learned much from Bob and the way in which he was able to so effectively communicate Aquinas' thought to undergraduates, most of whom were encountering the Angelic Doctor for the first time. At Baylor, I led a graduate seminar on Aquinas' *Treatise on Law* (Spring 2016) and taught an undergraduate survey of Aquinas' *Summa theologica* (Spring 2018). Since there is probably no better way to master a subject than to try to teach it to others, I am grateful to Bob and to the students in all three classes for allowing me to work through Aquinas with them.

Finally, a special thanks to Benjamin Rusch and David Skowronski who created the index for this book. Ben and David, both Baylor Ph.D. students in philosophy, served as my research assistants for the Spring 2019 semester.

Foreword

Fr. Thomas Joseph White, O.P.

When Pope Leo XIII released his famous encyclical *Aeteri Patris* in 1879, the Church's cultural situation in Europe was precarious. Following the widespread effects of the French Revolution and the Napoleonic Wars, much of the Church's infrastructure had been disassembled, including major losses of universities, religious orders, schools, and monasteries. The Italian revolutions of the nineteenth century had dissolved the papal states and set Italy on a path toward secular government and cultural de-Christianization. What Leo called for in his encyclical was a return to the study and promotion of Christian philosophy, after the example of the great scholastic authors of the High Middle Ages, and especially in the lineage of St. Thomas Aquinas. Aquinas, so Leo argued, is able to show the coordinated unity and distinctness of the various sciences, be they mathematical, philosophical, or theological. He also shows the inherent intelligibility of the mysteries of the Catholic religion, without either reducing these to mere products of human reason or casting them in opposition to the many legitimate discoveries of human reason.

Pope Leo's Thomistic Revival, as it is now called, was largely successful. In the twentieth century there were thriving centers of Thomistic study in Rome, Louvain, Paris, Cologne, and Toulouse but also Toronto, Buenos Aires, St. Louis, and Washington, D.C. Thomism contributed in its own way to the work of Vatican Council II and its aftermath, not least in the pontificate of Pope John Paul II (trained in

Roman Thomism), whose encyclical *Fides et Ratio* in 1998 on Christian philosophy serves as a kind of profound complement to *Aeterni Patris.*

At the same time, after Vatican Council II a reaction became widespread in the Church against the place of Aquinas in Catholic intellectual studies. Twentieth century neo-Thomism was seen by many as too ahistorical, too unengaged with contemporary questions, too intellectually restrictive or arbitrarily systematic. Instead, other forms of philosophy were promoted—from continental and eventually analytic traditions—as these were often seen as an alternative to Thomism and as a way of approaching philosophy that was more advanced, nuanced, and engaged with the times.

Happily, today a generation of Christian philosophers has emerged who have recaptured the original spirit of Leo XIII's encyclical as well as that of John Paul II. Those pontiffs wanted an engagement with Aquinas' thought that was rooted in the principles of his thought, historically alert to Aquinas' own views in their original context, but also deeply engaged with the living questions of our age. After all, philosophy is for Aquinas and in itself a study of the shape of reality, as best known by the use of our natural human intellectual capacities. To think through the problems of one's era is normal for any living philosopher and if a thinker like Aquinas has much to offer us in the analysis of reality (which he does), then that analysis should also help illumine the subjects that we confront in our own historical moment. The dual concerns for both actual "relevance" and historical "retrieval" are never at odds if rightly understood in relation to one another. And they are related to one another philosophically through a very simple thread: the search for the truth, the truth as discovered in the past and the truth as uncovered today.

This very fine book by Francis Beckwith embodies the kind of engaged living Thomism that Pope Leo saw as essential for the life of the Church and for Christian philosophy in our own era. What are some of the key issues that touch the heart of our age? The question of the existence of moral norms (or the possibility of moral relativism), the dignity of human life and the difference of genders, the question of the existence of God in a scientific age, the relations of Christians and Muslims, the relations and longstanding divisions between Catholics and Protestants, and the compatibility of the Bible with the discoveries of modern physics and biology. Professor

Beckwith engages with these key questions with intelligence, serenity, clarity, and purpose. He also does so by making judicious appeal to principles from Aquinas, those that help us resolve many of these key questions in effective and wise ways. Consequently, we stand in Professor Beckwith's debt for producing a short but illustrative work of Christian philosophy. May his example be only one of many who believe rightly in the message of Leo XIII: reflection on perennial principles, engagement with contemporary concerns. These are twin dynamisms of a living Thomism. Those who pursue such a project serve not only the Church, but the larger social good of the academy as a whole.

Fr. Thomas Joseph White, O.P.
Director, Thomistic Institute
Angelicum, Rome

1

Why Thomas Today

For even as it is better to enlighten than merely to shine, so is it better to give to others the fruits of one's contemplation than merely to contemplate.

St. Thomas Aquinas[1]

This is not an ordinary book about the thought of St. Thomas Aquinas (ca. 1225–1274). It is a book on how the work of Aquinas illuminates certain contemporary questions that are important to many serious believers across a variety of Christians traditions, including Protestant and Catholic. This book is also unusual insofar as it is born of the author's own journey from Catholic to Protestant and back again.[2]

My earliest recollection of hearing of the work of Aquinas was in 1973, when I was a twelve-year-old student at St. Viator Catholic Elementary School in Las Vegas, Nevada, the city in which I grew up. But it was not in the classroom that I first heard of Aquinas. It was across the street at the Parish Community Center, which was hosting a four-day retreat led by three Dominican Catholic priests from the Bay Area. My parents had encouraged me to attend, since they were concerned that my newfound interest in Evangelical Protestantism (by way of a Jesus People congregation in downtown Vegas) was drawing me away from the Catholic Church in which they had me baptized as an infant. As best as I can recall, I had apparently made a nuisance of myself in my seventh-grade religion class, frequently asking the teacher, Sister Bernardus, pointed questions about the Bible, Christ, and belief in God that she did not seem particularly interested in sparring over. I can easily imagine my Italian mother telling my father, "Perhaps the visiting Dominicans can help."

Carrying my Bible to each session, I had come prepared to do theological battle. So every evening, after many of the attendees had departed, I peppered the priests with a variety of questions. One priest in particular (whose name I do not remember) seemed eager to engage me. Looking back, I see him as remarkably patient and kind, especially given my take-no-prisoners apologetic case for the Evangelical Protestant understanding of the Bible and salvation that I had been appropriating over the previous six months. He suggested, among other things, that I did not know how to read Scripture (he was right, by the way) and recommended that I consult the works of a Dominican named St. Thomas Aquinas. Sadly, I did not take his advice. But I left that evening with great admiration (and envy) for the wonderful combination of deep spirituality and intellectual sophistication that I saw in those men. Although I found myself drifting away from the Church of my baptism, I was strangely warmed by what I saw in those Dominican priests.

Years later, while in college at the University of Nevada, Las Vegas (UNLV), I would encounter Aquinas yet again, this time in the works of the Evangelical philosopher Norman L. Geisler. While at a Christian bookstore, I came across, by happenstance, a book of Geisler's entitled *Philosophy of Religion*.[3] It addressed, among other things, some of the perennial questions in philosophy of religion, such as the relationship between faith and reason, the existence of God, the problem of evil, and the nature of religious language. Geisler, who had earned his PhD at Loyola University of Chicago, offered a conspicuously Thomistic approach to these questions, even though he was an Evangelical. I was completely mesmerized by this approach and soon came to consider myself a Thomist of sorts, though a Protestant one. It took me a couple of years, after I was in graduate school, to realize that Thomism was a distinctly minority view in the Evangelical world. But for me, it really did not matter. Aquinas just seemed to make sense.

After earning an M.A. at Simon Greenleaf University in 1984, I went on to Fordham University in New York City for Ph.D. studies in philosophy.[4] It was there that I took courses from Fr. W. Norris Clarke, S.J., and Fr. Gerald McCool, S.J., both of whom were leading scholars of Aquinas. Although my course work at Fordham focused primarily on the history of philosophy, philosophy of religion, and philosophy of science—which were important to the work of my doctoral dissertation on David Hume's argument against miracles[5]—I left New York City a more convinced Thomist than when I had arrived, even though I was neither an Aquinas scholar nor a consistent Thomist. I was a selective Thomist, taking from the "Angelic Doctor" what I thought was helpful to my Evangelical faith but largely ignoring writings that would force me to think more critically about my commitments on subjects such as grace, the sacraments, and the nature of the church. I was, in the words of the late Ralph McInerny (1929–2010), a peeping Thomist,[6] though in retrospect I would describe myself as a doting Thomist. I adored Aquinas, but I had not yet availed myself of his wider corpus.

Not only did I not consult Aquinas' wider corpus, but my reading of the Angelic Doctor was sometimes not faithful to the text, even in those areas in which I saw him as a theological ally. In retrospect, I think this was a consequence of the way in which virtually all of the leading lights in non-Catholic Christian philosophy—such as Alvin Plantinga, Nicholas Wolterstorff, William Lane Craig, and Richard Swinburne—had taught a generation of aspiring Evangelical philosophers how they ought to practice the discipline. To be sure, these thinkers were for me (and countless others) wonderful intellectual role models, exhibiting a philosophical rigor and thoughtfulness that has profoundly influenced how the wider world of academic philosophy approaches questions involving the rationality of religious belief and Christian faith in particular. But when it came to understanding Aquinas—a figure whose philosophical commitments seem difficult to classify under the categories of contemporary analytic philosophy[7]—I was confounded[8] by the dominant way in which these and most other Christian philosophers of religion generally conducted their business.[9] For this reason, despite my training at Fordham and my own reading of Thomas and his numerous interpreters, I did not take notice of what I did not know until well into my career as a philosophy professor.

Consider, as an example, my early work on how certain Christian philosophers (and other Christian academics) deal with the apparent conflict between Darwinian evolution and the doctrine of creation. Some of these thinkers argue for the existence of an intelligent designer (or God) by trying to show that there are certain

aspects of the natural world—for example, the information content of DNA, the bacterial flagellum—that cannot only not be
accounted for by evolution but exhibit such a high level of specified
complexity that they seem to have more in common with human-
made artifacts—for example, computer programs, mousetraps—
than they do with the other aspects of the natural world that can be
accounted for by chance, scientific law, or both.[10] Darwin's theory of
natural selection is just such an account. So, the intelligent design
(ID) advocate reasons that if we can exclude chance and law, whatever remains must be the product of an intelligent designer, just as
a detective investigating a card-counting scheme is able to infer the
intervention of an agent from a player's highly improbable winning
hands. This is a view I flirted with but never fully embraced.[11] What
ultimately moved me against ID was its diminished understanding
of God as creator, which was contrary to what had been taught by
classical Christian theists like Aquinas.[12] Here is what I mean. As a
theist, I believe that God is creator of everything, including not only
those natural objects that allegedly exhibit irreducible complexity,
but also every other natural object as well as the chance and the
law in which all objects in the universe operate. If, as St. Paul told
his audience on Mars Hill, it is in God that "we live and move and
have our being" (Acts 17:28), and if, as the author of Hebrews notes,
"before him no creature is hidden" (Heb 4:13), then to postulate
God as a theory to shore up what science cannot for the time being
answer is to treat God as if he were a part of the created order rather
than the source or ground of the created order itself. And yet, there
are some Christian philosophers—some of whom I count as dear
friends—who claim that if Aquinas were with us today, he would
be a defender of ID theory.[13] I think they are mistaken, and I will
explain why in chapter 4 of this book.

As I dug deeper into St. Thomas and the classical tradition that
he represents, I began to see that some of the other views attributed
to Aquinas by certain Christian philosophers and theologians were
off the mark as well. Some of these thinkers have been critical of
what they believe are Aquinas' beliefs about the natural moral
law and natural theology, often concluding that the Angelic Doctor held to an exaggerated, and thus unbiblical, view of the power
of human reason to know both morality (the natural law) and the

divine nature (natural theology) apart from what God has revealed in Scripture. To buttress this analysis, some critics point to the fact that natural law arguments have failed to convince skeptics of traditional moral views, while other critics maintain that because Aquinas (allegedly) believed that faith in God requires that one first have a rational argument for God's existence, true faith would be out of the reach of most ordinary people, and that seems inconsistent with the gospel message found in Scripture.[14] But, as I argue in chapter 2, these claims are false, as much of what Aquinas himself says about human reason—especially in relation to natural law and natural theology—is consonant with what his critics say about the deficiencies of human reason.

On the other hand, there are some Christian philosophers and theologians—highly sympathetic to Aquinas' views on the natural law and natural theology—who believe that his writings on the doctrine of justification are more Protestant than they are Catholic (or least they do not embrace the semi-Pelagianism these writers believe the Catholic Church affirmed at the Council of Trent, 1545–1563). These thinkers—all Evangelical followers of Aquinas—believe that if the Catholic Church had remained true to St. Thomas' views on justification (or at least what these writers suppose them to be), there would have likely been no need for a Reformation. But, as I argue in chapter 5, Aquinas' views are not only consistent with Trent, but consistent with what he inherited from his ecclesial predecessors (St. Augustine, Council of Orange) and with what the Catholic Church teaches in its modern catechism. Although Aquinas was no paleo-Lutheran, it is not difficult to imagine how a Protestant, enamored of Aquinas' intellect and theological acumen, can read the Angelic Doctor as a kindred spirit, since his writings were untainted by the salvos and countersalvos of the Reformation and Counter-Reformation. He was writing as a university teacher under the authority of a unified ecclesial body in which the issues that would divide the Western church nearly three centuries later were not yet in dispute. For this reason, reading Aquinas on justification is like being reintroduced to the question with fresh eyes. At least it was for me, when I was making my pilgrimage back to the church of my youth.

According to several of his biographers, as a small child, Aquinas often asked the question, "What is God?" As a mature scholar, he answers that question in a variety of places, including his two major works, *Summa theologica* and *Summa contra gentiles*. What stands out about Aquinas' approach is that he believes we can know that God exists through our natural reason, but it is only by way of special revelation (or Scripture) that we can know particular things about God that unaided reason cannot know—for example, that God is triune and that he loves us. This distinction—between general revelation and special revelation—as I argue in chapter 3, is instructive in helping us answer in the affirmative what has become a controversial question (mostly) among Evangelical Protestants: "Do Christians, Muslims, and Jews worship the same God?" Oddly enough, many Evangelical friends of Aquinas—that is, Evangelicals who believe, like Aquinas, in the efficacy of natural theology[15]—answer this question in the negative. I argue in chapter 3, *it cannot be the case* that if two atheists who come to believe in the same God because of Aquinas' arguments, and one of them later becomes a Christian and the other a Muslim, we should now say that they believe in two different Gods. This is because for Aquinas (and for all classical theists, Jews and Muslims included) there can in principle be only one divine nature that reason can deliver, regardless of what one may believe God has revealed specially through the Church, the Torah, the New Testament, or the Qur'an, even if those claims of revelation are inconsistent with each other. Given the acrimony toward Islam and Muslim immigrants that one finds in certain American Christian circles,[16] perhaps Aquinas' approach to the divine nature—a belief that traditional Muslims, Christians, and Jews hold in common—can lead to better understanding.

Who exactly was St. Thomas Aquinas?[17] Other than perhaps St. Augustine of Hippo (354–430), he is the most influential theologian and philosopher in the history of the Christian faith, and one of the most important thinkers in the history of philosophy. In addition to his two most important works, the eight-hundred-page *Summa contra gentiles* (written between 1259 and 1265) and the three-thousand-page *Summa theologica* (written between 1265 and 1274, though never completed), Aquinas authored scores of treatises and commentaries on a wide range of topics including the philosophy of nature, metaphysics, the human soul, the nature of truth,

Aristotle's *Nicomachean Ethics*, *The Sentences* by Peter Lombard (1100–1160), and the Bible.

He was born around 1225 into an aristocratic family in Rocca-secca, a city near Aquino on the Italian peninsula about halfway between Rome and Naples. In 1231, when he was five or six years old, his parents placed him in the Benedictine abbey in Monte Cassino, where he was educated and introduced to the monastic life. Eight years later Thomas was sent to study at the University of Naples, a secular institution founded by Frederick II, the emperor to whom Aquinas' family was in service. It was there—in the hustle and bus-tle of that seaport metropolis—that Thomas realized that he was not cut out for monastic life, though he still wanted to study and teach and serve the Lord. He found himself drawn to a new order of priests, the Dominicans, named after its founder, St. Dominic Guz-man (1170–1221). Like the members of another order that was new at the time, the Franciscans, the Dominicans take a vow of poverty and work among the people in urban centers. Both orders are typically called *mendicant orders*, because they rely on begging for financial support. ("Mendicant" simply means "beggar.") Also known as the "Order of Preachers," the Dominicans are committed to teaching and expounding the faith in the rough and tumble of city life.

Thomas' family was not too pleased with his choice to become a Dominican. In 1244, shortly after Thomas had joined the order, his mother, Theodora, attempted to visit him in Naples to try to change his mind, but he had already departed by the time she arrived. But this did not deter his family. Thomas was soon detained and cap-tured just north of Rome by a coterie headed by his brother, Rinaldo. Holding him in the family castle under what was tantamount to house arrest, his family released him after about a year when they realized that their deprogramming efforts had failed. They had hoped that he would become a Benedictine abbot, following in the footsteps of his uncle. But Aquinas would not budge. After being freed, he returned to Naples for a short time and went on from there for further training in Paris, and then to Cologne for four years (1248–1252) to study under and work with Albert the Great (1200–1280), perhaps the leading expositor of Aristotle (384–322 BC) in the Latin Church at the time. Albert's project to appropriate the insights of Aristotle into Christian thought was picked up by his prized pupil, Thomas, who would, in a sense, finish the job that had been initiated by his great teacher.

In or around 1252 he went to Paris, where he served as baccalaureate commentator (a kind of lecturer) on Scripture and Lombard's *Sentences*, which was the standard theological text of the day. (One could say it was the *summa* before the *Summa*). Prior to finishing his voluminous commentary on *The Sentences*—equivalent to a doctoral dissertation in the present day—Thomas was appointed in 1256 as a master of theology (which would be like becoming a full professor in our time). He stayed in Paris in his new appointment until 1259. During these Parisian years, he would not only write his commentary on Lombard's *Sentences*, but he would also begin work on the *Summa contra gentiles* and complete several other texts including *De ente essentia* (On being and essence) and his commentary on *De trinitate* (On the Trinity) by Boethius (477–524).

Over the next decade and a half, he would work in various capacities, including administrative posts for the Dominican order, teaching assignments, and service to the Church as an adviser. These duties took Thomas to diverse locales throughout Europe, including Naples, Rome, Viterbo, and Orvieto in Italy, and Paris. And yet his prodigious scholarship did not let up. Among the many writings he produced, completed, or began working on during this period are the *Summa contra gentiles*, *Summa theologica*, *Quaestiones disputatae de malo* (Disputed questions on evil), *De regno* (On kingship), commentaries on several works by Aristotle, and biblical commentaries on Isaiah, Job, Jeremiah, and St. Paul's epistles.

On December 6, 1273, he abruptly stopped writing after having a profound mystical experience. As he told Brother Reginald of Piperno, his devoted secretary, "I cannot do anymore. Everything I have written seems to me as straw in comparison to what I have seen."[18] Thomas died three months later, on March 7, 1274, while on his way to the Council of Lyons at the behest of Pope Gregory X. After suffering a head injury as a result of hitting his head on a tree branch, his health declined quickly, and he succumbed to death at the Fossanova Abbey, where he had requested to be taken when he realized that his demise was imminent. "If the Lord is coming for me, I had better be found in a religious house than in a castle."[19]

In the aftermath of the Protestant Reformation, Aquinas is often portrayed as a mere sectarian *Catholic* thinker, which suggests that his work, however influential it has been in shaping the theological trajectory of the Church of Rome, should carry little if any weight among non-Catholic Christians.[20] It is a judgment, I am happy to report, that is *not* shared by a wide range of non-Catholic philosophers and theologians, including Plantinga,[21] John Milbank,[22] Arvin Vos,[23] J. P. Moreland,[24] Norman Kretzmann (1928–1998),[25] David Bentley Hart,[26] Eric Mascal (1905–1993),[27] R. C. Sproul (1939–2017),[28] Catherine Pickstock,[29] James E. Dolezal,[30] Carl Trueman,[31] Charles Raith II,[32] and a host of others.[33] I suspect that the reason for this non-Catholic consensus is the increasing recognition that the fundamental point of Aquinas' ambitious lifelong project was to answer that seemingly simple question he often asked as a young boy— "what is God?"—within the confines of a theological tradition that he inherited from his predecessors, *a tradition to which non-Catholic Christians have as much claim as their Latin church brethren.* As Protestant scholars Manfred Svensson and David VanDrunen note, "Beside ecumenism in the strict sense, we find something which is not wholly unrelated and yet distinct: the fact that Protestants and Roman Catholics face many similar intellectual challenges, and that at least some of these challenges can be faced together while relying on their common tradition."[34]

Aquinas answers the question "what is God?" not only by trying to understand and describe the divine nature, but also by providing a metaphysical account of all that which has God as its ultimate source: the created order including those rational animals who are made in his image. Because our natural knowledge of God, however inchoate, arises from what we know about creation, answering the question "what is God?" requires, as a first step, an investigation into the nature of the beings that we encounter in the natural world. Aside from recognizing the existence of a Creator,[35] the most important thing that we discover, writes Thomas, is that the human longing for our ultimate end—"beatitude," as it is often called—cannot be consummated by anything in the natural world, including human nature itself.[36] It requires that the God that we may indirectly encounter through natural reason by way of the created order specially reveal to human beings both

the cause of our fallenness and the means of grace that will help us
to be "conformed to the image of his Son" (Rom 8:29) so that
we may be made worthy to live eternally with God as we were
designed to do (though incapable of achieving without his perpet-
ual divine cooperation).[37]

This story—of creation, fall, and redemption—and the tradition developed out of it, belongs to all Christians, not only Catholics.
For this reason, Aquinas, who was living and writing within that
tradition nearly three centuries before the fragmentation of Western Christianity at the Reformation, belongs to all Christians as
well. It is my hope that through this small book I can convince a
few doting (and even peeping and doubting) Thomists that the work
of the Angelic Doctor, when properly understood, can provide real
insight and help us to clarify some important issues over which
many Christians have been divided since those fateful days in the
sixteenth century.

Addendum: A Note about Notes

This book contains a lot of endnotes that include not only references
and citations, but also quotations (most of which are from Aquinas)
as well as clarifications of what I am addressing in the text. There
are two reason for this. First, I have *not* written this book for spe-
cialists in Aquinas, but for educated and interested nonspecialists,
both inside and outside the academy, who find themselves drawn to
the Angelic Doctor as I was as a young man. I do not want to bog
down those readers with too many excursions into technical issues
or extended quotations from Aquinas. Nevertheless, I do want
them to have some limited access to those materials at their finger-
tips in the endnotes. Second, on each of the issues covered in this
book—natural law and natural theology, the same God question,
intelligent design, and justification—I am challenging the conventional wisdom as to what Aquinas *really taught* or what Christians
have historically believed. For this reason, some critical readers
would not be satisfied with a few citations here and there. The endnotes, I hope, will provide just the resources they are looking for.

2

Aquinas as Protestant
Natural Law and Natural Theology

For the wrath of God is revealed from heaven against all ungod-
liness and wickedness of those who by their wickedness suppress
the truth. For what can be known about God is plain to them,
because God has shown it to them. Ever since the creation of the
world his eternal power and divine nature, invisible though they
are, have been understood and seen through the things he has
made. So they are without excuse.

Romans 1:18-20

Can we actually "know" the universe? My God, it's hard enough
finding your way around in Chinatown. The point, however, is: Is
there anything out there? And why? And must they be so noisy?

Woody Allen (1969)[1]

If St. Thomas Aquinas is known for anything, it is his belief that
human beings have the capacity to know by their natural reason, apart from the deliverances of Scripture or ecclesial authority,
that God exists and that there is a natural moral law. Most everyone who has taken an introductory philosophy class learns about
Aquinas' famous proofs for God's existence, sometimes called *the
five ways*,[2] though they are not the only arguments he defends.[3]
Arguments like Aquinas' are examples of what is often called *natural theology*. But even if one has never had the pleasure of for-
mally studying philosophy or Aquinas in particular, the idea that
the universe, as it appears to us, cannot explain itself and requires
a self-existent source outside of itself to account for its existence—a
point defended by Aquinas in several places[4]—has never ceased

to be a claim that even the most vociferous atheists believe they are obligated to answer.[5] The question—why is there something rather than nothing?—makes sense to a lot of people, even those who do not believe in God. After all, when some atheists claim that the universe is merely self-existent, thus making God superfluous,[6] or when others suggest that a so-called universe "from nothing" does really require something (e.g., the law of gravity),[7] they are in fact confirming Aquinas' point that in order for anything to presently exist, something self-existent, which does not require another being to bring it into or keep it in existence, must exist. It's clear that Aquinas was onto something that even we moderns and postmoderns cannot seem to shake.

Far more people have heard of the *natural law*, or at least the idea of it, from documents such as America's Declaration of Independence (1776)[8] or the Universal Declaration of Human Rights (1948),[9] each of which affirms that human beings are endowed with certain natural rights that their governments are obligated to honor. Whenever anyone asserts that a particular old law is unjust, or that there ought to be a new law to correct an injustice, they are engaging in a kind of natural law reasoning, implying that there is, as one scholar puts it, a "law above the law."[10] Such reasoning was central to the most important and consequential judicial tribunal of the twentieth century: the Nuremberg Trials (1945–1949). They were convened by the Allied victors soon after the Second World War for the purpose of prosecuting Axis power war criminals. The lead prosecutor, U.S. Supreme Court Justice Robert H. Jackson, seems to have had the natural law in mind when in his opening statement he charged the defendants with "crimes against humanity,"[11] and in the particular case of the Nazis, argued that "they took from the German people all those dignities and freedoms that we hold *natural and inalienable rights in every human being.*"[12]

However, the idea that we can know things about God and the moral law apart from divine revelation is controversial in some Christian circles, especially among certain Protestant groups. What many of them hold to is what I call the standard narrative, which goes something like this: the Catholic Church, taking its cue from Aquinas, teaches that human beings are capable of knowing by unaided reason the existence and nature of both God and his moral law. Protestantism, on the other hand, maintains that human cognitive powers, so corrupted by sin, cannot provide to human beings the power to know God and his moral law apart from special revelation. The Catholic Church, in step with Aquinas, teaches that the deliverances of natural theology are preambles to faith and thus implies that in order for faith to arise in the believer, she must first know that God exists by way of her natural reason. On the other hand, Protestantism maintains that it is perfectly rational to have faith in God without the evidence of natural theology.

This standard narrative, I argue in this chapter, is mistaken, and Aquinas' views, often cited as a justification of this narrative, are often misunderstood. Catholicism and Protestantism, as it turns out (or so I will argue), are not that far apart at all on the matters of natural theology and natural law.

Prior to the early 2000s, when I first began thinking more deeply about the Catholicism of my youth and entertaining the prospect of returning to it, I had largely accepted the standard narrative, though I took the position that the so-called Catholic side in the dispute was correct. But as I read Aquinas and the Catholic Catechism more carefully, I was struck by how the Catholic and Protestant views had far more in common than I had supposed, and that the differences, though important, were more perspectival and historically contingent than they were substantive.[13]

However, before I launch into my analysis, I want to issue a couple of caveats. First, because of the wide spectrum of views that come under the umbrella of "Protestantism," I am fully aware that there will be those who identify as Protestant who part ways with some of the critiques and views that I attribute to Protestantism. So, what I call "Protestantism" in this chapter is a cluster of beliefs that imply or affirm that the human intellect is completely incapable of knowing anything about God or morality apart from special revelation—that is, Holy Scripture. The advocates of this view typically connect their beliefs to the Reformed tradition. Second, because I am a philosopher and not a historical theologian, much of my focus will be on philosophical and theological concerns rather than on the historical development of doctrinal disagreement. Having said that, I will, when necessary, appeal to certain historical documents and figures in order to help illuminate contemporary debates. With these caveats in place, let's look at natural law and natural theology.

I. Natural Law

I.A. *What Is the Natural Law?*

To say that a human being has the capacity to know the natural moral law is to say that there are normative guidelines for human action that are at their root *not* artifactual, and in that sense they are "natural." To embrace the sort of natural law taught by Aquinas and the Catholic Church requires that one believe at least three propositions:

–There are some universal and immutable moral truths.
–Human beings have the capacity to know these truths.
–Human nature is the basis on which these moral truths are known.

So, for example, the belief that courage is a virtue (or cowardice a vice) is a universal and immutable truth of the natural law that human beings have the capacity to know, and we know this on the basis of human nature. We are rational creatures with natural inclinations to pursue what we believe is good, preserve our lives, beget and educate children, know truths about the divine, and live in a community at peace with our neighbors.[14] Consequently, certain types of ingrained habits—such as prudence, justice, temperance, and fortitude—seem fitting for a rational creature with such inclinations.

The natural law, the Catholic Church teaches, is the basis for legitimate human or positive law. This is why governments issue statutes that prohibit murder, theft, assault, and child abandonment and make policies that they believe advance the common good, such as compulsory public education, policing, and national defense. It is the natural law that Martin Luther King Jr. (1929–1968) had in mind when he wrote in his famous "Letter from a Birmingham Jail" that "an unjust law is a code that is out of harmony with the moral law,"[15] implying that there is a non-artifactual ethical standard by which we can judge our conduct as well as the civil and criminal laws of our nation. (By *non-artifactual* I mean "not an artifact, or human invention." But even artifacts like an automobile, the stock market, or an iPhone require non-artifactual realities, such as matter, numbers, and the laws of physics.) Without this sort of reasoning, it is difficult to make sense of documents such as the Declaration of Independence or the Universal Declaration of Human Rights, or some of the comments made in Justice Jackson's opening statement at the Nuremberg Trials.

Relying heavily on Aquinas' understanding of the definition of law, the Catholic Church explains where the natural law is situated as part of God's creation: "Law is a rule of conduct enacted by competent authority for the sake of the common good. The moral law presupposes the rational order, established among creatures for their good and to serve their final end, by the power, wisdom, and goodness of the Creator. All law finds its first and ultimate truth in the eternal law."[16] This means that the natural law participates in the eternal law—that is, the order of creation in the mind of God— because the natural law is made for rational creatures with a nature ordered toward certain good ends, including the virtues. However, as the *Catechism* states, "the precepts of natural law are not perceived by everyone clearly and immediately. In the present situation sinful man needs grace and revelation so moral and religious truths may be known 'by everyone with facility, with firm certainty and with no admixture of error.'"[17] In other words, as Aquinas puts it, the natural law—without the divine law (i.e., what God specially reveals in Scripture)—is inadequate in directing man to his final end, addressing the inherent shortcomings of human judgment, assessing a person's interior life, and punishing or forbidding all evil deeds by means of the human law.[18] Also, given humanity's fallen nature, the natural law, though knowable and incapable of being fully eradicated, may be embedded in laws and customs that also include mistakes, both moral and metaphysical.

Take, for example, a common precept of the natural law: it is morally wrong always and everywhere to kill an innocent person intentionally. Everyone seems to understand this and to accept it as true. Yet, many people believe that the positive laws of some nations permit the private killing of innocent persons under the "right to abortion."[19] But how is that possible if *everyone knows* by the natural

law that it is morally wrong always and everywhere to kill an innocent person intentionally? First, one can know that X is wrong while
still committing X. Some of my students know that it is wrong to
attribute to themselves authorship of someone else's intellectual
property. Yet they still do it. (By the way, I once had a student whose
plagiarism was so bad, not even his sin was original.) Why? Human
beings are not only rational, but also animals, meaning that they
possess what Aquinas called concupiscible and irascible appetites
that often draw them away from what they know they ought to do
or nudge them in the direction of what they know they ought not
to do.[20] The plagiarizing student knows it is wrong to plagiarize,
though he gives in to the temptation because the prospect of getting
away with it offers the promise of less mental anxiety and more free
time to pursue classes he actually enjoys and extracurricular activities that bring him pleasure.

Second, the human will can assent to beliefs that the intellect
does not get right, and yet it may correctly apply a precept of the
natural law to one of those mistaken beliefs. From the perspective of
natural law, this helps explain why there are many philosophers and
bioethicists who agree with opponents of abortion that it is always
and everywhere morally wrong to kill an innocent person intentionally while at the same time not believing that an elective abortion ever violates that precept.[21] They argue that the unborn human
being, genetically a *Homo sapiens*, is not a person (or lacks moral
status).[22] Just as some beings—like angels and perhaps Klingons
and Vulcans[23]—are persons but not human beings, some beings are
human beings but not persons. These thinkers maintain that what
makes any being a moral subject, or person, is its present ability
to exercise some or all of the powers and traits that we associate
with more mature human beings, such as reasoning, consciousness,
self-motivated activity, a capacity to communicate, a self-concept,[24]
organized cortical brain activity,[25] or the desire for a right to life.[26]
The Catholic Church,[27] in agreement with most every Evangelical Protestant group,[28] disputes this point of view and maintains
that a person is not reducible to what she does, since what she
does—engaging in personal acts—flows from what she is by nature,
a human person. Nevertheless, the defender of abortion choice, in
offering what he believes is a justification of his position, assumes

the correctness of the same precept of the natural law embraced by the abortion opponent: it is morally wrong always and everywhere to kill an innocent person intentionally. For the Church, this is not a surprise. As the *Catechism* affirms: "Application of the natural law varies greatly. . . . In the diversity of cultures, the natural law remains as a rule that binds men among themselves and imposes on them, beyond the inevitable differences, common principles."[29]

I.B. Protestant Critics

Although in recent years several Protestant defenses of the natural law have been published and well received,[30] opinion on the natural law still varies widely among Protestant scholars.[31] Nevertheless, two types of critics of the natural law seem to dominate the dispute. The first I call the *Frustrated Fellow Traveler*. He is critical of the natural law because it has, in his judgment, proved inadequate and unpersuasive in securing victory for social conservativism in the culture wars. The second critic I call the *Solo Scripturist*. She argues that Christians should eschew natural law thinking because it understates the authority of Scripture and the noetic effects of sin as taught in Scripture.

I.B.1. The Frustrated Fellow Traveler

One such critic is my friend and colleague Alan Jacobs.[32] Agreeing with the eminent Orthodox scholar David Bentley Hart,[33] Jacobs writes that "when it's time to persuade, arguments founded on the existence of natural law get no traction in the current intellectual climate."[34] For this reason Jacobs argues that "in the short term we need to find ways to commend our strongly held views without recourse to natural law arguments; and in the long term we need to think about how the existence of natural law can be made both plausible and appealing to people who now see nothing in it."[35]

I think that Jacobs is partly right. He is surely correct that on certain contemporary political issues—for example, the legal recognition of same-sex marriage—natural law arguments have not won the day, and many people find them unpersuasive. But natural law arguments on *specific questions* have rarely ever won unanimous and universal acclamation. This is because they often involve judgments about what Aquinas called the secondary precepts of the natural law, and such judgments are subject to all the vicissitudes of human fallenness that bedevil every individual and culture. As Aquinas notes, the secondary precepts of "the natural law can be blotted out from the human heart, either by evil persuasions, just as in speculative matters errors occur in respect of necessary conclusions; or by vicious customs and corrupt habits, as among some men, theft, and even unnatural vices, as the Apostle states (Romans 1), were not esteemed sinful."[36]

Nevertheless, because, as Aquinas puts it, *the general principles* of "the natural law, in the abstract, can nowise be blotted out from men's hearts,"[37] even those who hope to vindicate new customs historically proscribed by the natural law have to rely on it in one way or another. Take, for example, Justice Anthony Kennedy's majority opinion in *Obergefell v. Hodges* (2015), the U.S. Supreme Court case that affirmed that same-sex couples have a constitutional right for their unions to be recognized as marriages by the state. He does not claim, in the words of C. S. Lewis, that he is "inventing a new value."[38] Rather, Justice Kennedy is arguing that same-sex marriage is merely a just development of traditional marriage, a natural unfolding in history of a deeper truth of marriage's nature that no one had realized until the late twentieth century: "The ancient origins of marriage confirm its centrality, but it has not stood in isolation from developments in law and society. The history of marriage is one of both continuity and change. That institution even as confined to opposite-sex relations has evolved over time."[39]

He writes that "from their beginning to their most recent page, the annals of human history reveal the transcendent importance of marriage,"[40] conceding that "it is fair and necessary to say these references were based on the understanding that marriage is a union between two persons of the opposite sex."[41] This, of course, is the marriage of the natural law,[42] the one supported by the Catholic Church and most everyone else until recently.[43] Nevertheless, Justice Kennedy argues that the marriage he is vindicating in *Obergefell* is identical to this ancient institution, despite the fact that it seems to be missing the three conditions—permanence, exclusivity, and conjugality[44]—that natural law defenders of traditional marriage claim are essential for any institution to receive the designation "marriage."[45] To make his case, the justice appeals to certain accidental features of natural law marriage that also happen to be found in some nonmarital friendships and romantic unions. This makes for a not-so-implausible case that the view of marriage the court is establishing in *Obergefell* is in conceptual continuity with natural law marriage.

For example, Justice Kennedy correctly notes that partners in a same-sex relationship want the state to attribute to their unions the same dignity it affords to traditional marriages,[46] may adopt children for whom they seek to obtain legal protections,[47] are romantically and domestically involved with each other over extended periods of time,[48] and would acquire many government benefits if their unions were recognized by the state as marriages in the same fashion as it recognizes opposite-sex unions.[49] Nevertheless, these accidental attributes—state-imparted dignity, children, domestic life and romance, and government benefits—though regularly found in natural law marriages, are also found in nonmarital unions and are nonexistent in some traditional marriages, even though one of them, the begetting of and caring for children, is a proper accident of a natural law marriage (i.e., a perfection to which one of the essential features of natural law marriage, conjugality, is by nature ordered).[50] So, what we find in *Obergefell* is an account of marriage that is, to be sure, contrary to the natural law as traditionally understood, but in a very real sense not entirely, since it relies primarily on what Lewis called "fragments from the *Tao* [or the natural law] . . . arbitrarily wrenched from their context in the whole . . . yet still owing to the *Tao* [or the natural law] and to it alone such validity as they possess."[51] For this reason, Justice Kennedy's opinion seems to make the Catholic Church's point: "Even when [the natural law] is rejected in its very principles, it cannot be destroyed or removed from the heart of man. It always rises again in the life of individuals and societies."[52] That is, the truths of human nature embedded in the natural law are so fundamental to human flourishing that even those who attempt to support a practice traditionally condemned by the natural law must do so by deploying its moral grammar.[53]

Jacobs' concerns are understandable, given the way advocates of contemporary philosophical liberalism—for example, thinkers such as John Rawls and Ronald Dworkin[54]—have conceptualized the public square. They argue that the only politically legitimate coercive policies that touch on basic rights are those policies that can be supported by "public reason." That is, if one wants to pass a law restricting X (e.g., abortion, the distribution of pornography, euthanasia, or intimate relations between consenting adults), then one must justify the law with a reason (or reasons) that the citizens one is trying to coerce would be unreasonable in rejecting.[55] Roughly, this is how many philosophical liberals think of public reason. In response to this, some contemporary natural law advocates defend their support of such coercive laws by arguing in a way that *could be interpreted* to be saying something like this: "We can play this game and win. Here's our 'public reason,' and it's called 'natural law.'"[56] (But I think this is a caricature and not what contemporary natural law theorists are actually claiming.[57]) Because the expectation, given the ubiquity of liberalism, is that whatever is a good public reason should be nearly unassailable, the natural law's Frustrated Fellow Traveler is disappointed when he discovers that many otherwise rational secular compatriots find natural law arguments unpersuasive for positions with which he is sympathetic. So, he concludes that the natural law has failed in some way. But, as we have seen, the Catholic Church's understanding of natural law, as defended by such theologians as Aquinas, is not advanced as an answer to the concerns of political liberalism. It is offered as an account of the precepts that seem to underlie the diversity of practices, laws, and customs among human civilizations. So, like Johnny Lee's bar-hopping cowboy who was "looking for love in all the wrong places,"[58] the Frustrated Fellow Traveler is looking for a natural law in all the wrong sages.

I.B.2. THE SOLO SCRIPTURIST

The second type of Protestant critic of natural law I want to address is the *Solo Scripturist*, a variation on a term that was coined in 2001 by the Reformed theologian Keith A. Mathison.[59] Because the Solo Scripturist wants to defend the integrity and uniqueness of the Bible's message, he argues that natural law is a poor substitute for the sure and stable deliverances of divine revelation.[60] He also argues that when natural law advocates confidently claim to have established universal moral knowledge, they understate the noetic effects of sin as taught in Scripture. A leading defender of this view is the late Evangelical theologian Carl F. H. Henry (1913–2003), in a piece he published in 1995.

The three contentions of the Thomist doctrine of natural law that evoke evangelical criticism are: (1) that independently of divine revelation, (2) there exists a universally shared body or system of moral beliefs, (3) that human reasoning articulates despite the noetic consequences of the Adamic fall.[61]

But once one attends to what Aquinas actually taught (and with which the *Catholic Catechism* is in full agreement), the distance between what Henry and other Reformed thinkers believe about the natural law and what Aquinas and the Church believe seems almost negligible.

For Aquinas, there are two senses in which the natural law is not independent of divine revelation, or what he calls divine law. It is not independent in the sense that the natural law participates in the eternal law, which is also the source of the divine law (that is, the Old and New Testaments). As I have already noted, to say that the natural law *participates in* the eternal law simply means that God is the source of the natural law, since God's eternal law is the order of creation that eternally exists in the mind of God and thus includes within it the rational nature that all human beings possess.

The natural law is also not independent in the sense that the natural law is incomplete and inadequate given human nature and its ultimate end and fallen state. Writes Aquinas: "If man were ordained to no other end than that which is proportionate to his natural ability, there would be no need for man to have any further direction, on the part of his reason, in addition to the natural law and humanly devised law which is derived from it."[62] But human beings are designed for beatitude, or eternal happiness, which exceeds their natural abilities. For this reason, God must provide to human beings divine law in addition to natural and human law so that we can be directed to fulfill our divine purpose. Moreover, notes Aquinas, "because, on account of the uncertainty of human judgment, especially on contingent and particular matters, different people form different judgments on human acts; whence also different and contrary laws result."[63] That is, because the natural law, without the assistance of the divine law, results in doubts about what man "ought to do and what he ought to avoid, it was necessary for man to be directed in his proper acts by a law given by God, for it is certain that such a law cannot err."[64] One, for example, can figure out by the natural law that marriage is a good, but whether it is indissoluble or a sacrament requires divine guidance.

There is, of course, even another sense in which the natural law is not independent of divine revelation: the Bible itself teaches it, as many scholars, both Protestants and Catholics alike, have ably argued.[65] Because this is an exegetical question that I do not have the space to address in great detail, I am going to simply point out a few of the many places in Scripture in which the existence of a natural moral law— not known through special revelation—is presupposed. How did Cain know that it was wrong to murder his brother Abel (Gen 4:1-18)? (Given the absence of any written divine law at the time, perhaps Cain should have hired a better lawyer.) What does it mean to "honor your father and your mother" (Exod 20:12), if you do not already know what mothers and fathers are and what it means to honor them? Although David knew that adultery and murder were wrong, why did Nathan's story of the rich man taking the poor man's only lamb work so well to prick David's conscience, and why do those unacquainted with the biblical tradition seem to grasp the moral gravity of the wrongness implied in Nathan's telling of the story (2 Sam 12:1-13)? Why did Jesus believe that his audience would know that giving one's child a stone rather than a loaf of bread was not something a good parent would do (Matt 7:9)? The parable of the good Samaritan seems to work, even though the lesson that Jesus is trying to teach requires his audience to engage in a type of moral reasoning that leads them to the conclusion that the only person in this scenario who acted rightly, the Samaritan, is the one person who does not have the Mosaic law (Luke 10:25-37). What could St. Paul possibly mean in Romans 1 when he appeals to universal knowledge of the demands of the created order while noting that there are those "who by their wickedness suppress [this] truth" (Rom 1:18-19)? In that same letter (Rom 2:14-15), St. Paul writes, "When Gentiles, who do not possess the law, do instinctively what the law requires, these, though not having the law, are a law to themselves. They show that what the law requires is written on their hearts." Although Henry seemingly rejects what appears to many as the plain reading of this passage[66]—that St. Paul is in fact teaching that there exists a natural law accessible via unaided reason—Aquinas[67] and the great Protestant reformer, John Calvin (1509–1564),[68] disagree. Since I am not one to quibble when the doctrine of the perspicuity of Scripture is to my advantage, I am with Aquinas and Calvin on this.

Finally, for Aquinas, the natural law is not, as Henry states, "a universally shared body or system of moral beliefs," as if it were a complex collection of rules to which everyone has immediate and infallible access. To be sure, there are general first precepts of the natural law that everyone knows, but as Aquinas notes, these precepts may be applied differently given certain conditions or in particular cases obstructed by an unruly passion, such as the person who murders in a fit of rage, even though he knows murder is wrong. But when it comes to the secondary precepts, according to Aquinas, as I have already noted, "the natural law can be blotted out from the human heart, either by evil persuasions, just as in speculative matters errors occur in respect of necessary conclusions; or by vicious customs and corrupt habits, as among some men, theft, and even unnatural vices, as the Apostle states (Romans 1), were not esteemed sinful."[69] So it seems, contra Henry, that the Thomistic and Catholic view of natural law does in fact hold that the fall has had a deleterious effect on our noetic powers. In fact, without that belief, it would be nearly impossible for advocates of the natural law to account for disagreement and cultural diversity. Thus, one could say that the belief in humanity's fallenness makes the Thomistic and Catholic view of natural law more plausible, not less.

II. Natural Theology

II.A. What Is Natural Theology?

Natural theology[70] is a philosophical project that maintains that one can acquire knowledge of the existence and nature of God by means of one's rational faculties without the benefit of divine revelation. In the Catholic Church, this is a *de fide* dogma, meaning that it is an essential belief of the Church. As Vatican Council I teaches, "The same Holy Mother Church holds and teaches that God, the beginning and end of all things, can be known with certitude by

the natural light of human reason from created things: 'for the invisible things of him, from the creation of the world, are clearly seen,
being understood by the things that are made.'"[71] Notice that this
does not commit the Church to affirming that particular philosophical arguments for God's existence are sound, though the Church
does teach that we can know by reason that "the world, and man,
attest that they contain within themselves neither their first principle
nor their final end, but rather that they participate in Being itself,
which alone is without origin or end."[72] All that the Church is saying is that the human mind has *the capacity* to know with certitude
that God exists from his creation. One could, for a variety reasons,
not exercise that capacity. As Aquinas writes, "For many are unable
to make progress in the study of science, either through dullness of
mind, or through having a number of occupations, and temporal
needs, or even through laziness in learning, all of whom would be
altogether deprived of the knowledge of God, unless Divine things
were brought to their knowledge under the guise of faith."[73]

And neither does Vatican Council I commit the Church to the
claim that it is only by means of arguments that the natural light
of human reason may reveal that God exists. One could, for example, immediately become convinced of God's existence when one
first sees the majestic beauty of the Grand Canyon or the elegance
of a mathematical account of the movement of heavenly bodies in
the Milky Way galaxy. Technically, in each case, one is not *arguing
to* belief in God, as when one infers from particular premises the
conclusion "God exists," even though it is "by the natural light of
human reason" and not by special revelation that one comes to this
belief. This is because, as the Church also teaches, "the desire for
God is written in the human heart, because man is created by God
and for God; and God never ceases to draw man to himself."[74]

II.B. Protestant Critics

As in the matter of the natural law, Protestants hold a variety of
views on natural theology.[75] In fact, in contemporary Christian philosophy, some of the strongest proponents of natural theology are
Protestants, including William Lane Craig, J. P. Moreland, Robin
Collins, Charles Taliaferro,[76] Douglas Groothius, James F. Sennett,[77]

Richard Swinburne,[78] Stephen T. Davis,[79] and my Baylor colleague C. Stephen Evans.[80] There are, of course, many Christian critics, some of whom argue that natural theology arguments, even if some people find them convincing, depend on contested premises that do not seem intuitively correct to everyone.[81] Others maintain that the entire project of natural theology is, to quote Karl Barth, "an abstract speculation concerning a something that is not identical with the revelation of God in Jesus Christ."[82] These are certainly important objections, which have been adequately dealt with by others.[83] However, to address them here would take us far afield from the purpose of this book, which is to show how Aquinas' work, properly understood, illuminates some apparent misunderstandings between Catholics and Protestants. For this reason, I am going to focus on what I believe is the biggest misunderstanding about Catholicism's stand on natural theology. It goes something like this: the Catholic Church maintains that natural theology is a necessary precondition for authentic faith, which makes acceptance of the Gospel message seemingly out of reach for most ordinary people.

Carl F. H. Henry, for example, in his monumental six-volume *God, Revelation, and Authority*, writes the following:

> In developing the empirical case for theism Aquinas's larger aim was to prepare the natural man, once convinced of God's existence by his own reason and apart from divine revelation, to accept supernaturally revealed truth. . . . The Thomistic way broke with the Augustinian-Anselmic *Credo ut intelligam* as with the Tertullian *Credo quia absurdum*, and its *Intelligo ut credam* (understand in order to believe) made room for natural or philosophical theology as preparatory for revealed theology. While Thomas Aquinas approaches the existence of God both from man's ordinary experience and from supernatural revelation as starting points, he nonetheless invokes philosophical theology, or metaphysics, a natural type of knowledge open to anyone, to supply the foundations of faith. Aquinas considers the first use of philosophy in respect to theology to be the demonstration of "items that are preambles to faith."[84]

In a book highly influential in Evangelical circles in the 1970s and 1980s, *Philosophy and the Christian Faith*, theologian Colin

Brown argues that Aquinas (and by default the Catholic Church) is "adopting a two-step process in presenting the case for Christianity. The first step is to use philosophical arguments to lay the foundation; the second is to try to complete the job by appealing to Christian teaching. We might also call it the two-story view of philosophy and faith. The ground floor is built by reason, and the top floor by faith."[85] Earlier in his book Brown chastises the advocate of natural theology by pointing out that belief in God as creator and designer of the universe is "an article of faith based on an awareness of God over against ourselves—not a rational deduction to be drawn by those capable of following certain arguments."[86]

Ironically, one of Evangelical Protestantism's strongest proponents of Aquinas' metaphysics, Norman Geisler, seems to think that the purpose of natural theology is exactly what Henry and Brown believe it is.

> [Theistic] proofs can play a very practical role, indeed a crucial one. . . . It is as essential that men be convinced that there is a God before they trust in Him as it is essential that a groom be convinced that there is a girl standing at the altar before he says, "I do." . . . Religious experience reveals that men need God, and if reason can aid in assuring men that there is a God there to fulfill that end, so much the better. If, on the other hand, the theistic arguments turn out to be unreasonable, then there may be a God, but no good reasons for believing God exists have been provided.[87]

Even though Henry, Brown, and like-minded theologians are correct that there are those who see natural theology as a precondition of faith—as in the case of Geisler—that is not the position of the Catholic Church or Aquinas. The Church's understanding of natural theology *neither implies nor affirms* that everyone who has authentic faith in God knows God "with certitude by the natural light of human reason from created things."[88] And neither is the Church saying that faith *requires* that one must first prove that God exists by the natural light of human reason. As the *Catechism* teaches, "What moves us to believe is not the fact that revealed truths appear as true and intelligible in the light of our natural reason: we believe 'because of the authority of God himself who reveals them, who can neither deceive nor be deceived.'"[89] For those who may think this is a new teaching of the Church deployed in response to Protestant critiques of natural theology, they are mistaken. It can be found in Aquinas:

> The existence of God and other like truths about God, which can be known by natural reason, are not articles of faith, but are preambles to the articles; for faith presupposes natural knowledge, even as grace presupposes nature, and perfection supposes something that can be perfected. *Nevertheless, there is nothing to prevent a man, who cannot grasp a proof, accepting, as a matter of faith, something which in itself is capable of being scientifically known and demonstrated.*[90]

Thus, they are called preambles of faith—not because they are objects of reason required for faith, as Henry implies—but rather, because they are beliefs—though in principle knowable by reason—that are presupposed as true in the articles of faith to which the believer assents. As Aquinas notes, "Things which can be proved by demonstration are reckoned among the articles of faith, not because they are believed simply by all, but because they are a necessary presupposition to matters of faith, so that those who do not know them by demonstration must know them first of all by faith."[91]

Consider the following illustration. Imagine for a moment two individuals: Tony and Tina. Tony is an Uber driver in Las Vegas with no background in philosophy or theology, but he believes in God. He could not give you a philosophical argument as to why, and he typically tells people who ask him that he believes in God because, as he puts it, "that's what I was taught in Sunday School." So, as with most people, he simply believes, just as he believes that the sun is the center of the solar system, even though he could not give you an astronomical argument to prove it. And if you pressed him on what he means by God, he would tell you that he believes that there is only one God, and that God is the creator of the universe, without a body, all powerful, and the subject of the Irving Berlin song "God Bless America." But Tony does not embrace any religious faith. He does not attend church, synagogue, or mosque, though he does pray once in a while when he goes to Sam's Town

Hotel and Gambling Hall on Boulder Highway and puts money on his beloved New York Yankees. Tina, on the other hand, is professor of philosophy at the University of Nevada, Las Vegas, and an expert in medieval Christian, Jewish, and Muslim thought. She has studied and taught all of the arguments for God's existence offered by Aquinas, Moses Maimonides (AD 1135–1204), and Avicenna (AD 980–1037) and has come to the conclusion, based on those arguments, that there is only one God and that God is the creator of the universe, without a body, all powerful, and the subject of the Irving Berlin song "God Bless America." Like Tony, Tina subscribes to no religious faith. Suppose, however, that both Tony and Tina, after reading the New Testament and learning more about Christianity, are moved to be baptized and enter the Church. They then assent to the articles of faith required for baptism. According to Aquinas, what each believed about God prior to coming to faith, though true and consistent with the Catholic faith, was not believed as an article of faith. Tony just believed in God, though he had neither knowledge nor faith. Tina had knowledge of God, since she had an argument, but she had no faith. Thus, for Aquinas, the preambles of faith (*praeambula fidei*) *are not* preconditions of believing in the articles of faith in the sense that one must be convinced of certain philosophical arguments for God and his nature before one's assent to faith can be rational. Rather, the preambles of faith are simply those things that one can either presuppose (as in the case of Tony) or know (as in the case of Tina) about God and his nature without assenting to the articles of faith. In other words, when one assents to the articles of faith without having proof of the preambles of faith, one presupposes them (as in the case of Tony), but one is not *irrational* in doing so. As if he had Tony and Tina in mind, Aquinas writes, "Someone can begin to believe what he did not believe before but which he held with some hesitation. Thus, it is possible that, before believing in God, someone might think that God exists, and that it would be pleasing to God to have him believe that He exists. In this way a man can believe that God exists because such a belief pleases God, although this is not an article of faith, but preliminary to the article, since it can be proved by a demonstration."[92] That is why they are called preambles *of faith*, not faith's prerequisites of reason.

Consider the example of St. Paul's preaching in Acts 17. (This is a story to which we will return in chapter 3 when we cover the "same God" question.) In verses 1–9, Paul and Silas present the Gospel in a synagogue in Thessalonica to a predominantly Jewish audience, arguing that Jesus of Nazareth is the Messiah promised by God in the Old Testament. St. Paul does not need to make an argument for God's existence to an audience that presupposes the reality of the God that the apostle is proclaiming had sent his Son into the world for our redemption. However, in Acts 17:16-34, when preaching in Athens to a predominantly pagan audience, St. Paul realizes, given the proliferation of idols in the region, that he has the burden to first identify the God about which he is speaking. After mentioning an Athenian altar that has inscribed on it "to an unknown god," St. Paul tells his listeners about the true God that they do not know.

> The God who made the world and everything in it, he who is Lord of heaven and earth, does not live in shrines made by human hands, nor is he served by human hands, as though he needed anything, since he himself gives to all mortals life and breath and all things. From one ancestor he made all nations to inhabit the whole earth, and he allotted the times of their existence and the boundaries of the places where they would live, so that they would search for God and perhaps grope for him and find him—though indeed he is not far from each one of us. For "In him we live and move and have our being"; as even some of your own poets have said, "For we too are his offspring." (Acts 17:24-28)

In one fell swoop St. Paul introduces his audience to the one true God, creator of the universe, without a body, and all powerful. He then proceeds to tell his audience that "[God] has fixed a day on which he will have the world judged in righteousness by a man [Jesus Christ] whom he has appointed, and of this he has given assurance to all by raising him from the dead" (Acts 17:31). The lesson from how St. Paul addressed both groups is that the articles of faith—including the belief that Jesus is God's Son and rose from the dead for our salvation—require for *their content* the preambles of faith—including the belief that there is one God who is creator of the universe—which, as Aquinas argues, can either be presupposed or demonstrated.[93]

For Aquinas, although theology is a science (in the sense of an organized body of knowledge),[94] the data of theology comes from revelation and not unaided reason.[95] To be sure, reason can assist theology in helping us to better understand and explain what has been revealed by God,[96] though reason by itself cannot establish the articles of faith.[97] And although, as we have seen, reason can establish the preambles of faith, one does not have to know God's existence by rational argument in order to assent to the articles of faith. This is why Aquinas writes in his commentary on Boethius' *De trinitate*, "Error arises if, in matters of faith, reason has precedence of faith and not faith of reason, to the point that one would be willing to believe only what he could know by reason, when the converse ought to be the case: wherefore Hilary says: 'While believing [in a spirit of faith], inquire, discuss, carry through your speculation.'"[98] Even Geisler, the popular Evangelical defender of Aquinas, does not seem to see this. As he notes in his book on the Angelic Doctor, "Aquinas would argue that God must be believed in simply because he is God, and his revelations must be accepted simply because they come from his authority. That is the only adequate basis for Christian belief. On the other hand, he would agree we must have sound reasons for believing that there is a God and that the Bible is the Word of God, otherwise belief is without justification."[99] As we have seen, this is not quite what Aquinas teaches.

How could theologians as learned as Henry and Brown (and even Geisler, a friend of Aquinas) have missed all this? My hunch is that it is the result of interpreting the Catholic view of faith and reason through modern categories. What do I mean by this? Consider the work of the esteemed Reformed Christian philosopher Alvin Plantinga.[100] He defends the rationality of belief in God, not by suggesting that faith is a means by which one can acquire truth not accessible through reason, but rather, that modern views of reason—which he attributes to classical foundationalism—are the culprit. Classical foundationalism is the view that a belief only counts as rational if it is either properly basic or based on properly basic beliefs. A properly basic belief is, as it sounds, basic (or fundamental). For example, imagine I say to you, "I see Beaty fishing," and you reply, "How do you know that?" I respond, "Because I am seeing him fish right now," and yet you repeat your query with different words, "How do you know you are seeing it?" Exasperated, I would have to say, "I'm pretty sure my eyesight and cognitive faculties are working properly. I cannot give you any more reasons, since what is evident to my senses is just *basic*." According to the classical foundationalist, *evident to the senses* is one of three types of properly basic beliefs. The other two are *self-evident beliefs* and *incorrigible beliefs*. The first are beliefs that are true by definition (or necessary truths), such as 1 + 1 = 2, a bachelor is an unmarried male, and C = 2πr. The second are incorrigible beliefs, meaning that they are subjective beliefs that one cannot be wrong about, such as "I feel pain" or "I am being appeared to by the Ghost of Christmas Past," even if it turns out there is no physiological cause of the pain or the ghost is a hallucination. According to the classical foundationalist, all of our other beliefs, in order to be rationally held, must be derived or based on our properly basic beliefs. This is what we call evidence. Because belief in God is not properly basic (or so argues the classical foundationalist), it follows that it is rational to believe in God if and only if one has sufficient evidence for it. Short of that, belief in God is not rational.

Plantinga critiques classical foundationalism by first pointing out that its standard for what counts as a rational belief—that it must be either properly basic or derived from properly basic beliefs—is self-referentially incoherent.[101] For the standard itself is neither properly basic nor derived from properly basic beliefs. Plantinga then argues that there seem to be many ordinary beliefs that are perfectly rational to hold that we do not believe based on inferences drawn from evidence. We simply believe them immediately and do not argue to them by conscripting evidence to support them. These include our memories, the belief that other minds exist,[102] most of our moral beliefs (e.g., that it is wrong to torture children for fun), and so forth. If, for example, your friend Alex asks you why you believe that you had breakfast this morning, you can say, "I remember it." But suppose Alex then asks, "What's your evidence *for that?*" Where do you go from there? For it seems to be properly basic, even though it is neither self-evident (it is not true by definition), nor evident to the senses (you are not observing it right now), nor an incorrigible belief (your memories are defeasible). This is just as true about your belief in other minds as well as your moral beliefs. After all, it would not be irrational if you continued to believe that other minds existed and that it was wrong to torture children for fun even if you could not produce evidence to prove those beliefs. So, reasons Plantinga, it turns out that there are more properly basic beliefs than the classical foundationalist had suspected. But if that's the case, why not hold that belief in God is properly basic as well?

Taking his cue from Calvin, Plantinga argues that because all human beings have a built-in *sensus divinitatis*, belief in God comes naturally unless it has been significantly clouded by the noetic effects of sin. Explains Plantinga, "God has so created us so that we have a tendency or disposition to see his hand in the world about us. More precisely, there is in us a disposition to believe propositions of the sort *this flower was created by God* or *this vast and intricate universe was created by God* when we contemplate the flower or behold the starry heavens or think about the vast reaches of the universe."[103] Thus, because belief in God is properly basic, Plantinga argues that it is rational to believe in God without any evidence or argument to justify one's belief, just as it is reasonable or rational to believe in all sorts of other things for which one does not have an evidential justification.[104]

In this Reformed way of looking at things, the articles of the Christian faith are items of reason, just like other properly basic nontheological beliefs we may hold. The goal here for the Reformed philosopher is to rescue theological beliefs from the capricious and narrow criteria of what counts as rational that our academic culture has inherited from certain thinkers that come out of the Enlightenment—for example, John Locke, David Hume, Immanuel Kant. So, under the Reformed view, beliefs we attribute to faith we may confidently say are rational. Faith, it turns out, is a species of reason, even if one's coming to faith is initiated by the grace of God.[105] On the other hand, under the Catholic view defended by Aquinas, faith and reason are separate means by which the intellect may acquire beliefs, though sometimes they overlap, as in the case of the preambles of faith; and yet, as in the Reformed view, coming to faith is initiated by God's grace.[106] (More on this in chapter 5.) Thus, for the Catholic, the articles of faith *as articles of faith* are not known under a broad understanding of what counts as reason, as it seems to be the case with Reformed philosophers like Plantinga. As Aquinas puts it, "The knowledge proper to this science [that is, the knowledge of sacred theology] comes through revelation and not through natural reason."[107] For this reason, the Catholic Church teaches that how one comes to know of God by natural reason is not how one comes to know of God by faith. For the former, one begins with the first principles of ordinary reason and proceeds from them to demonstrate the preambles of faith, such as the existence of God, that he is one and creator. For the latter, one begins with Scripture and proceeds from it to show the articles of faith, which include not only that God is one and creator, but that he is Triune, has sent his Son to earth for our salvation, and so forth. Nevertheless, for the Catholic Church (and Aquinas), this does not mean that the articles of faith are *against reason*, since, as Aquinas notes, reason may be used to clarify and explain the articles of faith in response to certain challenges to them by unbelievers. Calling this *persuasive reason*, Aquinas distinguishes it from *demonstrative reason* (or *scientia*).[108] The latter, by which one may come to know the preambles of faith, is a deductive enterprise. One begins with first principles and then through careful and rigorous reasoning arrives at the preambles of faith. Thus, once one's intellect grasps the arguments and their soundness, one's will assents to the conclusions. Persuasive reason, on the other hand, cannot result in automatic assent, since by it one is merely showing that the articles of faith are credible by means of arguments, analogies, and so on—for example, that the Trinity and the incarnation are conceptually coherent, that belief in Christ's miracles is plausible,[109] and so forth. But "credibility arguments," as Fr. John Jenkins calls them, are "insufficient to move one to assent to the articles of faith."[110] For if they could, that would make faith—which must arise from the gift of God's grace—superfluous.

For those committed to finding a place for the articles of faith under the aegis of "reason," as the advocates of the Reformed philosophical project have tried to accomplish, it will seem to many of them that the mission of natural theology is a misguided attempt to support the rationality of one's faith by defending a rationally defensible prerequisite for faith that satisfies the conditions of classical foundationalism.[111] That, of course, may be why some Christian philosophers, as in the case of Geisler, defend the legitimacy (and perhaps necessity) of natural theology. But, as we have seen, that is not how Aquinas, or the Catholic Church, sees it. Nevertheless, it may explain why Evangelical writers such as Brown, Henry, and Geisler (as well as many others) read Aquinas the way they do.

slippery notion of "under the eyes
of reason"?

• Just as Catholic claims assent
of faith is not opposed to reason
i.e. not irrational ⟹ rational
within epistemic rights

Plantinga can argue belief in God
(nd great truths of Gospel) are
not irrational. i.e. rational

Aquinas as Protestant
⟿ Why choose that chapter
title and what do you agree?

⟿ what is natural law and why
should all Christians (Protestant
Orthodox,-- Catholic) be
open to it?

⟿ On pg. 25, you put forth
what some hold about Catholic's
view of natural theology and
call it "begs misunderstanding"?

3

Aquinas as Pluralist
The God of Judaism, Islam, and Christianity

Because therefore God is not known to us in His nature, but is
made known to us from His operations or effects, we name Him
from these . . . hence this name "God" is a name of operation
so far as relates to the source of its meaning. For this name is
imposed from His universal providence over all things; since
all who speak of God intend to name God as exercising providence over all. . . . Taken from this operation, this name "God" is
imposed to signify the divine nature.

St. Thomas Aquinas[1]

Ring them bells so the world will know that God is one

Bob Dylan (a.k.a. Robert Zimmerman) (1989)[2]

In December 2015 Wheaton College in Illinois was embroiled in a
controversy. One of its political science professors, Larycia Hawkins,[3] was put on administrative leave by the Evangelical college
after she wrote on her Facebook wall, "I stand in *religious solidarity*
with Muslims because they, like me, a Christian, are people of the
book. And as Pope Francis stated last week, we worship the same
God."[4] The school maintained that Professor Hawkins' claim that
Muslims and Christians worship the same God was contrary to
its statement of faith, to which all faculty members must assent.[5]
When I first heard about the controversy, I was surprised to learn
that the vast majority of Evangelical commentators—including
many college and seminary professors, some of whom I count
as friends—thought that the school was right in censuring her. I

was surprised because I had just assumed (at least since the mid-2000s) that it was obvious that Christians and Muslims (along with Jews) worshiped the same God,[6] even though I am convinced that Islam and Judaism get some things wrong about God. This led me to become a participant in the controversy, publishing a piece in the online magazine the *Catholic Thing*, "Do Muslims and Christians Worship the Same God?"[7] As you could imagine, this garnered thousands of comments, responses, likes, and sad face emojis throughout the internet and in social media. I followed up with another piece, "Why Muslims and Christians Worship the Same God," also published in the *Catholic Thing*.[8]

In both essays I defended Professor Hawkins, offering a brief philosophical case for what the Catholic Church teaches in one of the documents of the Second Vatican Council (1962–1965), *Nostra Aetate* (1965): "The Church regards with esteem also the Moslems. They adore the one God, living and subsisting in Himself; merciful and all-powerful, the Creator of heaven and earth, who has spoken to men; they take pains to submit wholeheartedly to even His inscrutable decrees, just as Abraham, with whom the faith of Islam takes pleasure in linking itself, submitted to God."[9] This teaching, contrary to what some have suggested, is not an invention of Vatican II. It can be traced back to comments made by Pope Gregory VII in a 1076 letter he wrote to the Muslim ruler of Bijaya, Al-Nasir, in an effort to forge peaceful relations.

> Almighty God, who wishes that all should be saved and none lost, approves nothing in so much as that after loving Him one should love his fellow man, and that one should not do to others, what one does not want done to oneself. You and we owe this charity to ourselves especially because we believe in and confess one God, admittedly, in a different way, and daily praise and venerate him, the creator of the world and ruler of this world.[10]

Notice that for Gregory, Muslims and Christians worship the one God who is creator, but each group does so in a different way, meaning that there are in fact dissimilarities between how Muslims and Christians conceptualize God. So, they worship the same God but nevertheless disagree about that God. One can find this way of thinking about the great Abrahamic religions decades before the Second Vatican Council. In the entry "Monotheism" in the 1911 *Catholic Encyclopedia*, Charles F. Aiken writes that "the God of Moses is no mere tribal deity. He is the Creator and Lord of the world. . . . Of Mohammedan Monotheism little need be said. The Allah of the Qur'an is practically one with the Jehovah of the Old Testament. . . . The influence of the Bible, particularly the Old Testament, on Mohammedan Monotheism is well known and need not be dwelt on here."[11] Thus, according to Aiken, Muslims share with Christians and Jews the belief that there is one God and Creator. In another entry in the same volume, "Mohammed and Mohammedanism," Gabriel Oussani argues that "the doctrines of Islam concerning God—His unity and Divine attributes—are essentially those of the Bible; but to the doctrines of the Trinity and of the Divine Sonship of Christ Mohammed had the strongest antipathy."[12] Here we are told about the specific differences between the Muslim and Christian understandings of God, though each group (along with Judaism) holds the same view about what constitutes a divine nature, which each derives from Scripture. The Church recognized this in *Nostra Aetate*, asserting that even though there are deep disagreements about God between their traditions,[13] Christians, Muslims, and Jews nevertheless share a common belief in the one true God. This was pivotal to the case I made in those two online essays. It is a case that relies on a distinction made by Aquinas between the preambles of faith and the articles of faith, something we covered in chapter 2 in our discussion of natural theology. As you recall, according to Aquinas, there are things about God one can know by reason—or just happen to correctly believe, even in an incomplete way—that are part of the content of the Christian faith, even if one has not assented to the articles of faith.

As I have already noted, and as the Church fully concedes, Judaism, Christianity, and Islam are religions that differ on a variety of theological questions. These include the doctrine of the Trinity (which Christians affirm and Muslims and Jews deny), whether Jesus of Nazareth is the Messiah (which Jews deny and Christians and Muslims affirm), whether God can beget (or has begotten) a Son (which Muslims and Jews deny and Christians affirm), and whether Mohammed is a true prophet of God (which Muslims affirm and Christians and Jews deny). But for most people—and for some very smart and sophisticated Christians[14]—it just seems implausible for one to admit on the one hand that these faith traditions embrace contrary things about God, while on the other hand also claiming, as I argue in this chapter and as the Catholic Church teaches, that Jews, Christians, and Muslims worship the same God. Nevertheless, I not only argue that it is not implausible, I argue that once one attends to Aquinas' distinction between the preambles of faith and the articles of faith, it is the most reasonable view to hold.

Here's my case in a nutshell: if one can show that there can in principle be only one God, and if it violates no canon of reason for two (or three or more) contrary accounts of God to be all referring to that same God, then it follows that these contrary accounts of God must all refer to the same God. In order to understand why this is so, we will cover three topics: (I) sense, reference, and God; (II) disagreements about God; and (III) objections. Under the first, I explain the difference between sense and reference and why, for Christians, Jews, and Muslims, there can in principle be only one God, and thus the three religions *refer* to the same God even though each embraces a different *sense* of that same God. Under the second, I explain how the disagreements between Christians, Jews, and Muslims about God do not count against the claim that they are worshipping the same God. And under the third, I respond to several objections to the kind of case I am making in this chapter.

I should note that the point of this chapter is to persuade my fellow Christians that we worship the same God as Jews and Muslims worship. I am not trying to persuade Jews and Muslims to believe that they worship the same God as Christians do. Although I think they should embrace that position, I will leave that task to the believers within those traditions.[15]

I. Sense, Reference, and God

I.A. Superman and Bob Dylan

When I was a kid I was a big fan of the comic book character Superman. As the story goes, he is born on the planet Krypton and given the name Kal-El by his parents Jor-El and Lara. Jor-El is a scientist who discovers that Krypton is heading for destruction because of the instability of the planet's core. By the time his skeptical colleagues realize that Jor-El is correct, it is too late for the planet's population to escape to another world. But Jor-El knows that he can save his infant son, Kal-El, by sending him to Earth in a small rocket. Narrowly escaping the gravitational pull of the imploding Krypton, the rocket heads toward its intended destination. It lands in an open field near the town of Smallville, Kansas. Jonathan and Martha Kent, a couple driving by, witness the vessel's descent. Taking a closer look, the Kents are astonished at what they find: a cylinder containing a small child wrapped in a blanket. They gently remove the infant and bring him to their home. A childless couple, the Kents give Kal-El the name "Clark" (Martha's maiden name) and adopt him as their own. Over the following months and years, they discover his incredible properties and powers, including invulnerability, X-ray vision, superhuman strength and eyesight, extraordinary intelligence, and the ability to fly and move at a velocity "faster than a speeding bullet." Realizing the enormous responsibility of rearing such a child, the Kents try their best to keep Kal-El's abilities secret and provide a home life in which virtue is lived, praised, and rewarded.

While attending high school, Clark begins dating a fellow student, Lana Lang. It is during this time that Kal-El dons the iconic blue and red caped costume, announcing to the world the existence of Superboy, though no one, except his adoptive parents, knows that this new superhero is in fact a teenager from Smallville named Clark Kent. From that point forward, as far as the rest of the world knows, Clark Kent and Superboy (who becomes Superman) are two different people. After high school, Clark attends and graduates from Metropolis University. He is soon hired as a reporter by the local newspaper, the *Daily Planet*, which also employs the award-winning journalist Lois Lane. Now known as Superman, our caped hero goes about doing what superheroes do: saving the world from imminent destruction, foiling the malevolent plots of Lex Luther, and building alliances with peers, such as the Flash, Green Lantern, Batman, and Wonder Woman, in order to combat the world's seemingly endless supply of evil villains. Lois is assigned by her editor, Perry White, to the Superman beat. After several years, Lois and Superman begin dating, and yet Clark has never technically broken up with Lana,

who lives in a suburb of Metropolis. With his incredible superpow-
ers Kal-El is able to easily date both Lois and Lana without raising
either woman's suspicions. (Apparently, Jonathan and Martha did
not cultivate in Clark *every* virtue.) As far as Lois is concerned, she
is the girlfriend of a person named Superman, a nonhuman son of
the planet Krypton, and one of her colleagues at work is a gentleman
named Clark Kent, who is dating his high school sweetheart, Lana
Lang. As far as Lana is concerned, she is the girlfriend of her high
school sweetheart, Clark Kent, a human son of the planet Earth, and
one of her fellow Metropolitans is a gentleman named Superman,
who is dating Lois Lane, a woman who works with Lana's boyfriend
at the *Daily Planet*.

It is clear that Lois and Lana are dating the same person, even
though each of them holds false and incomplete beliefs about their
boyfriends. Lois and Lana mistakenly believe that Superman and
Clark Kent are two different people. Lana "knows" that her boyfriend
is human and was born on the planet Earth, while Lois "knows" that
her boyfriend is nonhuman and was born on the planet Krypton.
Lana "knows" that her high school sweetheart is not the man cur-
rently dating Lois, while Lois "knows" that her colleague Clark Kent
is not her boyfriend. Although Kal-El, Clark Kent, and Superman
are really identical to each other, the beliefs that the Kents, Lana,
and Lois hold about Kal-El, Clark Kent, and Superman are not identical (though some of them are true and some of them are false).

If you have understood this story so far, then you have understood an important philosophical distinction: sense is not the same
as reference. The expressions "Kal-El," "Clark Kent," and "Superman" all have the same *reference*, since they all refer to the same
thing, the son of Jor-El and Lara who was adopted by Jonathan and
Martha Kent. But each of the expressions—"Kal-El," "Clark Kent,"
and "Superman"—has different *senses* for the Kents, Lana, and Lois.
For the Kents, these expressions have identical senses and the same
reference, since they know that Kal-El, Clark Kent, and Superman
are the same person, in much the same way that many of us know
that Muhammed Ali, Bob Dylan, Mark Twain, and Marilyn Mon-
roe are identical to Cassius Clay, Robert Zimmerman, Samuel Cle-
mens, and Norma Jean Baker, respectively. But for Lana and Lois,
"Kal-El," "Clark Kent," and "Superman" have different senses, even

though they have the same reference. Both women correctly believe that Kal-El is Superman, but both incorrectly believe that Clark Kent is not Superman and Superman is not Clark Kent. Aquinas, though not using the language of sense and reference, seems to make this distinction when he writes that "to know that someone is approaching is not the same as to know that Peter is approaching, even though it is Peter who is approaching."[16] That is, two people can have the same reference—"that man who is approaching"— though one may think (or have the sense) that it is Peter while the other may think (or have the sense) that it is not Peter (or mistakenly think that it's Paul).

Let us now move from fictional characters to a real one. Suppose your friend Pauline is a 1959 graduate of Hibbing High School in Minnesota. One of her high school classmates is Robert Zimmerman (b. 1941), a Jewish boy whose family had moved from Duluth to Hibbing when he was six years old. In the mid-1960s Pauline becomes a huge fan of the singer-songwriter Bob Dylan (b. 1941), but for some reason she never comes to know that in 1962 her former classmate Zimmerman had changed his name to Bob Dylan, the same Bob Dylan whose music she now enjoys. From 1962 until 2019 Pauline goes on her merry way through life thinking that Zimmerman and Dylan are two different people. As far as she is concerned, Zimmerman may have fallen off the face of the Earth, since in her mind she has learned nothing new about him. She believes that the last time she saw Zimmerman was at their 1959 graduation. On the other hand, she has learned much about Dylan, including the fact that, though born into a Jewish family, he had converted to Christianity in 1978 and has a son named Jakob, founding member of the band the Wallflowers. She has no reason to think that these facts about Bob Dylan's life are facts about Robert Zimmerman's life. So, when Pauline walks into the Hibbing High gym at her sixty-year reunion and sees Bob Dylan, she points at him and turns to her husband, Dewey, and asks, "What's *he* doing here?" Dewey then explains that Bob Dylan *is* Robert Zimmerman, Hibbing class of '59. Although for Pauline the expressions "Bob Dylan" and "Robert Zimmerman," up until 2019, had different senses, in reality they have always had the same reference—even though Pauline did not know it.

Now let us move from the mundane to the transcendent.

II.B. Abdullah, Baruch, and Catherine

Imagine there are three philosophy majors at Princeton University (a.k.a. College of New Jersey),[17] all of whom are freshmen: Abdullah, who was raised Muslim; Baruch, who was raised Jewish; and Catherine, who was raised Christian. In their sophomore year, after each one reads Richard Dawkins' book *The God Delusion*, they all become atheists. However, one of their philosophy professors, Dr. Socrates, catches wind of this, takes these students aside, and tells them that if they are to abandon their faith they should at least do so for good reasons. "*The God Delusion*," she argues, "is—no offense to Professor Dawkins—sophomoric."[18] Although she is not a believer in God, Dr. Socrates is concerned with the intellectual integrity of her students. So she recommends that they first read what she thinks are the best arguments for God's existence. She suggests works by a Muslim philosopher, Avicenna (980–1037),[19] a Jewish philosopher, Moses Maimonides (1135–1204),[20] and a Christian philosopher, St. Thomas Aquinas (1225–1274).[21]

After reading these works, Abdullah, Baruch, and Catherine tell Dr. Socrates that they are now convinced that God exists. Abdullah confesses that he found Aquinas' argument most persuasive. Baruch explains why he thought Avicenna's case was compelling. And for Catherine, it was Maimonides' reasoning that changed her mind. When they sit down and compare notes, they discover, much to their surprise, that they all believe more or less the same thing about God, even though the arguments of Aquinas, Avicenna, and Maimonides are different, and even though the theological traditions (Christianity, Islam, and Judaism) of these three great medieval philosophers clash in important and significant ways. Abdullah, Baruch, and Catherine agree that each of these arguments correctly concludes that God exists and that he is *the uncaused, perfect, rational, unchanging, self-subsistent, eternal Creator and sustainer of all that which receives its being from another.* (Anything that might not have existed—like you, me, the planet Jupiter, or my dog Phydeaux—exists only because of something else that caused or causes it to exist, and thus "receives its being from another.")

What follows from this is that God is one, but not in the sense that God is a unique individual in the way that Bob Dylan is a unique individual. Rather, God is one in the radical sense that God *is not one of a kind*. Here is a way to think about it. You, Bob Dylan, and I are indeed unique individuals, but we are three of the kind "human being." Now suppose a plague killed every human being on Earth except Dylan. He would now be one of a kind. But since there is nothing about human nature that makes it impossible for there to be more than one human being, Dylan's oneness is not the same as God's oneness, even though there is now only one Dylan and one God. How can that be? If there could be two or more "Gods," like there could be two or more human beings, the two "Gods" would have to differ in some way. But to say that two things of the same kind differ from each other (e.g., Jerry Lewis and Dean Martin, Spock and Jim Kirk, Carole King and Gerry Goffin) means that one lacks what the other has and vice versa, that each has the potential for change,[22] and that there is a cause that accounts for that difference. But if God is uncaused, perfect, unchanging, self-subsistent, and eternal, it means that he is the fullness of being, and thus lacks nothing, cannot be an effect, has no potential, and depends on nothing for his existence. (As far as existence goes, you cannot really do better than the fullness of being. A "second fullness of being" makes about as much sense as a second number 1 or a four-sided triangle.) So, if God exists, there can only be one, not in the sense that the last saber-tooth tiger was the only one of its kind, but rather, in the sense that because God is *not* one *of a kind*, there can in principle be only one God.

It must also be the case that it is God's nature to exist. For it is not the nature of any created thing to exist, since every created thing may have failed to exist if something that exists had not existed to bring it into and keep it in existence. If God were like that, then God would be creaturely and thus would, like all creatures, require a source for his existence, something that would bring him into, and/or keep him in, existence. As Aquinas notes, a being that receive its being from another is "a being by participation," meaning that it cannot be the ultimate source of all existence. "He will not therefore be the first being—which is absurd. Therefore God is His own existence."[23]

To recap: after abandoning the religions of their births and becoming atheists for a brief time, Abdullah, Baruch, and Catherine return to theism. As a result of serious intellectual reflection, prompted by Professor Socrates, each comes to believe there exists only one God and that he is *the uncaused, perfect, rational, unchanging, self-subsistent, eternal Creator and sustainer of all that which receives its being from another.* Although Abdullah, Baruch, and Catherine have not returned to the faiths in which they were brought up, it seems uncontroversial for us to say at this point in their lives the former Muslim, the former Jew, and the former Christian, who are all former atheists, are now theists who *believe in the same God.* Returning to the concepts mentioned earlier, we can say with confidence that when Abdullah, Baruch, and Catherine speak of God they are using the term "God" in the same sense and with the same reference.

Now suppose that each student is not content with *mere theism.* They want something more than intellectual satisfaction. (A good argument is one thing; the beatific vision is quite another.) Given their own biographies, they are curious about whether a case can be made that the one true God has specially revealed truths about himself and the ultimate end of human life that are not accessible by the exercise of the natural reason that had led them back to theism. Given the conflicting revelatory claims of the world's great religions, each student embarks on a rigorous and prayerful study of those differing traditions, reading with a critical though open mind the Jewish Bible, the Qur'an, and the New Testament as well as a variety of commentaries, critiques, and apologetic works. After about two years, Abdullah, the former Muslim, becomes a Christian; Baruch, the former Jew, becomes a Muslim; and Catherine, the former Christian, becomes a Jew. But none considers himself or herself a former theist. Each sees his or her religious conversion, not as a change in "Gods," since there can only in principle be one God, but rather as an exercise of faith in what each believes the one true God has specially revealed in salvation history, sacred scripture, or sacred tradition. So, when Abdullah participates in the divine liturgy, when Baruch recites his five daily prayers (*salat*), and when Catherine attends synagogue, they are all worshipping the same God.

II. Disagreements about God

As I noted at the beginning of this chapter, the religions of Abdullah, Baruch, and Catherine—Christianity, Islam, and Judaism—do not say the same things about God. This is because each of these religious traditions has a different view of what counts as specially revealed truth, and it turns out that those revelations affirm incompatible, though sometimes overlapping, beliefs about God and salvation history. Christians, just as Jews and Muslims, believe that God made a covenant with Abraham and that he called Moses to lead the children of Israel out of Egypt. But Christians, along with Muslims, believe that Jesus was the promised Messiah, while Jews do not. Moreover, Christians believe that Jesus is God's Son, something denied by both Jews and Muslims. Christians and Jews do not believe that the Qur'an is divinely inspired or that Muhammed is God's prophet, though these beliefs are central to Islam. Christians hold that God, though one, is triune, that he has revealed himself in the New Testament as Father, Son, and Holy Spirit. Both Jews and Muslims reject the doctrine of the Trinity.

These are not minor matters for observant members of these faiths. A "Christian" who denies that Jesus is God's son is not really a Christian, just as a "Muslim" who rejects the prophetic authority of Muhammed is not really a follower of Islam. Although some Jews who have converted to Christianity have claimed to be practitioners of "Messianic Judaism," this designation has been nearly universally condemned by Judaism's leading rabbis as well as the state of Israel.[24] These are, indeed, deep differences, but none of them is a defeater to the claim that Christians, Muslims, and Jews worship the same God. This is because each tradition's understanding of "God" has the same reference—the one, uncaused, perfect, unchanging, self-subsistent, eternal Creator and sustainer of all that which receives its being from another.[25]

To return to the illustrations employed earlier in this chapter: Lana Lang is mistaken in her belief that her boyfriend, Clark Kent, is human, but "Clark Kent" refers to the same being that Lois Lane is dating, Superman, a son of the planet Krypton. Pauline attributed differing properties to Robert Zimmerman and Bob Dylan, since she believed that they were two different people, though she was in fact mistaken. In the same way, although Christians, Muslims, and Jews hold differing beliefs about God that entail that the other faith traditions get some important things wrong, the disagreements are at the level of sense, not reference (though one of the senses may in fact be entirely correct). This is so for three conjoined reasons, each of which, as we have seen, we have very good grounds to believe: (1) in principle there cannot be more than one God; (2) each of these faiths must be referring to that same one God; and (3) the differences between Christians, Muslims, and Jews arise as a consequence of what each group considers authoritative special revelation. This is why it makes perfect sense to say that the serpent in the garden is talking about the one true God even though what he allegedly reveals to Eve about that God is false, "'You will not die; for God knows that when you eat of it your eyes will be opened, and you will be like God, knowing good and evil'" (Gen 3:4b-5).

Assuming Christianity, Islam, or Judaism must be the one true faith, Abdullah, Baruch, or Catherine knows more about God than he or she knew as a mere theist. But *none of them knows less.* For this reason, despite their deep differences on issues like the Trinity, the incarnation, and so forth, it must be the case that Abdullah, Baruch, and Catherine worship the same God.

For Aquinas, prior to their conversions, Abdullah, Baruch, and Catherine knew and believed the preambles of faith, "the existence of God and other like truths about God."[26] However, after their conversions, only the Christian Abdullah by the movement of God's grace assented to the articles of faith,[27] of which there are fourteen.[28] The first seven concern the nature of the Godhead, while the second seven concern the human nature of Christ: God is (1) one, (2) the Father, (3) the Son, (4) the Holy Spirit, (5) the creator, (6) the source of grace for our sanctification, (7) he who will raise us from the dead and grant us everlasting life; and Christ (8) was conceived by the Holy Spirit, (9) born of the Virgin Mary, (10) suffered death and was buried, (11) descended into hell, (12) was raised from the dead, (13) ascended into heaven, and (14) will come to judge the living and the dead.[29] If Christianity is true, then Abdullah's assenting to its articles of faith means that he knows more about God than he knew before his conversion. But he does not know less. Consequently, when he, Baruch, and Catherine embraced only the preambles of faith—"the existence of God and other like truths about God"[30]—they all believed in the same God. When each came to believe more about that same God—even if each judged the others' view of God as inaccurate—it did not mean that they now believed in different Gods. For if the preambles of faith truly refer to the one, true, and living God, and Abdullah's, Baruch's, and Catherine's additional beliefs about that God do not contradict the preambles of faith, then they still believe in the same God after their conversions, even if one or all of them are mistaken about their additional beliefs about God.

Now imagine that Abdullah, Baruch, and Catherine, instead of being philosophers, are geologists, led by their redoubtable teacher Professor Theo. In one of their travels they stumble upon a large, apparently unexplored, mountain named Zion. At the foot of Zion live three tribes: X, Y, and Z. A scout from each tribe approaches the geologists to welcome them to their land. When the geologists ask the scouts about what lies inside the mountain's caves, each scout tells their tribe's official story. X says, "nothing except bugs and mice." Y says, "nothing except dogs and cats." And Z says, "nothing except bricks of gold." After talking with each scout individually, the four geologists come to contrary conclusions about the contents of the caves. Abdullah believes the scout from X, Baruch believes the scout from Y, Catherine believes the scout from Z, and Professor Theo believes none of the scouts. Although the four geologists hold contrary beliefs about Zion, they are all talking about the same mountain. As should be evident, the geologists' first viewing of the mountain is analogous to what their philosopher counterparts know about God through natural reason (i.e., the preambles of faith). The "information" the geologists receive from the three scouts is analogous to "special revelation," since it is not something they directly know but is a claim delivered to them by a messenger in whom they have chosen to put their trust. (Professor Theo, of course, trusts none of the scouts and remains a mere mountain man.) Assuming that one of the scouts is correct about what is inside the mountain, one of the three students knows more about the mountain than he or she knew before questioning the scouts, but they all know they are talking about the same mountain.

Here is yet another way to think about it. All three religious traditions affirm that Moses encountered God in the burning bush,[31] at which this exchange occurred: "Then Moses said to God, 'If I come to the Israelites and say to them, "The God of your ancestors has sent me to you," and they ask me, "What is his name?" what shall I say to them?' God said to Moses, 'I AM WHO I AM.' And he

said, 'Say this to the people of Israel, "I AM has sent me to you."'"
(Exod 3:13-14). Christians have traditionally read this passage
as Moses being told by God that he is literally the "self-existent
one," the fullness of being, that which is the source of everything
that exists but itself requires no source for its existence.[32] Most
Christians read John 8:58 as Jesus revealing that he is in fact the
one Moses encountered at the burning bush:[33] "Jesus said to them,
'Very truly, I tell you, before Abraham was, *I am*.'" And yet, when
God told Moses that he was "I am," the self-existent one, he did not
reveal to Moses that he was Father, Son, and Holy Spirit. That would
come later, as Christians understand God's progressive revelation.
For this reason, it would seem odd to say that because Moses (or for
that matter, Abraham, Isaac, or Jacob) did not believe that the self-
existent divine nature included the Son, that he (and they) did not
worship the same God that Christians worship today.

This, it turns out, is the God to which St. Paul refers in his
famous sermon preached on the Areopagus in Athens to his predominantly pagan critics.

> Athenians, I see how extremely religious you are in every way.
> For as I went through the city and looked carefully at the objects
> of your worship, I found among them an altar with the inscrip-
> tion, "To an unknown god." What therefore you worship as
> unknown, this I proclaim to you. The God who made the world
> and everything in it, he who is Lord of heaven and earth, does
> not live in shrines made by human hands, nor is he served by
> human hands, as though he needed anything, since he him-
> self gives to all mortals life and breath and all things. From one
> ancestor he made all nations to inhabit the whole earth, and
> he allotted the times of their existence and the boundaries of the
> places where they would live, so that they would search for God
> and perhaps grope for him and find him—though indeed he is
> not far from each one of us. For "In him we live and move and
> have our being"; as even some of your own poets have said, "For
> we too are his offspring." (Acts 17: 22b-28)

But, as we know, St. Paul does not end his teaching there. He goes
on to tell his audience about what this God has specially revealed
in history: "[God] has fixed a day on which he will have the world

judged in righteousness by a man [Jesus Christ] whom he has appointed, and of this he has given assurance to all by raising him from the dead" (Acts 17:31). Earlier in the same chapter of Acts we are told of the visit of St. Paul and Silas to the Jewish synagogue in Thessalonica, where St. Paul offered arguments for a suffering and resurrected Messiah and identified him as Jesus of Nazareth. Some listeners were converted, though many others were displeased (Acts 17:1-9). But unless St. Paul supposed that the Jews believed in the same God as he did, it would make little sense for him to try to convince them that Jesus was God's Messiah. So, one sees in Acts 17 two groups—pagans and Jews—that include listeners who either accepted or rejected the Christian message. But in neither case does St. Paul suggest that he is preaching the Gospel so that his listeners would be convinced to "change Gods." Quite the opposite: he introduces Christ to the pagans after first establishing the correct reference to God—"in him we live and move and have our being"— while with the Jews he establishes the correct reference to God by preaching that Jesus is the Messiah promised by the God of Abraham, Isaac, Jacob, and Moses, none of whom believed in the Trinity. So, it is clear that some of those who walk away from these encounters unconverted did not cease to believe in the same God in which St. Paul believed. Rather, they rejected St. Paul's claim that the coming of Jesus into the world is a true revelation from that same God.

Consider now the controversy in church history over Arianism. In the fourth century, the Christian church was divided over how best to understand Christ's status as the Son of God in relation to God the Father. Some bishops took the side of Arius of Alexandria (256–336), who argued that the Son of God, incarnate as Jesus, was made by the Father and had not always existed, and thus could not be God.[34] Other bishops took the side of Athanasius of Alexandria (296–373), who argued that Christ, the Son of God, as the Word mentioned in the beginning of John's gospel (John 1:1), is God.[35] There is no doubt that Arius and Athanasius had a deep disagreement about the nature of God's Son. Was he "begotten, not made, consubstantial with the Father,"[36] or was he made, not begotten, of a different substance from the Father? As it turns out, Athanasius's position prevailed at the First Council of Nicaea (AD 325), at which Arianism was declared a heresy. Although Arius and Athanasius disagreed about the nature of God's Son, they were no doubt both referring to the same God, since their dispute was over whether the Son of *that God* was a creature. In a sense, then, Arius' understanding of God's internal life (that it is not triune) does not differ from that held by Avicenna or Maimonides. Thus, if Athanasius and Arius believed in the same God, and if Arius, Avicenna, and Maimonides believed in the same God, then it stands to reason that Athanasius, Avicenna, and Maimonides believed in the same God. How could it be otherwise?

III. Objections

As I noted earlier, the type of case I make in this chapter has its origin in two online articles I published in December 2015 and January 2016 in response to a controversy at Wheaton College in Illinois. Much ink (both cyber and actual) was spilled in response to my case. What follows are four of those objections and my replies to them.

Objection 1: Why should the idea of God as creator—which Christians have in common with Muslims and Jews—take precedence over distinctly Christian beliefs about God, such as the Trinity, the incarnation, and so forth? My friend, the philosopher and literary scholar Lydia McGrew, raises this objection while comparing Islam to Christianity: "Islam says more than that God doesn't happen to be triune or that God didn't in fact come down as man. Islam insists God cannot be triune or incarnate. It denies Jesus could be the Son of God, much less God himself. Why is the fact that Allah (as conceived in Islam) is the Creator more important to the question at hand than the fact that he cannot be triune or incarnate?" [37]

Lydia is not entirely incorrect: these contrary understandings of God's internal life (whether or not he is or could be triune) and his revelation in salvation history (whether or not Jesus is or could be God's Son) are essential to both Islam and Christianity as religions. But to the question at hand, whether or not Muslims and Christians (and Jews) worship the same God, they are not more important. Here is why.

As we have seen, there can in principle be only one God and Creator. To deny this is tantamount to embracing atheism, since such a "God" would be less than the fullness of being and thus creaturely.

cf. Feser's "Simply irresistible"

This would be the case even if the followers of such a creaturely God claim they believe that God is triune and Jesus is God's Son. Imagine, for example, someone who identifies as a Christian and claims that God is a Trinity, but what he really means is that the "Godhead" actually consists of three separate finite beings of incredible strength and power named Father, Son, and Holy Spirit. Someone who embraces this view and worships that "Godhead" would not be worshipping the God of Christianity, despite the fact that he may confess that God is a Trinity and that Jesus is God incarnate. This is why the Catholic Church accepts virtually all Protestant baptisms as valid but not Latter-day Saint baptisms. It is because the LDS Church, though confessing belief in the Trinity[38] and the incarnation,[39] denies that there is only one God and that he is the uncaused, unchanging, self-subsistent, eternal Creator and sustainer of all that which receives its being from another.[40] This means that Trinitarianism, as understood in the Catholic creeds, requires God's oneness, and thus, to answer Lydia, getting the divine nature right is in fact more important. This is why St. Paul in Acts 17 first establishes the correct reference to God before he moves on to share the gospel.

After all, you cannot come to believe that God is a Trinity or that Jesus is God, as articulated by the Nicene Creed, unless you first "believe in one God, the Father almighty, maker of heaven and earth, of all things visible and invisible."[41] Without this first principle (or preamble of faith), the revelation of God's internal life that the Creed articulates makes little sense: "I believe in one Lord Jesus Christ, the Only Begotten Son of God, . . . begotten, not made, consubstantial with the Father; through him all things were made. . . . I believe in the Holy Spirit, the Lord, the giver of life, who proceeds from the Father and the Son, who with the Father and the Son is adored and glorified."[42] The revelation of the eternal processions (origin of the Son and Holy Spirit from within God)[43]—unknowable apart from Scripture—presupposes knowledge of the existence of one divine nature, either by way of natural theology or through ordinary use of the term "God." Thus, Jews and Muslims who reject the Christian revelation do not believe in a different God. They believe in the same God, though, from a Christian perspective, they hold mistaken beliefs about that God—for example, that he is not triune, that he cannot beget a Son, and so forth.

Objection 2: Just because Christians, Muslims, and Jews worship one God does not mean they worship the same God. In an article that appeared in the academic journal *Faith and Philosophy*,[44] philosopher Tomas Bogardus and his student Mallorie Urban offer the following counterexample to support this objection: "Perhaps fans of Democritus, fans of Plato, and fans of Aristotle agree that *only one* of those three can be the greatest philosopher. It hardly follows that these three groups of fans celebrate *the same* philosopher as the greatest. Similarly, the fact that Muslims, Christians, and Jews all believe in *only one* God does not prove that they all worship *the same* God."[45] Bogardus and Urban would have a point *if* the God worshipped by Muslims, Christians, and Jews were one of a kind, as Democritus, Plato, and Aristotle are each one of a kind. But, as we have seen, if God is the uncaused, perfect, rational, unchanging, self-subsistent, eternal Creator and sustainer of all that which receives its being from another, as Judaism, Christianity, and Islam teach about God, then there must exist only one God and he cannot in principle be one of a kind.

In fairness to Bogardus and Urban, they offer this objection to an argument that they admit I technically do not defend. What they are critiquing is a "retooled" version of my argument that does not depend on the claim that Christianity, Judaism, and Islam share a belief in classical theism, but rather, on the premise that each faith is monotheistic. Bogardus and Urban maintain that because it is doubtful that many Christians, Muslims, and Jews even know what classical theism is, let alone accept it, it would have been better if I had just said that the three faiths are monotheistic. But if I had done that, then I would have had to address the Democritus-Plato-Aristotle counterexample, which they think is a defeater to my case. As should be evident by my response, I stick with classical theism to defeat the Democritus-Plato-Aristotle counterexample. I do this because monotheism per se does not require that the one God who exists is the only God that can exist in principle, which is an essential belief to Christianity, Judaism, and Islam. Exodus 3:14 and Deuteronomy 6:4 would make little sense if this were not true. As for the other objection—that it is doubtful that all Christians, Muslims, and Jews accept classical theism—I respond to that below, in response to objection 4.

Answers to the "same God" question may diverge along the lines of those who hold to C.T. or not → e.g. WLC says not the same God.

Objection 3: Even if the Christian God, the Muslim God, and the Jewish God all refer to the same being, it does not mean that Christians, Muslims, and Jews worship the same God. My friend, William Lane Craig, argues this:

> A further wrinkle is that "worships x" is what philosophers call an intensional (as opposed to extensional) context, where the term "x" need not refer to anything at all (as in, *e.g.*, "Jason worships Zeus"). In an intensional context co-referring terms cannot be substituted without impacting the truth value of the sentence. For example, even though "Jupiter" may refer to the same god as "Zeus," still Jason, a Greek, does not worship Jupiter and may have never even heard of the Roman god. So one cannot say that Abdul, a Muslim, worships Yahweh, even if "Yahweh" and "Allah" are co-referring terms.[46]

The difference between intensional and extensional contexts is a technical philosophical question that we need not explore in order to adequately address Bill's objection. It will suffice for our purposes here to simply say that the intensional context is more or less the same as "sense" and the extensional context, "reference."

What exactly is Bill's point? It is simply that even if the God worshipped by Muslims is in reality the same being as the God worshipped by Christians, the term "Muslim God" in the sentence "Abdul worships the Muslim God" cannot be replaced with the term "Christian God" without changing the meaning of the sentence, since in Abdul's mind "Muslim God" does not have the same sense as "Christian God." After all, the Muslim concept of God includes "non-triune" whereas the Christian concept of God includes "triune." So, "Abdul worships the Muslim God" and "Abdul worships the Christian God" do not have the same truth-value, even if "Muslim God" and "Christian God" in reality refer to the same being.

But it is not precisely clear how this "wrinkle" defeats the position I am defending in this chapter. Consider a stock example often employed to show the difference between sense and reference. Every morning Harold gets up and sees the morning star, and at night before he goes to sleep Harold sees the evening star. He believes for his entire life that the morning star and the evening star are different stars with differing properties and characteristics. So, "Harold sees the morning star" and "Harold sees the evening star" do not have the same truth-value. Yet, we know that the morning star and the evening star are in fact the planet Venus. So, even though, for Harold, "morning star" and "evening star" have different senses, in reality they have the same reference. To turn this example into a question analogous to the one this chapter is trying to answer, we can ask, "Does Harold in the morning and Harold in the evening see the same star?" The answer is obviously, "yes."

Consequently, the terms "Muslim God" and "Christian God" no more have the same sense for a Muslim like Abdul than do the terms "Clark Kent" and "Superman" have the same sense for Clark's girlfriend Lana Lang or for Superman's girlfriend Lois Lane. Nevertheless, "Muslim God" and "Christian God" (along with "Jewish God") have the same reference—the uncaused, perfect, rational, unchanging, self-subsistent, eternal Creator and sustainer of all that which receives its being from another—even though the concept of God embraced by each faith tradition, shaped by what each believes is authentic deliverances of special revelation, differ in some very significant ways. So, just as it is true that Lana and Lois are dating the same man (though each has in her mind a different concept of that same man), it is also true that Mohammad Mostafa Ansari and Francis Beckwith worship the same God (though each in his mind has a different concept of that same God).[47]

Objection 4: It is doubtful that all Christians, Muslims, and Jews accept classical theism. The term "classical theism" is the name of the view of God embraced by orthodox Christianity, Islam, and Judaism,[48] for which I have already offered this shorthand description: God is the uncaused, perfect, rational, unchanging, self-subsistent, eternal Creator and sustainer of all that which receives its being from another. Philosopher Brian Davies writes:

> Classical theism is what you can find endorsed in the writings of people like the Jewish author Moses Maimonides, . . . the Islamic author Avicenna, . . . and the Christian author Thomas Aquinas. . . . Classical theism is what all Jews, Christians, and Muslims believed in for many centuries (officially, at least). And numerous philosophers have taken it for granted that God is as defenders of classical theism take him to be. From the time

of St. Augustine of Hippo (354–430) to that of G. W. Leibniz (1646–1716), philosophers almost always worked on the assumption that belief in God is belief in classical theism. And their understanding has been shared by many theologians. The major tenets of classical theism are part of the official teaching of the Roman Catholic Church. They were also taught by most of the major sixteenth-century Protestant reformers and by heirs of theirs, such as Jonathan Edwards, the famous eighteenth-century American Puritan divine.[49]

But according to Borgadus and Urban, it is probably the case that many Jews, Christians, and Muslims today would not explicitly identify as classical theists (or even know what that means): "One may reasonably wonder whether all members of these religions really are classical theists worshiping the God of the philosophers in the way Avicenna, Maimonides, and Aquinas did, or even a sufficient number to ground the claim that Christians and Muslims worship the same God. Have all or even most or even ten thousand of these folks heard of divine simplicity, for example, let alone understood it, let alone endorsed it? It's a heavy hike from the prayer hall to the lecture hall, and few make it."[50] (Divine simplicity is the view held by classical theists that God has no composition. Since all created things by nature must be composed in some way— whole/parts, substance/accidents, essence/existence—and God is not a creature, God must be simple. This is why for the classical theist, God's attributes, though conceptually separable in our intellects, are not separable in God.)[51]

Bogardus and Urban are no doubt correct in implying that most Christians, Jews, and Muslims—only a tiny percentage of whom are professional theologians or philosophers—have not even heard of the term "classical theism," let alone possess the ability to explain it. But it is not clear why that matters to my thesis, since I am not arguing that all or even most Christians, Muslims, and Jews understand, grasp, or fully realize the implications of the creeds and confessions that give meaning to their theological traditions. Take, for example, my late grandmother, Frances Guido (1913–2002). She was a devout Catholic, who every Sunday at Mass (prior to 1967) would recite these words in Latin: "Credo . . . in unum Dominum Iesum Christum, Filium Dei unigenitum, ex

Patre natum ante omnia saecula. Deum de Deo, Lumen de Lumine, Deum verum de Deo vero, genitum non factum, consubstantialem Patri; per quem omnia facta sunt" ("I believe . . . in one Lord Jesus Christ, only begotten Son of God, born of the Father before all ages, God from God, Light from Light, true God from true God, begotten not made, consubstantial with the Father; through whom all things were made"). Could she have told you the meaning of "consubstantial with the Father" or why "begotten" is not the same as "made"? Unlikely. And yet she said, every Sunday, "credo in," affirming that she believed what those words mean, even though she could not tell you what they mean as the fathers at Nicaea understood them. Whether or not she personally could give you a coherent account of these theological terms of art, let alone the elements of the classical theism presupposed by the AD 381 ecumenical council that issued this creed,[52] is beside the point. What is far more important is that she had what Aquinas called "implicit faith."[53] That is, she was baptized, and later at confirmation she assented to remain in a faith that was committed to classical theism, whether or not she was conspicuously aware of it.

What is true of Catholicism is true of Protestantism as well. How many pew-sitting Evangelicals on Sunday morning can explain the doctrine of the Trinity, the incarnation, or the inspiration of Scripture, let alone provide the historical background, theological arguments, and philosophical categories that resulted in the confessional dogmas that their respective churches officially accept?[54] And yet we do not say that this widespread ignorance on the part of most Evangelical believers means they are not true members of the Body of Christ. Billy Graham (1918–2018), for example, did not require that those who accepted his invitation to receive the Lord at his crusades first undergo a theological examination before saying the sinner's prayer. What happens at conversion is that you are received into an already established tradition, one in which virtually all of the heavy lifting on the nature of God, doctrine, Scripture, and so on has been done for you well in advance.

And what is true of Christianity is also true of Judaism and Islam. What matters is not the theological and philosophical sophistication of its individual members or particular groups of members, but rather, what the religion as an institution teaches.[55] What do its leaders, paradigmatic thinkers, creeds, confessions, holy books, and so on claim about God and his fundamental nature? This is also true of issues outside of religion. Imagine you are an American citizen and thus by default are under the authority of all the laws of the United States—federal, state, and local—but are incapable of giving an account of what the free speech and press clauses of the First Amendment teach or mean. In fact, your ignorance is so severe that you mistakenly believe that if the government were to prohibit hate speech, such a ban would be consistent with the two clauses. Suppose a scholar of American constitutional law from the United Kingdom were to cite your ignorance (as well as the ignorance of many of your fellow citizens) as proof that the United States has no normative understanding of the First Amendment. Your informed compatriots would rightfully think this an odd argument, since it would be overlooking what the nation as an institution actually teaches.[56]

There are, of course, sophisticated self-identified philosophical theists who have been critical of certain aspects of classical theism, including Craig,[57] Alvin Plantinga,[58] and Richard Swinburne.[59] Such thinkers, nevertheless, make their arguments *within* their respective traditions, each of which, as we have seen, is rooted in classical theism. (Although Craig, Plantinga, and Swinburne happen to be Christians, the same analysis can be applied to Muslim or Jewish philosophers who may depart slightly from the classical theism of their inherited traditions.) Sometimes called theistic personalists,[60] they have no problem describing God in language nearly indistinguishable from that employed by classical theists—for example, uncaused, perfect, rational, unchanging, self-subsistent, eternal Creator and sustainer of all that which receives its being from another[61]—albeit with certain controversial caveats that some classical theists believe are fundamentally misguided.[62] Nevertheless, because theistic personalists and classical theists are both trying to provide a coherent account of the same reality—the self-existent ultimate source of all contingent existence[63]—they are referring to the same God, just as Ptolemy and Galileo were referring to the same sun, even though their disagreements about it were indeed profound.

Although I have made a case for why Christians ought to believe that Jews, Muslims, and Christians worship the same God, I am not arguing for a kind of interreligious philosophical ecumenism. For to do so would be to diminish the seriousness of our dogmatic disagreements, to treat them as insignificant to what each faith tradition believes is essential to determining our ultimate destiny. As the Catholic theologian David B. Burrell, C.S.C., puts it, "To understand an apparently philosophical conclusion, then, one does best to try to identify the religious strands of which it is woven. Monotheism, once again, is not a confession but an abstraction. However convenient it may appear, one is ill-advised to assume it describes a common faith."[64] Consequently, although Christians, Jews, and Muslims worship the same God, they do not share the same faith.[65]

Ch. 3
↳ Christians & Muslims worship the same God?
↳ Bogardus objections about classical theism?

4

✦

Aquinas as Theologian
God and Intelligent Design

Now these two—namely, eternal and temporal—are related
to our knowledge in this way, that one of them is the means
of knowing the other. For by way of discovery, we come through
knowledge of temporal things to that of things eternal, according
to the words of the Apostle (Romans 1:20), "The invisible things
of God are clearly seen, being understood by the things that are
made": while by way of judgment, from eternal things already
known, we judge of temporal things, and according to laws of
things eternal we dispose of temporal things.

St. Thomas Aquinas[1]

However our question today is: in the age of science and tech-
nology does speaking of creation still make sense? How should
we understand the narratives in Genesis? The Bible does not
intend to be a natural science manual; rather, it wishes to make
the authentic and profound truth of things understood. The fundamental truth that the accounts of Genesis reveal to us is that
the world is not a collection of forces that clash with each other;
it has its origin and its permanence in the *Logos*, in God's eternal
Reason which continues to sustain the universe.

Pope Benedict XVI[2]

On July 1, 2003, I became associate professor of church-state
studies and associate director of the J. M. Dawson Institute for
Church-State Studies at Baylor University. The Dawson Institute is
named after one Joseph Martin Dawson (1879–1973),[3] legendary
Baylor alumnus and one of the founding members of Protestants

and Others United for the Separation of Church and State (POU), which is known today as Americans United for the Separation of Church and State (AU).

Eight days later, on July 9, I walked into a firestorm, but I had no idea I had done so until it was too late. On that day I testified before the Texas State Board of Education on the matter of the content of science textbooks that deal with the topic of evolution. I was invited by a member of the board to testify because of the academic work I had done on Darwinism and public education[4] that stems from my 2001 law school dissertation.[5] In those works I make the case that the teaching of intelligent design (ID) in public school science classes would not violate the establishment clause of the U.S. Constitution as had its predecessor "creationism" or "creation science."[6]

When I walked into the giant room in which the hearing took place, I was astounded at the size of the crowd and all the media that were present. At that point, I should have known that this was a big deal and that I should probably turn around and drive back home to Waco. But having just moved to Texas eight days earlier, I was blissfully clueless. When it was my turn to address the board, I introduced myself and said the following:

> According to TEKS [Texas Essential Knowledge and Skills], students should be taught how to "analyze, review, and critique scientific explanations, including hypotheses and theories, as to their strengths and weaknesses using scientific evidence and information." I am here to make the modest suggestion that this principle be applied to the contents of textbooks that cover the subjects of biological and chemical evolution, that these textbooks appropriately convey to students some of the critical questions raised about aspects of evolutionary theory in general and neo-Darwinism in particular.[7]

I went on to speak for about another three minutes, extolling the academic credentials and publications of some of these critics of Darwin, explaining why teaching criticisms of Darwinism (including ID) does not violate the establishment clause, and ending by briefly making a distinction between unconstitutional creationism and the views defended by these new and more respectable scholars. I handed the board members a copy of an open letter addressed to them that had been signed by some of these very same scholars along with a number of other Texas professors who agreed with what I was suggesting to the board that afternoon. After my time was up, I then went on my merry way back to our new home in Waco.

Within a couple of weeks I received a letter from Alice Baird, one of the granddaughters of J. M. Dawson, at whose namesake institute I held my academic appointment. She was not only displeased with my testimony, but also troubled by my association with the Discovery Institute, the Seattle-based think tank that housed a center that is at the forefront of funding ID advocacy and research.[8] In 1999 I had accepted an invitation to become a fellow of the institute, because it would allow me to apply for financial assistance on research projects. Eighteen months later Discovery awarded me a modest $9,000 grant to write what would eventually become my law school dissertation. The award covered only about 15 percent of my law school expenses. I never applied for another Discovery grant, and I resigned as a fellow in 2007.

Soon after the Fall 2003 semester began, Alice and twenty-seven other descendants of Dawson wrote an open letter to Baylor's then-president Robert Sloan, requesting that the university remove me as associate director of the Dawson Institute, since my views on church and state—which they thought they had accurately surmised from my legal scholarship on ID—did not adequately reflect Dawson's strict church-state separationism. In a sense, they were right. But they were right not because of my legal views on ID, but because I had learned that Dawson had harbored an anti-Catholic prejudice that he shared with his friend[9] and cofounder of POU, the notorious Paul Blanshard.[10] Even though I was an Evangelical Protestant at the time, I was deeply skeptical of the Dawson-Blanshard understanding of Catholicism, and thus I was suspicious that their church-state philosophy was born more of anti-Catholic animus than principled reflection.[11] On matters of church and state, my views were more in line with the moderate separationism found in Vatican II's *Dignitatis Humanae*[12] and the works of Catholic authors Fr. John Courtney Murray, Robert P. George, and Fr. Richard John Neuhaus[13] and non-Catholic writers Stephen V. Monsma, Daniel Driesbach, Stephen D. Smith, Michael W. McConnell, and Philip Hamburger.[14]

Because the Dawson letter went to scores of media outlets, it
was not long before it became a national story. I would be lying if
I did not say that I was shell-shocked by the negative attention. It's
one thing to have one's views critically assessed by one's peers in an
academic journal; it's quite another to have one's views offered as a
reason to challenge the legitimacy of one's academic appointment.
And yet I am partially to blame for how I was received at Baylor.
I had quickly, and uncritically, become a champion for the legal
permissibility of teaching ID in public schools without having first
carefully thought through ID's *theological* and *philosophical* implications for the classical Christian understanding of creation and
divine action. ID had become, with the 1991 release of *Darwin on
Trial* by University of California, Berkeley, law professor Phillip E.
Johnson[15] and the subsequent publications of academic monographs
by the philosopher and mathematician William A. Dembski and
the biochemist Michael J. Behe,[16] a cause célèbre for many Christian
professors who saw ID as a sophisticated way to combat philosophical naturalism without being saddled with all the anti-intellectual
baggage that comes with creationism.[17] At the time I was enthusiastic to enter the fray. Although I had *some* reservations about ID
as a view, I never wrestled with them. My deeper commitment was
to the project of unseating a particular school of political liberalism from its cultural dominance.[18] That was the focus of most of
my academic writings on the subject.[19] For this reason, the Dawsons
were largely correct in believing that I had hitched my wagon to
the star of the Discovery Institute because it offered me access to an
academic community that could assist me in advancing a philosophical perspective contrary to the church-state position defended
by their ancestor. Although it is a perspective I still hold, whatever
sympathies I had for ID at the time have waned considerably.[20]

The controversy that greeted me when I first arrived at Baylor—
led as it was by the descendants of a vitriolic anti-Catholic—
forced me to rethink both where I belonged in the Christian
world—was I Catholic or Protestant?—as well as what ID means for
someone who calls himself a Thomist. It was around mid-2005 that
I started to think more critically about ID as a view. This was two or
three months before I was invited to participate by the *Legal Times*
in an online debate on the topic of ID and public education with

the esteemed legal scholar Douglas Laycock.[21] Even though in my contributions to that debate my claims about ID were more modest than they had been just two years earlier, I was still conceptualizing the issues in a way that was contrary to the Thomism to which I thought I was committed. Take, for example, this paragraph:

> Intelligent design (or ID) is not one theory. It is a short-hand name for a cluster of arguments that offer a variety of cases that attempt to show that intelligent agency rather than unguided matter better accounts for apparently natural phenomena or the universe as a whole. Some of these arguments challenge aspects of neo-Darwinism. Others make a case for a universe designed at its outset, and thus do not challenge any theory of biological evolution.[22]

This is an accurate summary of what ID arguments are trying to do. But would Thomas Aquinas, or any of his pupils, use such arguments? Would, for example, Aquinas argue that God's intelligent agency "guides matter" in lieu of scientific laws, chance, and so on? That is, would Aquinas think of God's agency as in some sense in competition with scientific theories such as neo-Darwinian evolution and its claim that all life on Earth has a common ancestor and that the biological diversity and complexity in the natural world arose from natural selection working on random mutation? I eventually answered no to each of these questions. What led me to that conclusion were the works of several authors—all serious Christian thinkers,[23] and as far as I can tell, all Thomists—who had remained resolute in not joining other Christian intellectuals in advancing the cause of ID. But they held their views not because they were enthusiastic about aligning themselves with atheists such as Richard Dawkins[24] and Daniel Dennett,[25] who advocate the view that neo-Darwinian evolution is nearly fatal to belief in the Christian God. Rather, they are critical of ID because they believe that the view teaches us the wrong lessons about the relationship between God and creation—lessons that, ironically, concede too much intellectual real estate to Dawkins and Dennett. Among the authors I consulted over several years were Etienne Gilson, William Carroll, Stephen Barr, Edward Feser, Sr. Damien Marie Savino, Ric Machuga, Brad S. Gregory, and Thomas Tkacz.[26] In what follows I explain what went into the reasoning that pushed me away from ID and toward a Thomistic account of creation. But to accomplish that we will first review what exactly ID is, and then we will move on to what Aquinas teaches about God, design, and creation.

I. Intelligent Design

The theoretical underpinning of the contemporary ID movement can be found in a 1984 book, *The Mystery of Life's Origin: Reassessing Current Theories*,[27] authored by scientists Walter Bradley, Charles Thaxton, and Roger L. Olsen. It is in this book that one finds some of the earliest presentations of ideas that are central to the arguments offered by ID advocates today.[28] For example, Bradley and colleagues appeal to the *specified complexity* of certain natural phenomena in order to show that they exhibit characteristics that we typically attribute to artifacts we believe are designed.[29] Years later Dembski would appropriate *specified complexity* in his own work,[30] while Behe would employ a similar idea which he calls *irreducible complexity*.[31] Following Bradley, Thaxton, and Olsen, Dembski and Behe would appeal to the Search for Extraterrestrial Intelligence (SETI) project with this line of argument: SETI provides specified complexity criteria as to what would constitute an intelligible message from non-human rational aliens; thus, it stands to reason that if anything in the natural world exhibits specified complexity, one is warranted in attributing an intelligent cause to that as well.[32] These ideas would also find their way into the work of another ID theorist, philosopher Stephen Meyer.[33]

As I noted in my 2003 book *Law, Darwinism, and Public Education*,[34] the contemporary ID movement is inexplicable without an understanding of the critical reception to Darwinian evolution among large segments of American Protestant Christianity in the early twentieth century.[35] Those citizens saw Darwinism, as Dawkins and Dennett do today, as a defeater to what they understood to be the biblical view of creation described in the book of Genesis. According to this account, God created the universe in six literal days, and on each day following the first he added to his creation what he had brought into being the prior day. On the sixth day, the author of Genesis writes, "God created humankind in his image, in the image of God he created them; male and female he created them" (Gen 1:27). In the next chapter, we are told that "the LORD God formed man from the dust of the ground, and breathed into his nostrils the breath of life; and the man became a living being" (Gen 2:7), and that the man's female helpmate was formed by God out of a rib taken from the man after God had caused him to fall asleep (Gen 2:20-22). Suppose you believe, as many American Fundamentalists and Evangelical Christians do, that this biblical account should be read literally.[36] If you do, you are not too keen on accepting the Darwinian story, that all the diversity and complexity of biological life on planet earth arose from a one-celled common ancestor. For according to that story, all that was necessary for our present biological world to have arisen is natural selection working on random mutation. This allows for the descendants of our common ancestor to adapt, survive, acquire new characteristics, and pass them on to their offspring. This, over the eons of time, produces new species. But in such a story, as the likes of Dawkins and Dennett never tire in pointing out, there is no room for God, or at least the God that many American Fundamentalists and Evangelical Christians believe is depicted in Genesis.

In order to protect and defend this biblical account of creation from the Darwinian critique, these Christians begin developing in the early twentieth century their own "science and faith" subculture, consisting of colleges, institutes, publishing houses, and so on committed to what would come to be called creationism or creation science.[37] Although there is a sense in which anyone who believes that God created the universe is a "creationist," the creationism discussed here is a term of art, referring to a way of looking at the biblical account of creation that is literalist and interventionist. This view comes to dominate the fundamentalist and evangelical worlds to such a great extent that many of their colleges and universities require their faculty to subscribe to it as a condition of employment. Take, for example, the doctrinal statements of some of these institutions. Patrick Henry College in Virginia affirms that "humans and each kind of organism resulted from God's distinct and supernatural creative intervention and did not result from a natural evolutionary process, nor from an evolutionary process that God secretly directed. In particular, God created man in a distinct and supernatural creative act, forming the specific man Adam from non-living material, and the specific woman Eve from Adam."[38] Ohio's Cedarville University states that "we believe that the Scriptures provide a literal and historical account of God's creation of all things. The climax of the six days of creation was the special, immediate, and personal creation of human life. The first humans, Adam and Eve, were directly created, not evolved from previous life forms."[39] Biola University in Southern California teaches that "the existence and nature of the creation is due to the direct miraculous power of God. The origin of the universe, the origin of life, the origin of kinds of living things, and the origin of humans cannot be explained adequately apart from reference to that intelligent exercise of power. A proper understanding of science does not require that all phenomena in nature must be explained solely by reference to physical events, laws and chance."[40] However, any "creation models which seek to harmonize science and the Bible should maintain [that] . . . God providentially directs His creation . . . [and] specially intervened in at least the above-mentioned points in the creation process."[41]

What stands out about these doctrinal statements is how they place divine action seemingly in competition with the deliverances of science, as if our scientific accounts of natural phenomena must in some sense be incomplete in order to make room for God to act. This is why one finds in these statements language that suggests that absent divine intervention what remains is a kind of autonomous creation: in the beginning every living thing was the result of "God's distinct and supernatural creative intervention," "Adam and Eve . . . were directly created . . . [and did not evolve] from previous life forms," "God providentially directs His creation . . . [and] specially intervened," and there are aspects of creation that *can* "be explained solely by reference to physical events, laws and chance."

With this understanding of Scripture and divine action in place, it is not difficult to see why *both* creationists *and* atheists like Dawkins and Dennett maintain that if Darwinian evolution is true, it is unlikely that the Christian God exists. This is why, starting with the 1925 Scopes trial in Tennessee,[42] the teaching of evolution in public schools became such a contested question in certain regions of the United States. For a vast majority of Evangelical and

Fundamentalist Christians, teaching their children that evolution is true (or at least the best theory of the origins of biological life) is tantamount to teaching them atheism.[43] For this reason, in some places, including Tennessee and Arkansas,[44] the teaching of evolution in public schools was prohibited by law. After the U.S. Supreme Court struck down one such law as unconstitutional,[45] the creationists went back to the drawing board and supported so-called balanced treatment laws, statutes that required school districts to teach creationism if evolution is taught and vice versa.[46] Soon after those statutes were struck down by the courts in the 1980s—largely on the grounds that creationism is a religious view and thus teaching it in public schools would constitute an establishment of religion[47]—ID arrived on the scene. Although, as I have argued elsewhere,[48] ID is in many significant ways qualitatively different than creationism, it is similar insofar as its advocates seem to assume creationism's view of divine action and interventionism.

This clearly comes out in the work of Dembski and Behe, ID's two leading theorists. Dembski's project focuses on what he calls the Explanatory Filter (EF), a standard by which he claims one can reasonably infer that an aspect of the natural world (or the natural world as a whole) has an intelligent cause. We, of course, recognize intelligent causes as producing certain artifacts—for example, houses, bridges, stained-glass panels, coherent sentences, computer code. But how do we distinguish those artifacts from those things that do not seem to have resulted from an intelligent cause, as Dembski understands that term—for example, a pile of rocks, dropped Scrabble letters that happen to spell "Bill," a puddle of rain? This is where the EF comes in. According to Dembski, "When called to explain an event, object, or structure, we have a decision to make—are we going to attribute it to *necessity, chance,* or *design*?"[49] Necessity refers to scientific laws. For example, if I let go of a Scrabble letter tile I am holding in my hand, gravity necessitates that it falls to the earth. Now suppose I toss nineteen of these tiles into my backyard and a gust of wind carries them onto my neighbor's lawn. As you would guess, the tiles land in such a way that they exhibit no identifiable pattern. Some of them are face up, others upside down. You can see only twelve of the letters: M N A O A S Y S I C I N. Although necessity is certainly present in this result, since without gravity or the scientific laws governing the wind, the tiles would not have landed in the places they did, from my neighbor's perspective and mine, my undirected tossing of the tiles makes their landing a product of chance, just as the results of a coin toss or a roll of the dice is a product of chance. What about design? Suppose my neighbor finds on his lawn the same nineteen Scrabble tiles, except they are arranged in this way: MY OWNER IS A PHYSICIAN. This, according to Dembski, would be an example of design, because it exhibits what he calls *specified complexity*. You get there, reasons Dembski, by going through each step of the EF. That is, when trying to figure out whether an object, event, or structure is designed, regardless of whether it is artifactual or natural, one must first exclude necessity and chance. How does one do that? Consider the dropping of the Scrabble tile. That is no different than a leaf falling from a tree or an asteroid heading toward Earth. Each of these, like the gravity-governed tile, given certain scientific laws, moves by necessity. It is specified. But in the case of the tossed tiles moved by the wind, things are a bit different. There is complexity to the configuration of tiles that results, since it involves a multitude of objects, each of which is indifferent to the others. (Indifferent means that there is nothing intrinsic to the tiles that inclines them to be part of an intelligible sentence. To create that requires an intelligent agent to choose the right letters and put them in the right order.) So, on Dembski's account, the configuration of the tossed tiles on the lawn is complex, but it is not specified. But in the third scenario, the pattern of letters on the lawn, MY OWNER IS A PHYSICIAN, is both complex and specified. Because this pattern is highly improbable to have arisen by necessity or chance, and because it is *detachable*—by which Dembski means that it is a pattern that we could know apart from encountering the Scrabble sentence on my neighbor's lawn—we conclude that the pattern was produced by an intelligent agent. The configuration of tiles after the random toss is *not* detachable, since it is not a pattern that we could know apart from having first encountered it right after the tiles landed. Think, for example, of the blackjack card counter who is detected by the conscientious pit boss in a Las Vegas casino. The pit boss knows that the player's odds of winning so often are highly improbable, and the pit boss also has in mind a pattern of what "cheating" looks like. The card counter's intelligent intervention in an otherwise random enterprise is the best explanation for his improbable accumulation of casino chips at the blackjack table. Thus, absent the card counter's mischief, whatever sequence of winnings or losses the pit boss observes at the blackjack tables is not detachable.

Dembski takes the reasoning of the EF and applies it to natural non-artifactual objects, events, and structures—for example, DNA and the bacterial flagellum—and argues that one can reasonably conclude that these are designed and thus are as much a product of intelligence as the Scrabble sentence and the card counter's winnings. Dembski writes that "the method applies quite generally: the position of Scrabble pieces on a game board is irreducible to the natural laws governing the motion of Scrabble pieces; the configuration of ink on a sheet of paper is irreducible to the physics and chemistry of paper and ink; the sequencing of DNA bases is irreducible to the bonding affinities between the bases; and so on." [50] In other words, the arrangement of the parts of a DNA molecule can no more be accounted for by chance and scientific laws that govern the matter of which DNA is composed than can the arrangement of the tiles forming a word on a Scrabble board or the shapes and configurations of the ink that make up this sentence be accounted for by appealing to the chance and scientific laws that govern their physical parts. Although Dembski maintains that one can be agnostic about the identity of the designer-cause of DNA (or other systems and entities in nature that exhibit specified complexity),[51] it "is compatible with the creator-God of the world's major monotheistic religions, such as Judaism, Christianity, and Islam," as well as "the watchmaker-God of the deists, the Demiurge of Plato's Timeaus and the divine reason (i.e., *logos spermatikos*) of the ancient Stoics." [52]

Behe's case for ID relies on a concept he calls irreducible complexity, which is similar to Dembski's specified complexity. Behe argues that something is irreducibly complex if it would have no function without all its parts being already in place, and thus if it is an organic thing (or system), it could not have any precursors from which it evolved. But, notes Behe, this would be contrary to the evolutionary story, as Charles Darwin (1809–1882) himself admits: "If it could be demonstrated that any complex organ existed which could not possibly have been formed by numerous, successive, slight modifications, my theory would absolutely break down."[53] Behe's stock example is the standard mousetrap you can purchase in virtually any hardware store. It consists of several parts. Yet if any one of them is missing, the result is not just a poorly functioning mousetrap, but a complete failure. There is no such thing, reasons Behe, as a mousetrap with a missing part that works "half as well as it used to, or even a quarter as well. It does not catch mice at all. It is irreducibly complex."[54]

Behe argues that there are aspects of the biochemical world that seem irreducibly complex, though their structures are far more intricate and complex than a mousetrap. His two favorite examples are the cilium and the bacterial flagellum. Calling them "molecular machines,"[55] they are parts of cells that function like motors in order to perform a variety of tasks. Citing the relevant scientific literature,[56] Behe maintains that the cilium and bacterial flagellum are irreducibly complex like the mousetrap, since in order for either one of them to function, all of its parts must be in place. But in that case, "its gradual production in a step-by-step Darwinian fashion is quite difficult to envision."[57]

Like Dembski, Behe moves from these empirical observations to the conclusion that the best way to account for these "molecular machines" is to postulate that they are products of intelligent design rather than neo-Darwinian evolution.[58] Behe writes that because "design is simply *the purposeful arrangement of parts*,"[59] and we know from our experience that irreducibly complex entities, like mousetraps, require a purposeful arrangement of parts,[60] we can reasonably conclude that certain natural entities, like the cilium and the bacterial flagellum, are intelligently designed as well. But who is the designer? According to Behe, it could be an alien or even God,[61] but the latter is rarely if ever entertained by those in the scientific community. Behe attributes this to a philosophical prejudice, harbored by many scientists, that excludes a priori supernatural causes from the domain of science.[62] Dembski's name for this alleged prejudice is *methodological naturalism*, "the view that science must be restricted solely to undirected natural processes."[63]

It is important to note here that both Dembski and Behe see science's commitment to methodological naturalism as a kind of epistemic exclusionary rule that prevents one from rationally believing in a God who designed the universe. In fact, that is how Johnson describes it: "A methodological naturalist defines science as the search for the best naturalistic theories. A theory would not be naturalistic if it left something out (such as the existence of genetic information or consciousness) to be explained by a supernatural cause." Therefore, "all events in evolution (before the evolution of intelligence) are assumed attributable to unintelligent causes. The question is not *whether* life (genetic information) arose by some combination of chance and chemical laws, to pick one example, but merely *how* it did so."[64] But this assumes, as I have already noted, that natural causes are in competition with divine action, the very assumption made by ID's creationist predecessors. It is an assumption, as we shall see, that the classical Christian theist (in continuity with Aquinas), would not make. For it implies that those aspects of the natural world that do not exhibit specified or irreducible complexity—necessity and chance, to use Dembski's expressions—may not be rationally attributed to the handiwork of God since they have not been confirmed by "design theory." So, ironically, ID's fight to displace methodological naturalism in science is tantamount to forfeiting all the philosophical real estate to the purveyors of scientism, the view that all knowledge claims must pass the bar of science. I cannot imagine why any theist would want to do that.

Before we move on to discuss Aquinas and his view on God and creation, I should note that there is a massive body of literature critical of Behe's and Dembski's arguments,[65] much of which focuses on the technical aspects of the cases they make (though, unfortunately, portions of some of these otherwise important works are peppered with unnecessary rhetorical potshots). I will not address those critiques here, since my purpose in this chapter is not to assess ID arguments as arguments, but rather, to show that the view of divine action and its relation to the created order implied in the ID project is contrary to the view held by classical theism.

II. Aquinas, Creation, and Design

As a Catholic, Aquinas affirmed, as all Christians confess, that God is "maker of heaven and earth, of all things visible and invisible."[66]

He also believed, as all Christians believe, that the universe exhibits an underlying order that our intellects have the capacity to know. Why then do many of us maintain that Aquinas would not be an ID advocate if he were alive today? To answer that question, we have to see what Aquinas believed about the nature of God and his relation to the universe he created. According to Aquinas, God is the first cause of everything that receives its being from another. Take, for example, yourself. You are a being that receives its being from another. You are right now kept in existence as a consequence of a variety of causes, each of which exists as a consequence of other things that cannot exist on their own. To be sure, you were brought into existence by your parents, but you no longer need them to presently exist. For this reason, it is not essential for your existence at this moment that your parents exist right now. But to exist at this moment you do need other things, such as a hospitable environment, your molecular structure, a planet with an intact atmosphere so many miles from the sun, and so forth. But each of these things requires yet other things to keep them in existence. Because the world of finite, dependent things—which is the world in which we live—consists exclusively of composite things, that is, things that have parts, that may or may not have existed, that do not exist essentially, and so forth, they require other things to ensure that they remain in existence and do not fall apart. The wine in the glass next to my keyboard did not pour itself, and neither is it holding itself up. It is held in place by a glass that rests on my desk, that sits on my floor, that is supported by my home's concrete foundation, that is upheld by the Earth, and so on. Because, reasons Aquinas,[67] each of these things is an intermediate (or instrumental) cause, there must be a first cause, a cause that does not receive its being from another. To employ a stock example used by the Angelic Doctor, the stone is moved by the stick which is moved by the hand.[68] The stick is the intermediate cause that moves the rock, if you think of the hand as the first cause. Thus, if there is no first cause, then there is no intermediate cause (the moving stick), and the stone is never moved. Because the hand is essential for the movement of the rock, this is an example of an essentially ordered series of causes. (This is in contrast to the causal relationship between you and your parents, which Aquinas calls an accidental series, since your parents' existence is not essential to your existence right here and now).[69] Of course, the stick example is merely an illustration, since in reality the hand is itself an intermediate cause for the person to which it belongs, and even that person is the effect of a variety of causes that keep her in existence. But those causes in turn are also intermediate, since they receive their being from another as well, and so on. Because, argues Aquinas, there cannot be an infinite regress of intermediate causes, there must be a first cause, and that cause is God.

Consider this illustration. My colleague, the philosopher John Haldane, tells the story of a new faculty-reviewing system that had been instituted while he was a professor at the University of St. Andrews in Scotland. It included these instructions: "The reviews of colleagues who have not been reviewed previously but are to act as reviewers will also have to be arranged . . . so that all reviewers can be reviewed before they review others."[70] So, imagine a philosophy department with ten faculty members sitting around an oval table, none of whom has been reviewed. Because no one can qualify as a reviewed reviewer, no one reviews or gets reviewed. The policy cannot in principle be instituted, since there has to be at least one unreviewed reviewer to get the ball rolling. On the other hand, imagine all ten faculty members claim that they qualify as reviewers, thus implying (under the policy) that each is a reviewed reviewer. But, as we have seen, that is impossible, since without an unreviewed reviewer, no one gets reviewed. In that case, if each faculty member does in fact have the authority to be a reviewer, you know immediately that one of them *must be* an unreviewed reviewer (in violation of the policy). As Haldane notes, the university, realizing the impossible situation it had placed its faculty, eventually designated someone as an unreviewed reviewer. In the same way, argues Aquinas, any being that must derive its causal power from another (i.e., any faculty member that is not an unreviewed reviewer) requires a first cause (i.e., an unreviewed reviewer). Not every cause can be intermediate, just as not every faculty member can be a reviewer that must derive her reviewing power from another. And it does not matter whether the number of intermediate causes (or faculty members) is finite or infinite, just as it does not matter if the universe has always existed. If the causal power of a cause is derived, then there must be a first cause. As Caleb Cohoe explains, "If there were only intermediate and derivative causes, then there would be no source from which the causal powers of the intermediate causes could be derived, regardless of whether there were a finite or an infinite number of intermediate causes."[71]

So, for Aquinas (and the classical theism he is defending), God is the first cause not merely in a chronological sense—like your parents are your "first cause"—but also, and more importantly, God is the first cause right here and now, keeping the entire universe, and all the intermediate causes in existence. As St. Paul told his audience on Mars Hill, God "is not far from each one of us. For 'In him we live and move and have our being'; as even some of your own poets have said, 'For we too are his offspring'" (Acts 17:27-28). Because Aquinas did not believe that one could prove philosophically that the universe began to exist, that it had a temporal beginning—as defenders of the kalām cosmological argument believe[72]—he argued for a first cause of the universe *even if the universe had always existed*,[73] though he did believe in a finite past based on the testimony of Scripture.[74] (To employ a distinction we covered in chapter 2, for Aquinas, belief in a temporal beginning of the universe is an article of faith, while knowledge of a first cause is a preamble of faith.) So when Aquinas writes of God as first cause, he is referring to God as the primary or fundamental cause of the universe, not the first cause in a chronological series of accidental causes, as in the case of Adam begetting Cain, and Cain begetting his children, and so on.

According to Aquinas, once we recognize God as first cause, there are many things that follow from it. For one thing, God is unlike any being in the causal nexus of the created order. He is the Being from which all created beings derive their existence and are kept in existence. He is not the being with maximal greatness who exists in every possible world, as Alvin Plantinga puts it,[75] and neither is he the ultimate brute fact and comprehensive hypothesis that best explains everything else in the universe, as Richard Swinburne affirms.[76] If either were the case, it would make God a being among beings, albeit the greatest one. But that is not the God of Aquinas and classical theism. In that tradition—the one universally embraced in the creeds and confessions of the Christian, Jewish, and Muslim faiths and by virtually all of its leading thinkers up until recently—*God is Being itself*, that which requires nothing for his existence but imparts existence to all that which receives its being from another. God does not *have maximal greatness in* every possible world, and neither is he the ultimate explanatory brute fact. He is the eternal, unchanging, and simple source of any world that is actualized as well as what constitutes greatness in that world,[77] and he is not *a* fact, brute or otherwise, but the underived subsistent being in which all facts must participate in order to exist.

This means that all causality within the universe and between the beings in it is under the providence of God.[78] But given God's omnipotence, he has the power to create a universe that consists of a wide variety of beings with their own natures, both animate and inanimate, that are able to function as real causes that bring about real effects. That is, as first cause, God can bring into existence a universe of real secondary causes without compromising his own providential control over the end to which the universe is ordered.[79] Consequently, on classical theism, when natural selection works on random mutation that results in a change within a species or an entirely new species, those are real secondary causes that are nevertheless under the providence of God. As Aquinas notes, "The same effect is not attributed to a natural cause and to divine power in such a way that it is partly done by God, and partly by the natural agent; rather, it is wholly done by both, according to a different way, just as the same effect is wholly attributed to the instrument and also wholly to the principal agent."[80] For this reason, according to Aquinas' account, it would be wrong to think of the secondary causes as either illusory or in competition with God's primary causality. To affirm the former would be to fall into some form of occasionalism,[81] but to assert the latter would be to fall into popular deism.[82] Because the causality of God requires that he be always present as first cause in every corner and crevice of his creation,[83] the idea that there are large swaths of nature from which his handiwork is absent—such as the parts that do not seem to exhibit specified or irreducible complexity—is to acquiesce to a view of the natural world intrinsically hostile to belief in the God of classical theism. As Brad S. Gregory notes.

> Advocates of intelligent design posit that ordinary biological processes of natural selection and genetic mutation can account

for much but not everything in the evolution of species, the remainder requiring recourse to God's intervention. Insofar as proponents of intelligent design posit normally autonomous natural processes usually devoid of God's influence, they share important assumptions with the New Atheists [like Dennett and Dawkins] . . .

The intelligent design proponents scramble to find remaining places for supernatural intervention; the New Atheists claim there are none left. Both assume that God, conceived in spatial and quasi-spatial terms, needs "room" to be God—which is precisely what traditional Christian theology says God does not need.[84]

Perhaps this is the reason why most ID advocates hesitate to explicitly claim that God is the intelligent designer, though it's not clear how this helps their cause against methodological naturalism's alleged reinforcement of undermining belief in God. For by suggesting that irreducible and specified complexity in nature may be attributed to God or aliens is to imply that God is not a first cause as classical theists hold, but rather, more like another causal agent in the universe.[85]

Thus, ironically, ID supporters such as Dembkxi and Behe, and advocates of naturalism such as Dawkins and Dennett, seemingly agree that absent "gaps" in nature, one is not justified in believing that there is design in nature. The design theorists think they can seal those gaps by appealing to intelligent agency (whether it be God or aliens); the naturalists see no reason to abandon fruitful theories because of a few anomalies for which they think they can someday account. Dembski, despite protestations to the contrary, accepts this narrative, but is confident that the naturalists will not be able to "explain" everything.

The "gaps" in the god-of-the-gaps objection are meant to denote gaps of ignorance about underlying physical mechanisms. But there is no reason to think that all gaps give way to ordinary physical explanations once we know enough about the underlying physical mechanisms. The mechanisms simply do not exist. Some gaps might constitute ontic discontinuities in the chain of physical causes and thus remain forever beyond the capacity of physical mechanisms.[86]

Nevertheless, as Aquinas notes, God does not always work through secondary causes, as when He acts directly in the cases of creation itself,[87] "justification of the unrighteous,"[88] some miraculous events,[89] and the creation of each and every human soul.[90] But these cannot be, under Thomism, examples of God "intervening" in an otherwise autonomous created order, as when ID advocates point to irreducible or specified complexity as evidence of intelligent intervention in an otherwise unintelligent natural world. For God, on classical theism, is present throughout all of creation as the first cause of all the secondary causes as well. This is why it is a mistake for my friends Rob Koons and Logan Gage to suggest that ID can be Thomistic in the sense that the detection of irreducible or specified complexity in nature is akin to detecting some "miracles" or other cases of God's primary causality.[91] For if ID's purpose is to "unseat naturalism"[92] or "to defeat scientific materialism,"[93] as its leading advocates assert, does not Koons and Gage's claim imply that absent the detection of irreducible or specified complexity or other apparent "designed" anomalies in the created order, naturalism wins? If the answer is yes, then ID advances a mistaken view of divine action, for it implies that God acts only in those places in nature where law and chance presently appear to be impotent. If the answer is no, then ID advocates should cease claiming that "design theory" is our best and perhaps only hope against the hegemony of unbelief in the culture and the academy,[94] or as Dembski once put it, "Naturalism is the disease. Intelligent design is the cure."[95] This is why, from the perspective of classical theism (and Thomism), the problems with ID have less to do with whether particular arguments offered by Behe, Dembski, and Meyer "work," but whether in fact ID teaches us the right lessons about divine action.

Here is what I mean. The late Lynn Margulis (1938–2011) championed endosymbiotic theory,[96] a non-Darwinian evolutionary account that may explain irreducible complexity in biological organisms without requiring a design inference (as understood by Behe and Dembski). Paleontologist Simon Conway Morris[97] has argued that apparently irreducibly complex organisms are perfectly "natural" because the development of nature requires a goal-directness, a teleology if you will (though the biological sciences as sciences do not require final causes for theory making).[98] If, as some believe, either Margulis or Morris offers an account that can adequately answer the concerns of Dembski and Behe while at the same time not undercutting evolution, are we now supposed to believe that because there is now no room in nature for a "design inference," then it is no longer rational to believe that God exists or that the universe exhibits his creative power? As I noted in my book, *Taking Rites Seriously*, if you combine the exaggerated claims of ID theorists about their modest publishing accomplishments and their self-proclaimed role in the restoration of Western civilization[99] "with the ubiquitous propagation of ID within Evangelical Protestantism and its churches, seminaries, and parachurch groups (and even among some Catholics) as a new and improved way to topple the materialist critics of Christianity, . . . you have a recipe for widespread disappointment (and perhaps disillusionment with Christianity) if the ID ship takes on too much water in the sea of philosophical and scientific criticism."[100] This is why teaching the right lessons about divine action is far more important to the integrity of the Christian intellectual life than is winning an argument about a tiny sliver of nature that happens to stump Darwinians at this moment in the history of science.

Aquinas, of course, believed that God's creation is designed, but not in the way in which ID advocates conceive of design. For Aquinas, there is an underlying order to the universe, since everything in it is the result of four causes: material, efficient, formal, and final. Imagine, for example, a marble statue of King David. Its material cause is the marble; its efficient cause is the sculptor who carved the marble; its formal cause is the image of King David that the marble takes on after the sculptor has done his work; and the final cause is the purpose for which the statue was made, to honor a great figure of the Christian Old Testament. According to Aquinas, every substance in the universe is a result of these four causes, not just artifactual entities like statues of King David. Consider now a cockroach. Its material cause is the organic matter of which it is made; its efficient cause is its parents; its formal cause is its nature that organizes the matter in a way that distinguishes it from other creatures like spiders and dolphins; and its final cause is to actualize the perfection of its nature, to be a mature, healthy, cockroach that does what cockroaches do. Although when we hear the word "cause" today, we usually think of material and efficient causes—largely because contemporary science focuses almost exclusively on them—Aquinas believed that one cannot make sense of material and efficient causality without formal and final causality. This is because for Aquinas, as Edward Feser notes, "efficient causality is just the actualization of a potency. But a potency is always for some specific outcome or range of outcomes, and in that sense entails finality or directedness."[101] That is, a thing's potency—what it can do or have done to it—depends on the sort of thing that it is, its form. Suppose you come home one day and find your home flooded. You discover that it was caused by a broken water main located at a higher elevation up the street. You also find out that the water main break itself was caused by corrosion of the pipes. Corrosion, given its nature (or form), has the potency to damage pipes, which have the potency to be damaged by corrosion. For this reason, one can say that corrosion, the efficient cause of the broken water main, has a finality (or directedness) to damage pipes. And, of course, given the nature (or form) of water, we know that it has the potency to run downhill. So, the efficient cause of your house's flooding—the water—depends on water's inherent directedness that may be actualized by certain geological objects, such as inclines, hills, or mountains. Whether an efficient cause is a sculptor, cockroach parents, corrosion, water, or anything else for that matter, it is able to bring about a certain effect or effects because of the sort of thing that it is (its form) and the finality to which it is ordered.

So, for Aquinas, the design we observe in the natural world is intrinsic to nature, arising in our minds as a consequence of our intellectual power to know the four causes of a thing. For Aquinas, design is not a scientific hypothesis for which we seek confirmation (e.g., specified or irreducible complexity), but rather, a metaphysical truth about the natural world that is practically undeniable. To be sure, what is intrinsic to nature, including a thing's final causality, ultimately depends on God for its being and continued existence. But this is an inference from the nature of material substances as material substances, and not an appeal to apparently inexplicable gaps in nature about which necessity and chance cannot account.

This is precisely how Aquinas argues from final causality to the existence of God in the fifth of his famous five ways.[102]

> The fifth way is taken from the governance of the world. We see that things which lack intelligence, such as natural bodies, act for an end, and this is evident from their acting always, or nearly always, in the same way, so as to obtain the best result. Hence it is plain that not fortuitously, but designedly, do they achieve their end. Now whatever lacks intelligence cannot move towards an end, unless it be directed by some being endowed with knowledge and intelligence; as the arrow is shot to its mark by the archer. Therefore some intelligent being exists by whom all natural things are directed to their end; and this being we call God.[103]

To repeat, Aquinas is not appealing to specified or irreducible complexity in order to detect design in nature. Rather, he is appealing to the very order of nature itself, a condition that must be present once something exists. Consider the claim made by some thinkers that the truth of neo-Darwinian evolution is a defeater to the belief that the order of nature requires a mind to account for it. Dawkins, for example, writes that evolution "is close to being terminally fatal to the God Hypothesis."[104] But under a Thomist philosophy of nature, it is not at all clear how that follows. After all, for natural selection to work on random mutation, living beings must be ordered toward self-preservation and efficient reproduction. That is, without final causality, it's difficult to see how any scientific account of the origin of species, neo-Darwinian or otherwise, can even get off the ground. Any sort of randomness or chance presupposes an underlying order, since it involves material entities, things that have natures and thus have final causes, just as the result of a dice roll requires two cubed material objects of a certain nature. This is why you cannot correctly calculate the chances of rolling snake eyes without the existence of an underlying order. So, as long as there are material things there will be final causes, and thus the major premise of Aquinas' fifth way stands, with the truth or falsity of neo-Darwinian evolution being entirely beside the point.

Final causality is so inescapable that even those who deny it cannot help but rely on it. Take, for example, Dawkins' comments about Kurt Wise, a Harvard-trained paleontologist who did his undergraduate degree in geology at the University of Chicago. Wise grew up in a Fundamentalist Christian home where he was taught that because the Bible's creation account should be read literally, the earth is less than 10,000 years old. When Wise realized that he could not become a professor at a major research university without abandoning this way of reading Scripture, he made a very painful choice and "accepted the Word of God and rejected all that would ever counter it, including evolution." As Wise notes, in a passage quoted by Dawkins, "with that, in great sorrow, I tossed into the fire all my dreams and hopes in science."[105] In assessing Wise's decision, Dawkins writes the following:

> As a scientist, I am hostile to fundamentalist religion because it actively debauches the scientific enterprise. It teaches us not to change our minds, and not to want to know exciting things that are available to be known. It subverts science and saps the intellect. The saddest example I know is that of the American geologist Kurt Wise. . . . The wound, to his career and his life's happiness, was self-inflicted, so unnecessary, so easy to escape. All he had to do was toss out the bible. Or interpret it symbolically, or allegorically, as the theologians do. Instead, he did the fundamentalist thing and tossed out science, evidence and reason, along with all his dreams and hopes.[106]

There is no doubt that Dawkins has a point, one with which many theists, including Christian theists, would agree. But his point depends on final causality, an idea that Dawkins seems to confuse with the type of artifactual design implied in William Paley's (1743–1805) famous "watchmaker" argument for God's existence.[107] In that argument,[108] Paley likens the design of natural objects to a watch that one comes upon in an open field. Although the watch's design is a type of final causality—a purpose imposed on an arrangement of bits of matter by an external mind (the watchmaker)—it is *extrinsic* to the matter. There is nothing intrinsic about metal that is ordered toward the formation of watches (though metal does have the potency to be used in the construction of watches if the right things are done to it). According to Dawkins, Darwin's theory showed that the design of biological species did not require the intervention of a "watchmaker," for natural selection working on random mutation was quite enough, and as a consequence Paley's design story lost its explanatory power.[109] But, as we have seen, final causality—for Aquinas and his followers—is not merely artifactual purpose. It is intrinsic to all material objects per se, including the metal used by the watchmaker to make the watch. (Unless metal has a certain potency—one not shared by cookie dough, water, or viruses, for example—it cannot be an adequate resource for making watches.) And this is precisely why Dawkins' assessment of the Kurt Wise case requires final causality. For when Dawkins laments Wise's career path, he seems to be saying that the human intellect has a certain potency, a final cause, that is ordered toward the acquisition of truth, and that anything that interferes with the intellect's finality, such as fundamentalist religion, ought to be avoided, for whatever the intellect really knows must conform to reality. Aquinas agrees: "Truth resides, in its primary aspect, in the intellect. Now since everything is true according as it has the form proper to its nature, the intellect, in so far as it is knowing, must be true, so far as it has the likeness of the thing known, this being its form, as knowing. For this reason truth is defined by the conformity of intellect and thing; and hence to know this conformity is to know truth."[110] And when Dawkins says that Wise made a choice that was contrary to his own happiness, Dawkins seems to be saying that the final cause of the human person as a whole is happiness, and that one has an obligation to act in ways that lead one to acquiring it. On this, Dawkins will get no argument from Aquinas, who affirms that "man's last end is happiness; which all men desire, as Augustine says (De Trin. Xiii, 3,4)."[111] Although Aquinas believed that God, the Sovereign Good, "is the object and cause of Happiness,"[112] one need not believe in God to recognize, as Dawkins does, that human beings by nature are ordered toward happiness. Aquinas, of course, maintained that nothing short of God could suffice for Perfect Happiness, since everything that gives us imperfect happiness—pleasure, bodily goods, wealth, honor, intellectual accomplishments—is fleeting and temporary.[113] Nevertheless, the point here is that Dawkins, despite his best efforts, cannot rid himself of the common sense reflexes that require the reality of final causality.

III. What about Exemplar Causality and
the Creation of New Forms?

Because ID, at least among a certain segment of Christian scholars, is hotly contested, it oftentimes results in friends finding themselves in opposing camps. For this reason, I take no pleasure in disagreeing with philosophers and theologians such as Koons, Gage, J. P. Moreland, Jay Wesley Richards, and C. John Collins.[114] Nevertheless, I owe it to my friends to respond to some of the criticisms that a few of them have leveled against the Thomistic view I am defending in this chapter. Because I have already briefly responded to one of Koons and Gage's criticisms, and because not all of them are germane to the case I am making here (or at least I do not think they are), I will conclude this chapter by responding to a second criticism offered by Koons and Gage.[115]

According to Aquinas, "God is the first exemplar cause of all things,"[116] meaning that because God is the ultimate source of all the form/matter composites that make up the universe, all the exemplars of those forms—for example, the ideas of humanness, frogness, or photonness—are in the mind of God. So, in a sense, all things in creation "attain to likeness to [God], ... forasmuch as they represent the divine idea, as a material house is like to the house in the architect's mind."[117] Koons and Gage argue that Thomist critics of ID emphasize immanent teleology (or intrinsic finality) to such a degree that they sometimes neglect the role that exemplar causality plays as an extrinsic cause in Aquinas's understanding of creation. For in the Darwinian scheme, the arising of a new species from a predecessor species—such as *Homo sapiens* evolving from *Homo heidelbergensis*[118]—would mean that nature would have to generate a new form, but according to Koons and Gage that is not possible under Aquinas' view.[119] For only like things can generate like things—only dogs can generate dogs, only frogs can generate frogs, and so forth—but only God can create a new form because he is the exemplar cause of all forms. (As I note elsewhere in this chapter, human beings cannot generate human forms [or souls], for those forms must be directly created by God.) As Koons and Gage claim, "Creatures do possess the causal powers proper to the nature God granted them, but creatures most certainly do not possess the power

to create the form of their (or any other) species."[120] The implication is that without God intervening in the evolution of species by
directly creating a new form at the proper time, nature by itself is
inadequate to the task: "Only God has the power to create novel
form. He is truly the creator 'of all things visible and invisible.'"[121]

Koons and Gage are correct that Thomist critics of ID should be
careful not to overemphasize immanent teleology to the neglect of
God's role as exemplar cause. But it is not clear how one can move
from making that metaphysical clarification to showing that ID is
consistent with Aquinas' thought. After all, as I have already noted,
for Aquinas, nature is never *by itself*.[122] For even events that seem
to us to be chance occurrences are under the direction of divine
providence,[123] since God wills the entirety of his creation and the
events within it—including the free actions of rational creatures,
the random, and the law-like[124]—in a single thought from all eternity,[125] and he keeps in existence all things in his creation at every
moment they exist.[126] Of course, among the events he wills from all
eternity are ones in which he does not employ secondary causes,
as in the cases of creation itself, "justification of the unrighteous,"
some miraculous events, and the creation of each and every human
soul. One could, I suppose, include in this list the direct creation of
new forms at the moment a new species arises in evolution when
matter is constituted in such a way that it may receive a new form.
But it is not clear how this supports ID theory, since under Thomism
God's direct creation of the human soul, when matter is ready to
receive it, appears indistinguishable from what occurs when a non-
human animal generates its offspring. So, if in the case of God's creation of the human soul it cannot be accounted for by the empirical
sciences by something like "design theory" (since it is a belief based
on a metaphysical argument, not a scientific one),[127] it stands to reason that God's creation of new forms in the process of evolution (if
in fact that's the way he does it) is outside the scope of the empirical
sciences as well.

Nevertheless, Aquinas does in fact believe that animal generation
can result in a new species with a new form. He writes that "animals
of new kinds arise occasionally from the connection of individuals
belonging to different species, as the mule is the offspring of an ass and
a mare; but even these existed previously in their causes, in the works

of the six days."[128] What Aquinas is saying here is that when a new spe-cies is generated by beings that are not of the same species as the new one, the form of the new species existed virtually (or eminently) in its progenitors. What a mule is—its form or nature—is not literally in either the ass or the mare, just as the cake's form or nature is not lit-erally in the flour, milk, sugar, or eggs. Nevertheless, the ingredients have the potency, when combined in the right way, for a baker to bring a cake into being, just as the germ cells of the ass and the mare have the potency, when combined in the right way, to bring a mule into being. But the form "mule" is no less created by God than are the forms "ass" or "mare," since, as Aquinas remarks, "though a natural thing produces its proper effect, it is not superfluous for God to produce it, since the natural thing does not produce it except by divine power,"[129] and though "the rational soul can be made only by creation; . . . [it] is not true of other forms."[130]

Intelligent design theorists want to defend the rationality of belief in God against the incursions of scientism in our academic culture. For this reason, at least from the perspective of this theist, their hearts are in the right place. However, the way in which they conceive of God's creative power and action concedes far too much to the scientism they want to defeat. It is my hope that they recon-sider their project in light of the insights of Aquinas and the classical theistic tradition that he represents.

5

Aquinas as Evangelical
Justification in Catholic Teaching

Amazing grace! How sweet the sound
That saved a wretch like me!
I once was lost, but now am found;
Was blind, but now I see.

'Twas grace that taught my heart to fear,
And grace my fears relieved;
How precious did that grace appear
The hour I first believed.

John Newton, "Amazing Grace" (1779)

In his 1946 book *Remaking the Modern Mind*, the late theologian Carl F. H. Henry (1913–2003), captures the near unanimous judgment about the thought of St. Thomas Aquinas by Henry's Evangelical contemporaries: "The acceptance of Thomism at the University of Paris in 1275 marks the real break from historic Christianity in the medieval Church."[1] Others voicing negative judgments about the Angelic Doctor and his intellectual legacy include a veritable who's who in Evangelical theology and philosophy including Edward John Carnell (1919–1967),[2] Cornelius Van Til (1895–1987),[3] Francis Schaeffer (1912–1984),[4] Bruce Demarest,[5] and Colin Brown.[6]

Times, however, have changed. Over the past several decades, as I already noted in chapter 1, a growing number of Evangelical philosophers and theologians have described their views, on a variety of issues and arguments, as *Thomistic*.[7] That is, they claim to be, on certain questions, followers of Aquinas. Although many of these thinkers often claim to be Thomistic almost exclusively on questions in philosophical theology, metaphysics, philosophical anthropology, and apologetics, a few of them have gone so far as to claim that Aquinas' views on justification are either (1) consistent with, or not obviously opposed to, a Protestant perspective, or (2) inconsistent with the doctrine of justification expounded by the Catholic Church at the Council of Trent and in the 1994 *Catechism of the Catholic Church*. Among the thinkers who embrace this understanding of Aquinas are Norman L. Geisler, R. C. Sproul (1939–2017), and John Gerstner (1914–1996). I will call these thinkers Proto-Protestant Thomists. In this chapter, I argue that their reading of Aquinas is mistaken and that in fact Aquinas' soteriology is nearly indistinguishable from both the Council of Trent's and the *Catechism*'s accounts of the doctrine of justification.

After concluding that analysis, we will move on to a further clarification of Aquinas' view of justification by taking a critical look at Jerry Walls' defense of purgatory. Walls, an Evangelical philosopher who has coauthored a book critical of Catholicism,[8] is, believe it or not, a defender of the doctrine of purgatory, though he rejects what he takes to be Aquinas' view. I argue that Walls, like Geisler, Sproul, and Gerstner, misreads Aquinas.

Although this chapter touches on some of the central issues over which the sixteenth-century fragmentation of Latin Christianity was initiated, I have no intention of refighting the Reformation in these pages. My purpose, I am happy to report, is embarrassingly modest. It is to offer a correction of certain ways of reading Aquinas—though no doubt born of a deep respect and appreciation of the Angelic Doctor—that cannot be reconciled with what Aquinas actually believed.[9]

In my own journey back to Catholicism, there were four doctrinal issues with which I had great difficulties: apostolic succession, the sacrament of penance, Eucharistic realism, and justification.[10] I could not in good conscience return to the Church without first being convinced that the Catholic perspectives on these doctrines were at least plausible accounts of them. When it came to changing my mind on justification, it was my reading of the Evangelical Thomists and their account of Aquinas, combined with an eye toward Aquinas' predecessors and successors in the Church, that helped me to see that the Catholic view was actually Aquinas' view, and that Aquinas' view was the view of St. Augustine of Hippo (ca. 354–430), the Council of Orange (529), and the Council of Trent (1545–1563). The Evangelical Thomists tell a different tale, one that I argue is mistaken.

I. The Proto-Protestant Thomas

The champions of Proto-Protestant Thomism make their case by both citing Aquinas' writings as well as arguing that there is a historical continuity between Aquinas' view of justification and those of his predecessors, like St. Augustine, and his successors in the Reformation.

In part 1 of his 1995 book *Roman Catholics and Evangelicals: Agreements and Differences*, Geisler and his coauthor Ralph McKenzie review in several chapters those areas on which Catholics and Evangelicals agree. One of the issues is "salvation." Quoting extensively from Aquinas, Geisler concludes that Aquinas "clearly believed that salvation is completely dependent on God's grace." Qualifying his comments by saying that Aquinas' work is "not infallibly normative for Catholics," Geisler explains that what the Angelic Doctor means is that our salvation "is by grace alone (*sola gratia*) in the sense that every human action connected with salvation is not only prompted by but is produced by God's grace. Grace is operative, not merely cooperative, in effecting our salvation." [11] Geisler concedes that Aquinas, unlike the Protestant Reformers, did not write of forensic justification in his account of salvation. And thus Aquinas did not distinguish between forensic justification and progressive sanctification as did the Reformers. Nevertheless, writes Geisler, "this does not mean that the Reformers' distinction is incompatible with Aquinas' view, but simply that Aquinas did not state it that way." [12] Although, as Geisler points out in a footnote, Aquinas' embracing of "the doctrine of merit and the necessity of good works" means that "he would fall short of the Protestant understanding of salvation by faith alone," nevertheless, "some Evangelicals have embraced Aquinas as 'Protestant'" because "these good works come in the overall context of God's operative grace." [13] Gerstner goes so far as to claim that "with Augustine" Aquinas "taught the biblical doctrine of justification so that if the Roman

Church had followed Aquinas, the Reformation would not have been absolutely necessary." [14]

In volume 3 of his *Systematic Theology*, Geisler argues that there is a pre-Reformation historical basis for the Protestant belief that "works are not a *condition* of salvation." [15] This claim is echoed by both Sproul and Gerstner. [16] As the Proto-Protestant Thomists see it, what the Protestant Reformers were attempting to do was to help return the Church to the proper view of justification that Western Christianity had largely abandoned by the time of the late Middle Ages. Thus, the burden for the Proto-Protestant Thomists is to show that there is a historical continuity between Scripture, the early church fathers, medieval writers like Aquinas, and the Protestant Reformers on the matter of faith, works, and justification. [17] In making his case, Geisler contrasts this apparent Christian consensus with the view he claims is presently held by Roman Catholics, who "argue that performing good works is a *condition* for salvation rather than a *consequence* of it," [18] the latter of which he attributes to both the sixteenth-century Council of Trent [19] as well as the present teaching of the Catholic Church. [20] Sproul mentions both Trent and the 1994 *Catechism* as unequivocal evidence [21] that the "Roman Catholic Church . . . [has] denied the gospel and ceased to be a legitimate church." [22] But Aquinas, according to Sproul, stands in the tradition of those who now stand on the outer shore of the Tiber, those who embraced the biblical doctrine that "regeneration precedes faith." [23] And the reason for this, writes Sproul, is that "Aquinas insisted that regenerating grace is operative grace, not cooperative grace. Aquinas spoke of prevenient grace, but he spoke of a grace that comes before faith, which is regeneration." [24]

Gerstner, offering greater detail, makes a similar claim when he argues that "Aquinas taught a doctrine of *iustifactio impii*, a justification of the impious," which Gerstner says "means that a sinner is justified while yet in himself he is a sinner," echoing Luther's proclamation that "redeemed man is *simul justis et peccatore*, at the same time just and sinner." Not surprisingly, Gerstner maintains that "justified" for Aquinas means "'reckoned just' based on union with Christ" and not "made just." But, writes Gerstner, like the Protestant Reformers, Aquinas believed that once the "the justified impious" are justified they "begin the process of being 'made just,' or sanctification," and thus "it necessarily follows" that "our being reckoned just is fully and finally settled by Christ." Consequently, proclaims Gerstner, Aquinas' justification of the impious, "is essentially the biblical (and Reformation) doctrine." Although Gerstner admits that Aquinas did not employ the language of "the 'imputation' of Christ's righteousness," Gerstner nevertheless claims that it "is implied by the infusion of sanctifying grace which would never be infused into an unjustified soul."[25]

Although the Proto-Protestant Thomists disagree with each other on how close Aquinas came to a Reformation view of justification,[26] it seems fair to say that for all of them, Aquinas held a view of justification that was within the boundaries of legitimate Christian opinion as they understand it. That is, Aquinas may have gotten some things wrong about justification, but because he did not embrace the semi-Pelagianism that many Protestant writers claim would be taught by Trent and the *Catechism*, Protestants can rightfully claim Aquinas as an ancestor that contributed to the Reformers' theological patrimony.

Although an entire generation of Evangelical Thomists, influenced by Geisler, Sproul, and Gerstner, has largely accepted this narrative, it is spectacularly false. To explain why, I cover two topics: (1) Aquinas and his Catholic predecessors, and (2) Aquinas and his Catholic successors: Trent and the *Catechism*.

II. Aquinas and His Catholic Predecessors

There is little doubt that Aquinas' writings on justification were consistent with those held by his theological and ecclesiastical predecessors, especially St. Augustine.[27] In that sense, the Proto-Protestant Thomists are correct.[28] But, unfortunately, they often quote from these sources selectively, taking them out of the context of the ecclesiastical and liturgical infrastructures in which these writings were penned. In order to appreciate this problem, consider Geisler's use of the early church fathers to defend the idea that the Protestant Reformers were merely recovering what had been lost. The following are four patristic quotations that initially seem "Protestant" and thus can be read as if they support Geisler's case for Proto-Protestant patristics.[29]

St. Irenaeus of Lyons (ca. 140–ca. 202)

Vain, too, is [the effort of] Marcion and his followers when they [seek to] exclude Abraham from the inheritance, to whom the Spirit through many men, and now by Paul, bears witness, that "*he believed God, and it was imputed unto him for righteousness.*"[30]

St. Cyril of Jerusalem (ca. 318–386)

For as a writing-reed or a dart has need of one to use it, so grace also has need of believing minds . . . It is God's to grant grace, but thine to receive and guard it.[31]

St. John Chrysostom (ca. 347–407)

In order then that the greatness of the benefits bestowed may not raise you too high, observe how he brings you down: "*by grace you have been saved,*" says he, "*Through faith;*" Then, that, on the other hand, our free-will be not impaired, he adds also our part in the work, and yet again cancels it, and adds, "*And that not of ourselves.*"

For this is [the righteousness] of God when we are justified not by works (in which case it were necessary that not a spot even should be found), but by grace, in which case all sin is done away.[32]

St. Augustine of Hippo (ca. 354–430)

[Grace] is bestowed on us, not because we have done good works, but that we may be able to do them—in other words, not because we have fulfilled the law, but in order that we may be able to fulfill the law.[33]

If all one had were these quotes, one may be persuaded to accept Geisler's thesis, that the Reformation attempted to restore what the Church had once embraced, or at least implicitly held, from its earliest days through the Middle Ages and affirmed by Aquinas. One would, of course, be partly right, since, as some Catholic writers have noted, the Protestant Reformers did in fact attempt to retrieve something of that Catholic tradition that had been obscured by the abuses of late medieval Catholicism.[34] But the difficulty for Geisler is that the church fathers whom he quotes affirm beliefs and practices, uncontroversially and widely embraced in both the Eastern and Western Churches, that Geisler asserts elsewhere are contrary to the "biblical" doctrine of justification.[35] (Sproul says something similar.[36]) Consider just these passages, penned by the same church fathers just quoted:

St. Irenaeus of Lyons
This able wrestler, therefore, exhorts us to the struggle for immortality, that we may be crowned, and may deem the crown precious, namely, that which is acquired by our struggle, but which does not encircle us of its own accord (*sed non ultro coalitam*). And the harder we strive, so much is it the more valuable; while so much the more valuable it is, so much the more should we esteem it. And indeed those things are not esteemed so highly which come spontaneously, as those which are reached by much anxious care.[37]

St. Cyril of Jerusalem
For as a writing-reed or a dart has need of one to use it, so grace also has need of believing minds. You are receiving not a perishable but a spiritual shield. Henceforth you are planted in the invisible Paradise. Thou receivest a new name, which you had not before. Heretofore you were a Catechumen, but now you will be called a Believer. You are transplanted henceforth among the spiritual olive-trees, being grafted from the wild into the good olive-tree, from sins into righteousness, from pollutions into purity. You are made partaker of the Holy Vine. Well then, if thou abide in the Vine, you grow as a fruitful branch; but if thou abide not, you will be consumed by the fire. Let us therefore bear fruit worthily. God forbid that in us should be done what befell that barren fig-tree, that Jesus come not even now and curse us for our barrenness. But may all be able to use that other saying, But I am like a fruitful olive-tree in the house of God: I have trusted in the mercy of God for ever—an olive-tree not to be perceived by sense, but by the mind, and full of light. As then it is His part to plant and to water, so it is thine to bear fruit: *it is God's to grant grace, but thine to receive and guard it.* Despise not the grace because it is freely given, but receive and treasure it devoutly.[38]

Then, we pray [in the anaphora] for the holy fathers and bishops who have fallen asleep, and in general for all who have fallen

asleep before us, in the belief that it is a great benefit to the souls
on whose behalf the supplication is offered, while the holy and
tremendous Victim is present. . . . By offering to God our sup-
plications for those who have fallen asleep, if they have sinned,
we . . . offer Christ sacrificed for the sins of all, and so render
favorable, for them and for us, the God who loves man.[39]

St. John Chrysostom

Let us then give them aid and perform commemoration for
them. For if the children of Job were purged by the sacrifice of
their father, why do you doubt that when we too offer for the
departed, some consolation arises to them? [For] God is wont
to grant the petitions of those who ask for others. And this Paul
signified saying, "*that in a manifold Person your gift towards us
bestowed by many may be acknowledged with thanksgiving on
your behalf.*" (2 Cor. i.11.) Let us not then be weary in giving aid
to the departed, both by offering on their behalf and obtaining
prayers for them: for the common Expiation of the world is even
before us.[40]

Mourn for those who have died in wealth, and did not from their
wealth think of any solace for their soul, who had power to wash
away their sins and would not. Let us all weep for these in private
and in public, but with propriety, with gravity, not so as to make
exhibitions of ourselves; let us weep for these, not one day, or two,
but all our life. Such tears spring not from senseless passion, but
from true affection. The other sort are of senseless passion. For
this cause they are quickly quenched, whereas if they spring
from the fear of God, they always abide with us. Let us weep for
these; let us assist them according to our power; let us think of
some assistance for them, small though it be, yet still let us assist
them. How and in what way? By praying and entreating others to make prayers for them, by continually giving to the poor
on their behalf.[41]

St. Augustine of Hippo

We run, therefore, whenever we make advance; and our wholeness runs with us in our advance (just as a sore is said to run
when the wound is in process of a sound and careful treatment),
in order that we may be in every respect perfect, without any

infirmity of sin whatever result which God not only wishes, but even causes and helps us to accomplish. And this God's grace does, in co-operation with ourselves, through Jesus Christ our Lord, as well by commandments, sacraments, and examples, as by His Holy Spirit also; through whom there is hiddenly shed abroad in our hearts . . . that love, *"which makes intercession for us with groanings which cannot be uttered,"* . . . until wholeness and salvation be perfected in us, and God be manifested to us as He will be seen in His eternal truth.[42]

Some specific points from these quotes are worth singling out. St. John Chrysostom, for instance, writes of praying for the dead so that the living through their prayers and charity may affect the dead's purification in the afterlife. This is reinforced by St. Cyril's description of the Catholic Mass in which prayers are said for deceased bishops and fellow believers, because these prayers are "a great benefit to the souls on whose behalf the supplication is offered, while the holy and tremendous Victim [Christ's body and blood in the Eucharist] is present." The comments by both St. John and St. Cyril are consistent with the *Catholic Catechism*[43] and found deep in Christian history,[44] and thus it is not surprising, as Robert Wilken points out, that "all the ancient liturgies included prayers commemorating the 'faithful departed' . . . [who] were not simply remembered, they were welcomed as participants in the liturgy."[45] St. Cyril explains justification by the metaphor of being grafted onto a vine, bearing fruit, and continuing to abide in the vine, though he warns of the possibility of our ceasing to abide and being "consumed by the fire." And yet, St. Cyril clearly affirms that one's abiding is the result of grace "freely given" and that one should "receive and guard it" and "treasure it devoutly," which implies the believer's lifelong cooperation in justification, something we will see is affirmed not only by Aquinas but by St. Augustine, the Council of Orange, Trent, and the *Catechism*. St. Irenaeus refers to "the struggle for immortality" as a "crown" for which "we strive." St. Augustine echoes St. Irenaeus and St. Cyril when he speaks of our moving toward perfection by God's grace through Jesus Christ and "by the commandments, sacraments, and examples, as by His Holy Spirit."

Geisler[46] and Sproul[47] cite the canons of the Council of Orange (AD 529) as precursors to Protestantism and thus in line with Aquinas. Although they are right about the council's continuity with Aquinas, a careful reading of its canons reveals an understanding of grace, the sacraments, and the life of faith that is more Ratzinger than Reformed.

The council, with papal sanction, rejected Pelagianism and semi-Pelagianism as heretical doctrines. The first, having its origin in the Catholic monk Pelagius (ca. 354–ca. 420/440), affirms that human beings do not inherit Adam's sin (and thus denies the doctrine of original sin) and by their free will may achieve salvation without God's grace. On the other hand, semi-Pelagianism maintains that a human being, though weakened by original sin, may make the initial act of will toward achieving salvation prior to receiving the necessary assistance of God's grace. The Council of Orange, in contrast,[48] argued that Adam's original sin is inherited by his progeny and can only be removed by the sacrament of baptism. By the means of baptism God's unmerited grace is infused for the remission of sins.[49] According to the council, justification is not the consequence of our initiative and then God assisting us by extending to us his mercy.[50] Rather, "God himself," writes the council, "first inspires in us both faith in him and love for him without any previous good works of our own that deserve reward, so that we may both faithfully seek the sacrament of Baptism, and after Baptism be able by his help to do what is pleasing to him."[51] Thus, the Christian's inner transformation continues throughout his lifetime, entirely the work of the infusion of grace with which the Christian cooperates,[52] for the Christian "does nothing good for which God is not responsible, so as to let him do it."[53]

It is not surprising, then, that one finds in Aquinas an account of grace and justification that embodies what his predecessors, including St. Augustine and the Council of Orange, embraced. Like the council, Aquinas rejected Pelagianism and semi-Pelagianism and affirmed baptismal regeneration.

> According to the Catholic Faith we are bound to hold that the first sin of the first man is transmitted to his descendants, by way of origin. For this reason children are taken to be baptized soon

after their birth, to show that they have to be washed from some uncleanness. The contrary is part of the Pelagian heresy, as is clear from Augustine in many of his books.[54]

As the Apostle says (Romans 5:15-16), the sin of Adam was not so far-reaching as the gift of Christ, which is bestowed in Baptism: "for judgment was by one unto condemnation; but grace is of many offenses, unto justification." Wherefore Augustine says in his book on Infant Baptism (De Pecc. Merit. Et Remiss. I), that "in carnal generation, original sin alone is contracted; but when we are born again of the Spirit, not only original sin but also wilful sin is forgiven."[55]

Like the Council of Orange (along with St. Augustine), Aquinas maintains that regeneration is wholly gratuitous,[56] or in the words of Sproul, "regeneration precedes faith." But Aquinas does so in line with his predecessors' understanding of the role of sanctifying grace in both conversion and the Christian life. This means that infused grace is not only required for the Christian's entry into the family of God at baptism but also for her subsequent movement toward being conformed to the image of Christ. Consider, for example, Aquinas' explanation of sanctifying grace as "habitual grace." It has, writes the Angelic Doctor, "a double effect of grace, even as of every other form; the first of which is 'being,' and the second, 'operation.'" For example, "the work of heat is to make its subject hot, and to give heat outwardly. And thus habitual grace, inasmuch as it heals and justifies the soul, or makes it pleasing to God, is called operating grace; but inasmuch as it is the principle of meritorious works, which spring from the free-will, it is called cooperating grace."[57] Because God is the sole mover in the infusion of habitual grace, it is entirely attributable to him. This is called operating grace. But if habitual grace is supposed to heal and justify the soul, and the soul has by nature certain powers to think and act, then this healing and justification must manifest itself in the activities of the soul. Thus, these acts allow us to cooperate with God for our inward transformation. This is, Aquinas calls, cooperating grace, since any meritorious acts performed by a soul infused with habitual grace by God would lack merit without that grace and thus without God's cooperation. Writes Aquinas, "God does not justify us without ourselves, because whilst we are

being justified we consent to God's justification [*justitiae*] by a movement of our free-will. Nevertheless this movement is not the cause of
grace, but the effect; hence the whole operation pertains to grace."[58]

For Aquinas, justification refers not only to the Christian's initial
entrance into the family of God at baptism—which is administered
for the remission of sins—but to the intrinsic work of both the infusion of that grace at baptism and all the subsequent graces that work
in concert to transform the Christian from the inside out.[59] This is
possible only because the baptized Christian literally partakes in the
Divine Nature as a consequence of being infused with sanctifying
grace.[60] Consequently, for Aquinas, justification and sanctification
are not different events, one extrinsic and the other intrinsic, as the
Protestant Reformers taught.[61] Rather, "sanctification" is the ongoing
intrinsic work of justifying, or making rightly ordered, the Christian
by means of God's grace, the same grace that intrinsically changed
the believer at the moment of her initial "justification" (i.e., at baptism) into an adopted child of the Father.[62] Writes Aquinas, "Augustine says (De Gratia et Lib. Arbit. Xvii): 'God by cooperating with us,
perfects what He began by operating in us, since He who perfects by
cooperation with such as are willing, beings by operating that they
may will.' But the operations of God whereby He moves us to good
pertain to grace. Therefore grace is fittingly divided into operating
and cooperating."[63] For Aquinas, justification is as much about getting heaven into us as it is about getting us into heaven.[64]

Not only is Aquinas' account of justification consistent with the
accounts proffered by St. Augustine, the Council of Orange, St. Ire-
neaus, and St. Cyril, one finds in the Angelic Doctor's writings a
place for praying for the dead,[65] the sacraments as means of grace,[66]
and belief in the Eucharist as the body and blood of Christ,[67] just as
we have seen are found in some of the church fathers quoted above
who are sometimes cited as Proto-Protestant in their soteriology.

III. Aquinas and His Catholic Successors:
Trent and the *Catechism*

Although it is clear that Aquinas' account of justification is in historical continuity with those of his predecessors, what about its continuity with his successors in the Catholic Church? According to

the Proto-Protestant Thomists, the accounts of justification artic-ulated by the Council of Trent and in the Catholic Church's 1994 *Catechism* are not only inconsistent with the views of the Protestant Reformers—as one would expect—they are also inconsistent with Aquinas' perspective. In fact, as I have already noted, Gerstner went so far as to say that Aquinas "taught the biblical doctrine of justifi-cation so that if the Roman Church had followed Aquinas the Refor-mation would not have been absolutely necessary." [68]

Sproul, for instance, claims that Trent's account of justification "appeared, at least to the Reformers, to retreat to the semi-Pelagian position that, though the human will is weakened by the fall, it still has the spiritual power to incline itself toward grace." [69] In making his case for Tridentine semi-Pelagianism, Sproul quotes the follow-ing passage from chapter 5 of Trent's sixth session:

> It is furthermore declared that in adults the beginning of that justification must proceed from the predisposing grace of God through Jesus Christ, that is, from His vocation, whereby, with-out any merits on their part, they are called; that they who by sin had been cut off from God, may be disposed through His quick-ening and helping grace to convert themselves to their own jus-tification by freely assenting to and cooperating with that grace; so that, while God touches the heart of man through the illumi-nation of the Holy Ghost, man himself neither does absolutely nothing while receiving that inspiration, since he can also reject it, nor yet is he able by his own free will and without the grace of God to move himself to justice in His sight. [70]

Commenting on this passage, Sproul writes, "Here Rome makes it clear that fallen man cannot convert himself or even move himself to justice in God's sight without the aid of grace. Again Pelagianism is repudiated." [71] Thus, it seems that Sproul is saying that Trent, like Aquinas and Orange, maintained that regeneration precedes faith. Nevertheless, Sproul goes on to claim, "This predisposing grace, however, is *rejectable*. It is not in itself effectual. Its effectiveness depends on the fallen person's assent and cooperation. This sounds very much like semi-Pelagianism, which had been condemned at Orange." [72]

As for the *Catechism*, Sproul offers this passage from it as evidence of its semi-Pelagianism: "God's free initiative demands *man's free response*, for God has created man in his image by conferring on him, along with freedom, the power to know him and love him."[73] Commenting on this passage, Sproul writes that "to avoid the Reformation and Augustinian view of the enslaved will, Rome speaks of the power of fallen man to assent to and cooperate with prevenient grace. That grace is not effectual without the sinner's response."[74]

Although what Sproul is affirming may be good Reformed theology, his reliance on Trent and the *Catechism* to make his case undermines his Proto-Protestant Thomism. First, the Council of Orange (AD 529), whose canons Sproul embraces as orthodox and biblical,[75] treats God's grace in a fashion almost identical to the way Trent understands it: "According to the catholic faith we also believe that after grace has been received through Baptism, all baptized persons have the ability and responsibility, *if they desire to labor faithfully, to perform with the aid and cooperation of Christ what is of essential importance in regard to the salvation of their soul.*"[76] This is because, according to Orange, "the freedom of will that was destroyed in the first man can be restored only by the grace of Baptism,"[77] which, like Trent[78] and the *Catechism*,[79] presents baptism as the instrumental cause of justification. So, if a free Adam can reject God, and our liberty has been restored to be like Adam's, then it makes sense for Orange to declare that the salvation of our souls is conditioned upon our "desire to labor faithfully, to perform with the aid and cooperation of Christ what is of essential importance in regard to the salvation of their soul." And yet, the council proclaims, "for as often as we do good, God is at work in us and with us, in order that we may do so."[80] And like Trent,[81] Orange employs the language of infusion to describe how grace works in baptism and the subsequent life of the believer, including his cooperation.[82]

Both Orange and Trent employ Jesus' vine and branches account of his relationship to his Church (John 15:1–17) in order to explain the connection between operating and cooperating grace and the role of faith and works in a believer's salvation. The Council of Orange writes, "Concerning the branches of the vine. The branches on the vine do not give life to the vine, but receive life from it; thus the vine is related to its branches in such a way that it supplies them with what they need

to live, and does not take this from them. Thus it is to the advantage
of the disciples, not Christ, both to have Christ abiding in them and
to abide in Christ. For if the vine is cut down another can shoot up
from the live root; but one who is cut off from the vine cannot live without the root (John 15:5ff)." And given that grace, we "have the ability
and responsibility, if [we] desire to labor faithfully, to perform with the
aid and cooperation of Christ what is of essential importance in regard
to the salvation of [our] soul." [83] Over a millennium after Orange, the
Church affirmed at Trent: "For since Christ Jesus Himself, as the head
into the members and the vine into the branches, continually infuses
strength into those justified, which strength always precedes, accom-
panies and follows their good works, and without which they could
not in any manner be pleasing and meritorious before God, we must
believe that nothing further is wanting to those justified to prevent
them from being considered to have, by those very works which have
been done in God, fully satisfied the divine law according to the state of
this life and to have truly merited eternal life, to be obtained in its [due]
time, provided they depart [this life] in grace." [84]

Not surprisingly, the *Catechism* offers an understanding of justification that is consistent with both Orange and Trent. Like the
two councils, the *Catechism* affirms the absolute gratuitousness of
God's movement of the human will: "The first work of the grace
of the Holy Spirit is *conversion*, effecting justification in accordance
with Jesus' proclamation at the beginning of the Gospel: 'Repent,
for the kingdom of heaven is at hand.' [Matthew 4:17]. Moved by
grace, man turns toward God and away from sin, thus accepting
forgiveness and righteousness from on high." [85] And like Orange
and Trent, the *Catechism* uses the language of cooperating grace
in its account of human merit and the role it plays in justification:
"The merit of man before God in the Christian life arises from the
fact that *God has freely chosen to associate man with the work of
his grace*. The fatherly action of God is first on his own initiative,
and then follows man's free acting through his collaboration, so
that the merit of good works is to be attributed in the first place
to the grace of God, then to the faithful. Man's merit, moreover,
itself is due to God, for his good actions proceed in Christ, from the
predispositions and assistance given by the Holy Spirit." [86] Oddly,
Geisler quotes a sliver of this passage—"*the merit of good works is*

attributed in the first place to the grace of God, then *to the faithful*"
(his emphasis)—and then concludes, "hence, it is grace *plus* good
works,"[87] even though in context that's not what the *Catechism* is
saying. It seems to me that Geisler's blind spot, one he shares with
Gerstner and Sproul, is the consequence of abandoning the idea of
participation in the Divine Nature, a view more explicitly taught in
the Eastern churches, though certainly essential to the West's idea
of justification as well.[88] According to the Catholic view, sanctifying
grace allows us to participate in the divine life. Thus, when we act in
charity, we do not contribute to our justification, as if it were merely
a case of God adding up our deeds on a cosmic balance sheet. This
is why the *Catechism* teaches, "The merits of our good works are
gifts of the divine goodness."[89] (Does that *really* sound like "grace
plus good works"?) Consequently, one's cooperation does not take
away from the fact that justification is a work of God, just as Christ's
human nature does not take away from the fact he is 100 percent
divine, and just as the Bible being authored by human beings is not
inconsistent with it being God's Word.

Second, because neither Trent nor the *Catechism* departs from
Orange, and because Aquinas's account of justification is in line
with Orange as well (as I noted earlier in this chapter), it should not
surprise us to learn that Trent, the *Catechism*, and Aquinas are in
agreement on the doctrine of justification.

As we have seen, Aquinas held that one's entry into the Body of
Christ is the consequence of operating grace,[90] wholly the work of God,
while Trent[91] and the *Catechism*[92] maintain that position as well. The
effect of grace, according to Aquinas, is to heal and justify the will so
that the human being may freely partake in the Divine Nature and
undergo transformation.[93] Thus, any meritorious acts in which a soul
infused with God's grace freely engages could not be meritorious without that grace and thus without God's cooperation. (Hence, Aquinas
calls it "cooperating grace.") For this reason, as I have already noted
above, Aquinas writes that "God does not justify us without ourselves,
because whilst we are being justified we consent to God's justification
[*justitiae*] by a movement of our free-will. Nevertheless this movement
is not the cause of grace, but the effect; hence the whole operation pertains to grace."[94] Hence, Sproul's claim that such grace is "not effectual
without the sinner's response"[95] begs the question, since its intended

effect is to heal and justify the soul of a particular sort of being, one that is a moral agent with the intrinsic power to respond or not to respond. In that sense, the grace is most certainly effectual. Unsurprisingly, St. Augustine concurs with the *Catechism* and Aquinas,[96] but according to Sproul the purpose of the *Catechism's* account of grace was "to avoid the . . . Augustinian view of the enslaved will."[97] So, apparently, either it did not succeed or St. Augustine is not Augustinian.

Thus, it should come as no surprise that Aquinas (following St. Augustine[98]), Trent and the *Catechism* are aligned in their understanding of the relationship between justification, sanctifying grace, and the infusion of faith, hope, and charity. The *Catechism* declares, "Justification is at the same time *the acceptance of God's righteousness* through faith in Jesus Christ. Righteousness (or 'justice') here means the rectitude of divine love. With justification, faith, hope, and charity are poured into our hearts, and obedience to the divine will is granted us."[99] Consistent with this, Trent affirms, "Man through Jesus Christ, in whom he is ingrafted, receives in that justification, together with the remission of sins, all these infused at the same time, namely, faith, hope and charity. For faith, unless hope and charity be added to it, neither unites man perfectly with Christ nor makes him a living member of His body."[100] And for Aquinas, "charity denotes union with God, whereas faith and hope do not,"[101] and "grace is neither faith nor hope, for these can be without sanctifying grace."[102] Aquinas writes in his *Commentary on Romans*: "The act of faith, which is to believe, depends on the intellect and on the will moving the intellect to assent. Hence, the act of faith will be perfect, if the will is perfected by the habit of charity and the intellect by the habit of faith, but not if the habit of charity is lacking."[103] The indwelling of Christ "is not perfect, unless faith is formed by charity, which by the bond of perfection unites us to God, as Col 3(:14) says."[104]

And finally, Aquinas believed, like Trent[105] and the *Catechism*,[106] that one can lose the grace of one's justification—that it is, in the words of Sproul, rejectable. Writes Aquinas: "Now the effect of virtuous works, which are done in charity, is to bring man to eternal life; and this is hindered by a subsequent mortal sin, inasmuch as it takes away grace."[107]

IV. Conclusion

It is abundantly clear that Aquinas was more a Proto-Tridentine Catholic than a Proto-Protestant. What then accounts for this misreading of the Angelic Doctor? Love. No serious Christian—especially one with philosophical dispositions—can read Aquinas without being impressed by not only his intellect and philosophical acumen, but also his encyclopedic knowledge of Scripture, which permeates virtually every page of his monumental *Summa theologica*. This no doubt has enkindled even in the coolest of Protestant hearts a warm affection for Aquinas that one is reluctant to extinguish. Because love, in this case, is less than blind, since it sees through a glass darkly, the Proto-Protestant Thomist finds it difficult to believe that such a historically imposing figure whose work came to dominate Western Christendom during the Middle Ages, someone so theologically insightful, philosophically compelling, and intellectually attractive, could be so wrong about the doctrine on which Luther boldly claimed the Church rises or falls. Thus, these smitten scholars unconsciously find creative ways to make it seem as if a thirteenth-century Dominican friar was a lonely beacon in a papist fog destined to be vindicated by a sixteenth-century Augustinian monk. Unfortunately, or fortunately, it is not so.

Postscript: Aquinas, Catholicism, and Purgatory

According to Catholic doctrine, upon death one may not wind up in either heaven or hell, but in purgatory, a place in which those "assured of eternal salvation . . . undergo purification, so as to achieve the holiness necessary to enter the joy of heaven."[108] It is a view of the afterlife rejected by virtually all Protestants, who believe that heaven and hell are the only two options. Although Eastern Orthodoxy rejects purgatory as well, there seems to be a place in its theology for some posthumous development on the part of the believer that can be affected by the prayers of the living.[109]

Jerry Walls is one of the few Evangelical Protestants who defends the reality of purgatory.[110] He argues that purgatory is a legitimate and defensible option for Evangelicals, though they need not believe in it in order to remain Christians in good standing.[111] One of Walls' underlying motivations for his project is that it offers the wonderful and alluring possibility of building bridges between Christian traditions that many had thought had been burned centuries ago.[112] Walls' serious reexamination of purgatory within an ecclesial communion that has historically rejected it is a hopeful sign that those Evangelicals who increasingly claim the paternity of the ancient church have come to realize that they too are as entitled to its inheritance as those who call Rome or Constantinople their home.

Walls believes that the right way to think about purgatory is in terms of sanctification, not satisfaction. He maintains that a sanctification model is consistent with Protestant thought, and thus any model of purgatory that includes the notion of satisfaction is an impediment to the sort of ecclesial unity that he hopes his project would help facilitate. But Catholic theologians have at times offered each model or some combination of both in their accounts of purgatory.

Defenders of sanctification models argue that the pains and punishments of purgatory exist for the sole purpose of personal transformation. The point of purgatory, according to this understanding, is to cleanse the believer who died in imperfection so that he may be able to enter heaven. All of us, except for a few saints, will die with unconfessed venial sins and disordered desires, with some of us further away from perfection than others. The distance we have to travel determines the sort and length of punishment we will undergo in purgatory. We do not suffer because it will satisfy some demand of justice owed God. Rather, we suffer because heaven cannot include among its residents anyone who is imperfect. So, before you can get into heaven, heaven must get into you.

Defenders of satisfaction models, on the other hand, argue that the pains and punishments of purgatory exist for satisfying a demand of justice owed to God. Walls offers up as proponents of this view the Catholic theologians Francisco Suarez (1548–1617) and Fr. Martin Jugie (1878–1954). According to Suarez, as M. F. Egan notes, whenever a human soul enters the afterlife "bearing upon it the guilt of unrepentant venial sin, the 'remains' of mortal sin forgiven but not altogether purged, and imperfect or evil inclinations due to past sins, all these are completely obliterated by the act of divine love which that soul immediately elicits."[113] This is the view also held by Fr. Jugie.[114] So, for Suarez (and Jugie), after a believer dies and leaves his "mortal coil," he is instantly perfected. Nevertheless, unless he is that exceptional saint, he must undergo the agonies of purgatory. Why? Because, as Egan writes, "Nothing remains except the *reatus poenae*, the debt of justice."[115]

How widely satisfaction models may have been entertained by Catholic theologians I cannot say. Nevertheless, it seems to me that these models are not reflected in the Catholic Church's magisterial pronouncements on purgatory, as I understand them. What follows are some brief excerpts:

Second Council of Lyons (1274)

Because if they die truly repentant in charity before they have made satisfaction by worthy fruits of penance for sins committed and omitted, their souls are cleansed after death for purgatorial or purifying punishments.[116]

Pope Clement VI (1351)

We ask if you have believed and now believe that there is a Purgatory to which depart the souls of those dying in grace who have not yet made complete satisfaction for their sins. Also, if you have believed and now believe that they will be tortured by fire for a time and that as soon as they are cleansed, even before the day of judgment, they may come to the true and eternal beatitude which consists in the vision of God face to face and in love.[117]

Council of Florence (1439)

It has likewise defined, that, if those truly penitent have departed in the love of God, before they have made satisfaction by worthy fruits of penance for sins of commission and omission, the souls of these are cleansed after death by purgatorial punishments.[118]

Catechism of the Council of Trent (1566)

Amongst them is also the fire of Purgatory, in which the souls of just men are cleansed by a temporary punishment, in order to be admitted into their eternal country, "into which nothing defiled entereth."[119]

The Baltimore Catechism (1885)

Q. 1381. What is Purgatory?

A. Purgatory is the state in which those suffer for a time who die guilty of venial sins, or without having satisfied for the punishment due to their sins.

Q. 1382. Why is this state called Purgatory?

A. This state is called Purgatory because in it the souls are purged or purified from all their stains; and it is not, therefore, a permanent or lasting state for the soul.

Q. 1383. Are the souls in Purgatory sure of their salvation?

A. The souls in Purgatory are sure of their salvation, and they will enter heaven as soon as they are completely purified and made worthy to enjoy that presence of God which is called the Beatific Vision.

Q. 1384. Do we know what souls are in Purgatory, and how long they have to remain there?

A. We do not know what souls are in Purgatory nor how long they have to remain there; hence we continue to pray for all persons who have died apparently in the true faith and free from mortal sin. They are called the faithful departed.[120]

The Catechism of the Catholic Church (2000)

All who die in God's grace and friendship, but still imperfectly purified, are indeed assured of their eternal salvation; but after death they undergo purification, so as to achieve the holiness necessary to enter the joy of heaven.[121]

It seems, then, that what one finds in these pronouncements is an understanding of purgatory that emphasizes sanctification, though some of them include the language of satisfaction as well, while clearly not embracing the Suarez-Jugie model of satisfaction. As I have already noted, whether or not the Suarez-Jugie model (or something similar to it) has made significant inroads among Catholic theologians, I cannot say. One, however, should not be surprised that some Catholic theologians provide accounts of Catholic doctrine seemingly inconsistent with the Church's magisterial teachings.[122] Consequently, a Catholic can agree with Walls that the Suarez-Jugie model is an unacceptable account of purgatory.

Given the Church's use of both sanctification and satisfaction language in its magisterial presentations of purgatory, I would like to interact with Walls's assessment of what he calls a satisfaction/ sanctification model, one that "employs metaphors of cleansing and healing, along with debt and payment, to describe the purpose of purgatory, with accent on the former."[123] In presenting this model, Walls relies heavily on Aquinas' account of purgatory, which in fact uses the language of both sanctification[124] and satisfaction.[125] Walls raises several criticisms of it, four of which I believe can be answered in light of Aquinas' understanding of justification. (I am going to address only three of them here.)[126]

First, Walls suggests that "versions of the model that place the predominant emphasis on satisfaction over sanctification are certain to draw the most insistent accusations of 'works righteousness,' but any claim that the remission of sins requires suffering or the willing acceptance of discipline is sure to be met with similar suspicions."[127] If, of course, one understands justification as equivalent to purely forensic justification, then Walls has a point. But that's not the view of justification that Aquinas was operating under. As we have already seen, his understanding of justification, consistent with the deliverances of Orange and the work of St. Augustine, has a place for works in the formation of a rightly ordered self as a consequence of cooperating grace. Therefore, unless one wants to make the controversial claim that Orange and St. Augustine were defending Pelagian or semi-Pelagian accounts of grace, Aquinas' view is not an apology for "works righteousness." It is, to be sure, non-Protestant. But to embrace a non-Protestant view is not the same as embracing "works righteousness."

It follows then that "similar suspicions" about Aquinas' belief that the remission of sins requires suffering in purgatory are equally unwarranted. As Aquinas writes, "We must say with others that venial sin in one who dies in a state of grace, is remitted after this life by the fire of purgatory: because this punishment so far as it is voluntary, will have the power, by virtue of grace, to expiate all such guilt as is compatible with grace."[128] Because "the forgiveness of guilt and of the debt of eternal punishment belongs to operating grace, while the remission of the debt of temporal punishment belongs to cooperating grace,"[129] when one voluntarily undergoes the sufferings of purgatory one is in fact doing so as a consequence of grace. In line with this understanding, Joseph Cardinal Ratzinger (now Pope Emeritus Benedict XVI) writes, "[Purgatory] does not replace grace by works, but allows the former to achieve its full victory precisely as grace. What actually saves is the full assent of faith."[130]

Second, Walls writes that "it is altogether unclear . . . how a sentence to purgatory exactly proportioned to the demands of justice correlates with notions that purgatory is simultaneously a process of spiritual improvement and lasts as 'precisely' long as necessary to complete that process. . . . The demands of justice, it seems, are a different sort of requirement than the necessities of character growth and spiritual healing."[131] But the demands of justice in the Thomistic account are not distributive, as this criticism seems to imply. For Aquinas, as well as for the Church's magisterial pronouncements, the use of juridical language is tightly tethered to a teleological understanding of justice. For this reason, claims about "satisfaction" and "debt or punishment" refer to our obligation to properly appropriate God's grace for his purpose of working through us so that we may be conformed to the image of Christ. "Justice," writes Aquinas, "is so-called inasmuch as it implies a certain rectitude of order in the interior disposition of a man, in so far as what is highest in man is subject to God, and the inferior powers of the soul are subject to the superior."[132] Consequently, this answers Walls' follow-up criticism as well, since it depends on the same distributive understanding of justice.[133]

Third, Walls maintains that on Aquinas' model it is not clear how the living may provide assistance to the dead in purgatory by offering prayers, alms, Masses, indulgences, and so on without undermining the point of purgatory: "If such improvement and transformation is really necessary for a person to be in the presence of God and fully enjoy a relationship with him, then it cannot simply be foregone or remitted."[134] Again, the problem is thinking of the Thomistic model in terms of distributive justice, that the assistance of the living is a rival to the performance of the deceased as if the entire enterprise were a zero-sum game. It is a version of the problem of what happens when one reads Catholic thought through the lens of Protestant categories: if you think of grace as imputed and not as infused (and thus not a "divine quality"[135]), then cooperating grace vanishes and grace and "works-righteousness" become contrary accounts of how one is justified.

This is why, as I noted above, two Church councils—Orange[136] and Trent[137]—employ the metaphor of the vine and the branches (John 15:1-17) in order to express the relationship between the members of Christ's body—both living and dead—as they assist each other on the journey to paradise. So, however we may assist those in purgatory—through fasting, praying, almsgiving, masses, indulgences, and so on—it is the consequence of cooperating grace, God working through us so that we may express our love, the virtue of charity, to the entirety of Christ's body, both living and dead. As Pope St. John Paul II once put it, "Just as in their earthly life believers are united in the one Mystical Body, so after death those who live in a state of purification experience the same ecclesial solidarity which works through prayer, prayers for suffrage and love for their other brothers and sisters in the faith. Purification is lived in the essential bond created between those who live in this world and those who enjoy eternal beatitude."[138]

Consider, for example, Jesus' parable of the unforgiving slave (Matt 18:21-35). In response to St. Peter's question of how often one must forgive, Jesus tells the story of a slave who is in such significant debt to his lord that the lord orders that the slave, his family, and everything they own be sold so that the debt can be paid. The slave then begs his lord for mercy. This elicits his lord's pity, and thus he releases the slave and forgives his debt. However, when the slave must deal with a fellow slave who owes him a measly sum in comparison to what the slave owes his lord, the slave shows his fellow slave no mercy at all. He grabs his fellow slave's throat and demands payment after his fellow slave promises payment while asking for patience. Upon hearing of the incident, an outraged lord summons the unmerciful slave and says to him: "You wicked slave! I forgave you all that debt because you pleaded with me. Should you not have had mercy on your fellow slave, as I had mercy on you?" (Matt 18:32-33). Jesus then concludes, "And in anger his lord handed him over to be tortured until he should pay his entire debt. So my heavenly Father will also do to every one of you, if you do not forgive your brother or sister from your heart" (Matt 18:34-35).

This parable suggests that there is an organic relationship between forgiveness, charity, and gratitude that depends on the internal disposition of both the forgiver and the forgiven. As the lord's condemnation of his slave clearly teaches, the initial forgiveness was not followed by the slave's transformation, for he did not appropriate with gratitude the grace he received from his lord and offer the same to his fellow slave.

Consequently, unlike Walls, I am not convinced that another's charity cannot benefit a soul in such a way that results in character development that is just as real and legitimate (or perhaps more so) as the sort that would develop in the absence of such charity. Take, for example, a child, Xavier, growing up in a broken home. As a consequence, Xavier develops vices that lead him to a life of crime and debauchery. Suppose as a young adult he undergoes a conversion experience, though he finds it difficult to change his old habits. He often finds himself tempted to return to his former life, though he knows that it will destroy him. Fed up with this internal struggle, he pursues a cloistered life of spiritual discipline that includes rigorous fasting, prayer, studying, meditation, devotion to the poor, and self-flagellation. After many years, he has acquired a level of self-mastery that truly astounds him as well as the numerous friends he has made in the monastery. But then he has an epiphany that causes him to well up with tears of deep gratitude. For he looks around and sees, really sees for the first time, what he had taken for granted the past decade: the wonderful architecture, the mountains of books, the opulent sanctuary, the scores of friends he now calls family, all expressions of the love and selfless giving that made his journey possible. Although the donors, volunteers, and fellow monks that contributed to these magnificent surroundings are often described by others as helping relieve the burdens of its residents, it would not be accurate to think of this assistance in merely distributive terms, and in fact Xavier cannot bring himself to see it that way, or at least not anymore. Yes, there was pain and suffering, all deserved, of course, and Xavier knows that if not for this overabundance of charity his agony would have been worse. But he does not, indeed he cannot, view this charity as a mere amelioration of what could have been. Rather, he sees his experience as an organic whole, ordered toward both his good and the good of those with whom he lives in fellowship. The charity and the suffering worked in concert for a proper end.

What this example accentuates is how one's gratitude toward the Church's charity is itself a catalyst for total transformation. Because, as I have already noted, the debt owed in the sanctification/satisfaction model is not an obligation of distributive justice, the appropriation of God's grace by a soul in purgatory, through the Church and its members (whether by indulgences,[139] prayers, almsgiving, and so on), is not a case of forensic penal substitution, but rather, a case of gracious participation.

Given these clarifications of Aquinas' (so-called) sanctification/ satisfaction model, it seems that the distance between it and Walls' ecumenical version of purgatory—the sanctification model—depends on the degree to which one is willing to entertain the possibility that the view of grace that Aquinas' model presupposes is correct. But if one is willing to do that, then the ecumenical prospects of Walls' call for a reassessment of purgatory are even greater than he has imagined.

6

The Aquinas Option

Grant me, O Lord my God, a mind to know you, a heart to seek you, wisdom to find you, conduct pleasing to you, faithful perseverance in waiting for you, and a hope of finally embracing you.

St. Thomas Aquinas[1]

When I taught at the University of Nevada, Las Vegas, in the 1990s, I had a student who never hesitated to challenge me during my lectures. (This, by the way, is something I have always encouraged in my students, since serious learning is virtually impossible without critical engagement.) One day, after I had told the class that the primary point of studying philosophy is the pursuit of truth, she immediately asked the question, "Why is the truth important?" I responded without missing a beat, "Do you want the true answer or the false one?" In that rhetorical quip I was trying to make the point that sometimes the answers to our questions are right under our noses, but we often do not have the presence of mind to realize it or even to know where to look. I kind of feel that way about how Aquinas' thought can help the curious Christian to address the four issues that have been the focus of this book. These issues, as we have seen, typically divide Christians along denominational or theological lines, though the divisions seem less pronounced (or at least easier to navigate) when we examine them under the guidance of Aquinas' insights.

On the matters of natural law and natural theology (chapter 1), we saw that the standard Protestant narrative—that Catholicism (and Aquinas) has an exaggerated sense of human reason's capacity to acquire knowledge of morality and God apart from special revelation—is mistaken. On the natural law, Aquinas fully concedes its limitations, arguing that without the eternal law (the order of creation in God's mind) there can be no natural law, and that without divine law (special revelation) the natural law is woefully inadequate in providing us the details of morality and what is required for achieving the beatific vision. Ironically, Aquinas' explication of the natural law nearly echoes what some contemporary detractors consider good reasons to reject it! When it comes to natural theology, contrary to some Protestant critics, neither Aquinas nor the Catholic Church teaches that one must first know God by reason in order to have saving faith. In fact, Aquinas' understanding of the articles of faith and how one assents to them is guided by St. Paul's instruction: "It is written (Eph. 2:8, 9): 'By grace you are saved through faith, and that not of yourselves . . . that no man may glory . . . for it is the gift of God' . . . for, since man, by assenting to matters of faith, is raised above his nature, this must needs accrue to him from some supernatural principle moving him inwardly; and this is God. Therefore faith, as regards the assent which is the chief act of faith, is from God moving man inwardly by grace."[2] When all is said and done, Aquinas' claims about the natural law and natural theology are quite modest, and for that reason, the skeptical Protestant may find in the Angelic Doctor more of a fellow traveler than the overly rationalistic caricature portrayed by those who have relied more on rumored reputation than refined reading.

Aquinas begins both the *Summa theologica* and the *Summa contra gentiles* by offering a lengthy and detailed answer to the most fundamental question in theology, "What is God?"[3] It is a question, as I noted in the introduction, that his biographers claim he first and frequently asked as a little boy. It is, of course, a question that is still with us today, and especially so when Christians stake out differing positions on whether Muslims, Christians, and Jews worship the same God, which was the focus of chapter 2. Although Aquinas was emphatic in holding that Islam and Judaism are mistaken in different ways[4]—and in that sense he agrees with many today who argue that Muslims, Christians, and Jews do not share the same faith—his understanding of the preambles of faith—what we can know by reason or common sense about God's existence and his nature—ought to lead one to the conclusion that all three faiths, despite their deep differences, refer to the same God when they use the term "God."[5] This is not an acquiescence to a soppy, milquetoast interreligious ecumenism. Rather, it is a conclusion consonant with what Scripture teaches about the power and limitations of our natural reason and the necessity of what Aquinas called the divine law (Rom 1; Acts 17). For this reason, it should be welcomed by Evangelicals as an instance of what many Protestant writers call common grace.[6]

Most ordinary Christian believers are troubled by the rise of an aggressive secularism whose advocates claim that modern science in general, and Darwinian evolution in particular, places belief in God outside of the scope of rational discourse. This is why many of these believers either abandon their faith or gravitate to writers who claim that so-called new scientific theories, such as intelligent design, have the power to humble these overconfident secularists into intellectual submission. But, as we saw in chapter 3, if one thinks along with Aquinas on the nature of divine action, one will conclude that both the irascible infidel and the beleaguered believer hold the same mistaken view about how God creates and acts in nature. For God is not merely the greatest being whose interventions at certain points in the history of the natural world fill gaps for which an autonomous creation cannot account, but rather, God is existence itself, that transcendent first cause on which all contingent being depends, in whom "we live and move and have our being" (Acts 17:28). Moreover, once one attends to Aquinas' understanding of causality, there is no good reason to abandon the idea that design (in terms of final causality) is intrinsic to nature, and that even the secularist who claims that modern science has forever banished design from intellectual respectability must unwittingly rely on it. When, for example, the late atheist writer Christopher Hitchens claimed that "religion poisons everything,"[7] he assumed that at least certain things have intrinsic good ends with which one ought not to unjustly interfere. That is, you cannot say X is corrupting to Y unless you know Y's purpose. As Aquinas once remarked, "But the absence of good, taken in a privative sense, is an evil; as, for instance, the privation of sight is called blindness."[8]

Although the dispute over the nature of the doctrine of justification was what launched the Reformation, we saw in chapter 4 that several Evangelical Protestant thinkers find in the Catholic Aquinas a kindred spirit, a spiritual companion who sees the believer's justification as they do, as a consequence of God's unmerited grace. And yet, Aquinas' understanding of justification is nearly indistinguishable from the one held by his predecessors and his successors, such as St. Augustine (354–430) and the Council of Trent (1545–1563), the latter of which is often portrayed by these very same Evangelical Protestants as departing from what Aquinas had taught. This should not only give us pause about the accuracy of the popular depictions of the distance between Catholic and Protestant views on justification, but it should help incline us more generally to an intellectual modesty whenever we read thinkers and writers outside of our own traditions.

Having lived on both sides of the Tiber, I am keenly aware of the pitfalls of reading one's theological rivals—not to mention, one's ecclesial patrimony—without charity, inquisitiveness, or imagination. For this reason, it is fitting that we end this volume with these prayerful words penned by the Angelic Doctor: "Creator of all things, true source of light and wisdom, origin of all being, graciously let a ray of your light penetrate the darkness of my understanding."[9]

Notes

1: Why Aquinas Today

1   St. Thomas Aquinas, *Summa theologica* II–II.Q188, art. 6, 2nd rev. ed, literally translated by Fathers of the English Dominican Province (1920), online ed., http://www.newadvent.org/summa/index.html. All quotations of *Summa* are taken from this edition. For the remainder of the book, I will simply cite the *Summa* as *ST*.

2   Francis J. Beckwith, *Return to Rome: Confessions of an Evangelical Catholic* (Grand Rapids: Brazos, 2009); Francis J. Beckwith, "A Journey to Catholicism," in *Journeys of Faith: Evangelicalism, Eastern Orthodoxy, Catholicism, and Anglicanism*, ed. Robert L. Plummer (Grand Rapids: Zondervan, 2012), 81–114.

3   Norman L. Geisler, *Philosophy of Religion* (Grand Rapids: Zondervan, 1974).

4   SGU started in 1980 as a small Southern California Christian law school, the Simon Greenleaf School of Law. Founded by Lutheran theologian and attorney John Warwick Montgomery, it was renamed Simon Greenleaf University in the late 1980s to better reflect its broad graduate degree offerings outside of the J.D., such as religion, human rights, and Christian apologetics. In 1997 the school was purchased by Trinity International University (TIU), an institution in Deerfield, Illinois, and affiliated with the Evangelical Free Church of America. Still located in Southern California, it is now known as Trinity Law School. For many years after the merger, versions of the old SGU M.A. programs were offered on the law school campus under the auspices of TIU's graduate school. However, the institution no longer offers those degrees. Although I believe I received a good education at SGU, today I would never recommend that any of my undergraduate students attend a new and relatively unknown Christian graduate school.

I was fortunate that neither Fordham University (where I earned an M.A. and Ph.D. in philosophy) nor the Washington University School of Law, St. Louis (where I earned a Master of Juridical Studies), thought less of my credentials for taking that unconventional academic route.

5   Francis J. Beckwith, "David Hume's Argument against Miracles: Contemporary Attempts to Rehabilitate It and a Response," Ph.D. diss., Department of Philosophy, Fordham University (1988).

6   Ralph McInerny, *A First Glance at St. Thomas Aquinas: A Handbook for Peeping Thomists* (Notre Dame, Ind.: University of Notre Dame Press, 1989).

7   An example of this is the way in which contemporary analytic philosophers typically categorize moral theories. They often divide them into three categories: (1) virtue theories, (2) deontological theories, and (3) consequentialist theories. According to the conventional wisdom, virtue theories have to do with becoming a good person by developing certain good habits, deontological theories concern obeying moral duties for their own sake rather than their consequences, and consequentialist theories concern engaging in acts or generally obeying certain rules because they achieve desirable consequences. But where then do we put someone like Aquinas, whose view of ethics not only involves aspects of all three categories but also presupposes that the good one performs in an ethical act is understood in relation to the sort of being one is (for example, it is morally wrong for Y to murder X because X and Y are rational animals and the murder robs from X the good of self-preservation to which he is by nature ordered)? So, for Aquinas, ethics depends on metaphysics. This is a view rejected by most contemporary moral philosophers.

8   To cite a particularly embarrassing example, in 2001 I published a peer-reviewed academic article in which I defended a view I called "the Classical Christian Concept of God," even though the view I was defending was not technically, as understood by classical theists, the Classical Christian Concept of God. I should have known better, but none of the Christian philosopher or theologian referees caught the error, since they likely did not think it was an error. See Francis J. Beckwith, "Mormon Theism, the Traditional Christian Concept of God, and Greek Philosophy: A Critical Analysis," *Journal of the Evangelical Theological Society* 44, no. 4 (2001): 671–95.

9   Plantinga calls the model of theistic belief that he argues has warrant "the Aquinas/Calvin (A/C) model" (Alvin Plantinga, *Warranted Christian Belief* [New York: Oxford University Press, 2000], 167), even though he rejects the classical theism of Aquinas (see pp. 319–23; see also Alvin Plantinga, *Does God Have a Nature?* [Milwaukee, Wisc.: Marquette University Press, 1980]).

10   See, for example, Michael Behe, *Darwin's Black Box: The Biochemical Challenge to Evolution* (New York: The Free Press, 1996); Michael Behe, *The Edge of Evolution: The Search for the Limits of Darwinism* (New York: The

Free Press, 2008); William A. Dembski, *The Design Inference* (New York: Cambridge University Press, 1998); William A. Dembski and Michael Ruse, eds., *Debating Design: From Darwin to DNA* (New York: Cambridge University Press, 2004); Stephen C. Meyer, *Signature in the Cell: DNA and the Evidence for Intelligent Design* (New York: HarperOne, 2009).

11 My 2001 Washington University School of Law (St. Louis) Master of Juridical Studies (M.J.S.) dissertation—"Rethinking *Edwards v. Aguillard*? The Establishment Clause of the First Amendment and the Challenge of Intelligent Design"—gave a sympathetic account of ID in evaluating the constitutional question of whether ID could be taught in public schools without violating the establishment clause of the First Amendment. A revised version of this work was published as a book (*Law, Darwinism, and Public Education: The Establishment Clause and the Challenge of Intelligent Design* [Lanham, Md.: Rowman & Littlefield, 2003]), portions of which first appeared as law review articles: Francis J. Beckwith, "A Liberty Not Fully Evolved? The Case of Rodney LeVake and the Right of Public School Teachers to Criticize Darwinism," *San Diego Law Review* 39, no. 4 (2002): 1111–26; Francis J. Beckwith, "Science and Religion 20 Years after *McLean v. Arkansas*: Evolution, Public Education, and the Challenge of Intelligent Design," *Harvard Journal of Law and Public Policy* 26, no. 2 (2003): 456–99.

12 See Francis J. Beckwith, "Or We Can Be Philosophers: A Response to Barbara Forrest." *Synthese* 192, suppl. 1 (December 2015): 3–25; Francis J. Beckwith, *Taking Rites Seriously: Law, Politics, and the Reasonableness of Faith* (New York: Cambridge University Press, 2015), chapter 6.

13 See, for example, Robert C. Koons and Logan Gage, "St. Thomas Aquinas on Intelligent Design," *Proceedings of the American Catholic Philosophical Association* 85 (2011): 79–97; Logan Gage, "Can a Thomist Be a Darwinist?," in *God and Evolution*, ed. Jay W. Richards (Seattle: Discovery Institute, 2010), 187–202.

14 See, for example, the following texts: "Jesus answered them, 'Have faith in God. Truly I tell you, if you say to this mountain, "Be taken up and thrown into the sea," and if you do not doubt in your heart, but believe that what you say will come to pass, it will be done for you. So I tell you, whatever you ask for in prayer, believe that you have received it, and it will be yours'" (Mark 11:22-24). "No one can come to me unless drawn by the Father who sent me; and I will raise that person up on the last day. It is written in the prophets, 'And they shall all be taught by God.' Everyone who has heard and learned from the Father comes to me" (John 6:44-45). "Now faith is the assurance of things hoped for, the conviction of things not seen" (Heb 11:1). "You believe that God is one; you do well. Even the demons believe—and shudder" (Jas 2:19).

15 See, for example, William Lane Craig, "Do Muslims and Christians Worship the Same God?," Question of the Week (459), January 31, 2016, https://

www.reasonablefaith.org/writings/question-answer/do-muslims-and
-christians-worship-the-same-god#_ednref1.

16 See, for example, Paul Crookston, "Religious Freedom for Me but Not for
Thee?," *National Review Online*, February 21, 2017, https://www.nationalreview
.com/corner/russell-moore-muslim-mosques-religious-liberty-universal/.

17 Much of what follows I gleaned from the biographical accounts of Aquinas
found in the following works: Brian Davies, *The Thought of Thomas Aquinas* (New York: Oxford University Press, 1992), 1–20; Brian Davies, *Thomas
Aquinas' "Summa Contra Gentiles": A Guide and Commentary* (New York:
Oxford University Press, 2016), 3–8; Jason T. Eberl, *The Routledge Guidebook to Aquinas' "Summa Theologiae"* (New York: Routledge, 2016), 3–8;
Edward Feser, *Aquinas: A Beginner's Guide* (Oxford: Oneworld Publications, 2009), 3–7; Denys Turner, *Thomas Aquinas: A Portrait* (New Haven,
Conn.: Yale University Press, 2013), 8–46.

18 As quoted in Eberl, *The Routledge Guidebook*, 8.

19 As quoted in Davies, *The Thought of Thomas Aquinas*, 9.

20 See, for example, Dewey Roberts, "Aquinas Is Not a Safe Guide for Protestants," *The Aquila Report* (online), October 16, 2016, https://www
.theaquilareport.com/aquinas-is-no-safe-guide-for-protestants/.

21 As I have already pointed out in a prior note, Plantinga argues that "the
Aquinas/Calvin (A/C) model" is a model of theistic belief that has warrant
(Plantinga, *Warranted Christian Belief*, 167).

22 John Milbank and Catherine Pickstock, *Truth in Aquinas* (London: Routledge, 2001).

23 Arvin Vos, *Aquinas, Calvin, and Contemporary Protestant Thought* (Grand
Rapids: Eerdmans, 1985).

24 Moreland describes his version of mind/body dualism as "Thomistic."
See J. P. Moreland and Scott B. Rae, *Body and Soul: Human Nature and
the Crisis in Ethics* (Downers Grove, Ill.: InterVarsity, 2000). See also
J. P. Moreland, *The Recalcitrant* Imago Dei: *Human Persons and the Failure
of Naturalism* (London: SCM Press, 2009).

25 Norman Kretzmann, *The Metaphysics of Theism: Aquinas' Natural Theology in Summa Contra Gentiles I* (Oxford: Oxford University Press, 2002).

26 David Bentley Hart, *The Experience of God: Being, Consciousness, Bliss*
(New Haven, Conn.: Yale University Press).

27 E. L. Mascal, *He Who Is: A Study in Traditional Theism* (London: Longmans, Green, 1943).

28 R. C. Sproul, John Gerstner, and Arthur Lindsley, *Classical Apologetics: A
Rational Defense of the Christian Faith and a Critique of Presuppositional
Apologetics* (Grand Rapids: Zondervan, 1984).

29 Milbank and Pickstock, *Truth in Aquinas*.

30 James E. Dolezal, *All That Is in God: Evangelical Theology and the Challenge
of Classical Christian Theism* (Grand Rapids: Reformation Heritage Books,
2017).

31 Carl Trueman, *Grace Alone—Salvation as a Gift of God: What the Reformers Taught and Why It Still Matters* (Grand Rapids: Zondervan, 2017), 91–100. These pages make up the chapter entitled "Unexpected Ally: Thomas Aquinas."

32 Charles Raith II, *Aquinas and Calvin on Romans: God's Justification and Our Participation* (New York: Oxford University Press, 2014).

33 See, for example, the contributors to Manfred Svensson and David VanDrunen, eds., *Aquinas among the Protestants* (Oxford: Wiley Blackwell, 2018).

34 Svensson and VanDrunen, introduction to *Aquinas Among the Protestants,* 8.

35 "The Apostle [Paul] says: 'The invisible things of Him are clearly seen, being understood by the things that are made' (Romans 1:20). But this would not be unless the existence of God could be demonstrated through the things that are made; for the first thing we must know of anything is whether it exists." *ST* I.Q2, art. 2.

36 "To know that God exists in a general and confused way is implanted in us by nature, inasmuch as God is man's beatitude. For man naturally desires happiness, and what is naturally desired by man must be naturally known to him. This, however, is not to know absolutely that God exists; just as to know that someone is approaching is not the same as to know that Peter is approaching, even though it is Peter who is approaching; for many there are who imagine that man's perfect good which is happiness, consists in riches, and others in pleasures, and others in something else." *ST* I.Q2, art. 1.

37 "If man were ordained to no other end than that which is proportionate to his natural faculty, there would be no need for man to have any further direction of the part of his reason, besides the natural law and human law which is derived from it. But since man is ordained to an end of eternal happiness which is in proportionate to man's natural faculty, as stated above... therefore it was necessary that, besides the natural and the human law, man should be directed to his end by a law given by God (i.e., the Old and New Testaments)." *ST* I–II.Q91, art. 4.

2: Aquinas as Protestant

1 Woody Allen, "My Philosophy," *New Yorker,* December 27, 1969, 25–26.

2 See *ST* I.Q2, art. 3.

3 See, for example, St. Thomas Aquinas, *Summa contra gentiles,* book I: *God,* trans. Anton C. Pegis (Notre Dame, Ind.: University of Notre Dame Press, 1975), 13; St. Thomas Aquinas, *De ente et essentia* (On being and essence), trans. Joseph Kenny, O.P., 88–98, http://dhspriory.org/thomas/DeEnte&Essentia.htm.

4 See notes 2 and 3, this chapter.

5 For example, the renowned scientist, author, and well-known atheist Richard Dawkins writes, "Time and again, my theologian friends returned to

the point that there had to be a reason why there is something rather than nothing. There must have been a first cause of everything, and we might as well give it the name God. Yes, I said, but it must have been simple and therefore, whatever else we call it, God is not an appropriate name (unless we very explicitly divest it of all the baggage that the word 'God' carries in the minds of most religious believers). The first cause that we seek must have been the simple basis for a self-bootstrapping crane which eventually raised the world as we know it into its present complex existence." Richard Dawkins, *The God Delusion* (London: Bantam, 2006), 155.

6   In a famous BBC debate between two eminent philosophers, the Catholic Frederick Copleston, S.J., and the atheist Bertrand Russell, the latter asserts, "I should say that the universe is just there, and that's all." Bertrand Russell, "The Existence of God Debate between Bertrand Russell and Father F. C. Copleston, S.J.," as published in Bertrand Russell, *Why I Am Not a Christian (and Other Essays on Religion and Related Subjects)* (London: Routledge, 2004; first published 1957), 134.

7   For example, the late Stephen Hawking (1942–2018) writes, "Because there is a law such as gravity, the Universe can and will create itself from nothing. . . . Spontaneous creation is the reason there is something rather than nothing, why the Universe exists, why we exist." Stephen Hawking and Leonard Mlodinow, *The Grand Design* (New York: Bantam, 2010), 180. It seems to me that William Lane Craig is right when he says that "Hawking and Mlodinow have not even begun to address the philosophical question, 'Why is there something rather than nothing?' For 'nothing' in their vocabulary does not have the traditional meaning 'nonbeing' but rather means 'the quantum vacuum.' They are not even answering the same question. Like the philosophy student who, to the question, 'What is Time?' on his final exam, answered, 'a weekly news magazine,' so Hawking and Mlodinow have avoided the tough question by equivocation." William Lane Craig, "*The Grand Design*—Truth or Fiction?," Reasonable Faith (website), https://www.reasonablefaith.org/writings/popular-writings/science-theology/the-grand-design-truth-or-fiction/.

8   "When in the Course of human events it becomes necessary for one people to dissolve the political bands which have connected them with another and to assume among the powers of the earth, the separate and equal station to which the Laws of Nature and of Nature's God entitle them, a decent respect to the opinions of mankind requires that they should declare the causes which impel them to the separation. We hold these truths to be self-evident, that all men are created equal, that they are endowed by their Creator with certain unalienable Rights, that among these are Life, Liberty and the pursuit of Happiness." Declaration of Independence (1776), https://www.archives.gov/founding-docs/declaration-transcript.

9   "All human beings are born free and equal in dignity and rights. They are endowed with reason and conscience and should act towards one another

in a spirit of brotherhood." Universal Declaration of Human Rights (1948), article 1, https://www.ohchr.org/EN/UDHR/Documents/UDHR _Translations/eng.pdf.

10 That's the name of a book by the Lutheran theologian and legal scholar John Warwick Montgomery: *The Law above the Law* (Minneapolis: Bethany House, 1975).

11 Robert H. Jackson, "Opening Statement before the International Military Tribunal," November 21, 1945, https://www.roberthjackson.org/ speech-and-writing/opening-statement-before-the-international-military -tribunal/.

12 Jackson, "Opening Statement" (emphasis added).

13 By "historically contingent" I am referring to points of view on the matter of faith and reason that arise because of a particular challenge to the Christian faith unique to the era. I take note of this in the last pages of this chapter when I compare Alvin Plantinga's approach with Aquinas' approach.

14 This is a paraphrase of a list of Aquinas' primary precepts of the natural law. Here is how he puts it in *Summa theologica*.

> Since, however, good has the nature of an end, and evil, the nature of a contrary, hence it is that all those things to which man has a natural inclination, are naturally apprehended by reason as being good, and consequently as objects of pursuit, and their contraries as evil, and objects of avoidance. Wherefore according to the order of natural inclinations, is the order of the precepts of the natural law. Because in man there is first of all an inclination to good in accordance with the nature which he has in common with all substances: inasmuch as every substance seeks the preservation of its own being, according to its nature: and by reason of this inclination, whatever is a means of preserving human life, and of warding off its obstacles, belongs to the natural law. Secondly, there is in man an inclination to things that pertain to him more specially, according to that nature which he has in common with other animals: and in virtue of this inclination, those things are said to belong to the natural law, "which nature has taught to all animals" . . . such as sexual intercourse, education of offspring and so forth. Thirdly, there is in man an inclination to good, according to the nature of his reason, which nature is proper to him: thus man has a natural inclination to know the truth about God, and to live in society: and in this respect, whatever pertains to this inclination belongs to the natural law; for instance, to shun ignorance, to avoid offending those among whom one has to live, and other such things regarding the above inclination. (*ST* I–II.Q94, art. 2)

15 Martin Luther King Jr., "Letter from a Birmingham Jail," April 16, 1963, https://www.africa.upenn.edu/Articles_Gen/Letter_Birmingham.html.

16 *Catechism of the Catholic Church: Revised in Accordance with the Official Latin Text Promulgated by Pope John Paul II,* 2nd ed. (Washington, D.C.: U.S. Conference of Catholic Bishops, 2000), 1951. For Aquinas' definition of law, see *ST* I–II.Q90.

17 *Catechism of the Catholic Church,* 1960, quoting from Vatican Council I, "Dogmatic Constitution concerning the Catholic Faith" (April 24, 1870). The English translation in the *Catechism* differs from the one found in Denzinger's *Sources of Catholic Dogma:* "can. . . . be known readily by all with firm certitude and with no admixture of error." Henry Denzinger, ed., *The Sources of Catholic Dogma,* 13th ed., rev. Karl Rahner (1954), trans. Roy J. Deferrari (Boonville, N.Y.: Preserving Christian Publications, 2009), 444.

18 *ST* I–II.Q91, art. 4, *resp.*

19 Francis J. Beckwith, *Defending Life: A Moral and Legal Case against Abortion Choice* (New York: Cambridge University Press, 2007).

20 See, generally, *ST* I–II.Q22–64.

> A passion of the sensitive appetite cannot draw or move the will directly; but it can do so indirectly, and this in two ways. First, by a kind of distraction: because, since all the soul's powers are rooted in the one essence of the soul, it follows of necessity that, when one power is intent in its act, another power becomes remiss, or is even altogether impeded, in its act, both because all energy is weakened through being divided, so that, on the contrary, through being centered on one thing, it is less able to be directed to several; and because, in the operations of the soul, a certain attention is requisite, and if this be closely fixed on one thing, less attention is given to another. In this way, by a kind of distraction, when the movement of the sensitive appetite is enforced in respect of any passion whatever, the proper movement of the rational appetite or will must, of necessity, become remiss or altogether impeded.
>
> Secondly, this may happen on the part of the will's object, which is good apprehended by reason. Because the judgment and apprehension of reason is impeded on account of a vehement and inordinate apprehension of the imagination and judgment of the estimative power, as appears in those who are out of their mind. Now it is evident that the apprehension of the imagination and the judgment of the estimative power follow the passion of the sensitive appetite, even as the verdict of the taste follows the disposition of the tongue: for which reason we observe that those who are in some kind of passion, do not easily turn their imagination away from the object of their emotion, the result being that the judgment of the reason often follows the passion of the sensitive appetite, and consequently the will's movement follows it also, since it has a natural inclination always to follow the judgment of the reason. (*ST* I–II.Q77, art. 1, *resp.*)

21 It should be noted that there are some thinkers who argue that the permissibility of abortion does not hinge on whether the unborn human being is a person. They argue that even if it is a person, it does not have the right to use the pregnant woman's body without her explicit consent, just as an injured or ill adult does not have the right to use another adult's body without explicit consent even if the former will surely die without the use of the latter's body. See, for example, Judith Jarvis Thomson, "A Defense of Abortion," *Philosophy & Public Affairs* 1, no. 1 (1971): 47–66. Nevertheless, even here the abortion-choice advocate relies on an application of a precept of the natural law with which the opponent of abortion agrees: "Because in man there is first of all an inclination to good in accordance with the nature which he has in common with all substances: inasmuch as every substance seeks the preservation of its own being, according to its nature: and by reason of this inclination, whatever is a means of preserving human life, and of warding off its obstacles, belongs to the natural law" (*ST* I–II.Q94, art. 2, *resp.*). Of course, the prolife advocate is going to argue that an abortion, though a means to ward off "an obstacle" that imperils the pregnant woman's being (as the abortion-choice advocate understands it), typically requires the intentional killing of an innocent human being, which the natural law can never countenance.

22 On the question of moral status, see Tom Beauchamp and James Childress, *Principles of Biomedical Ethics*, 7th ed. (New York: Oxford University Press, 2013), chapter 3.

23 Vulcans and Klingons are extraterrestrial humanoid species in the popular science fiction franchise Star Trek.

24 These first five are offered by Mary Anne Warren, "On the Moral and Legal Status of Abortion Rights," *Monist* 57, no. 4 (1973): 43–61. She argues that a being need not possess all five to be considered a person, though the first two together are probably sufficient. But a fetus, she argues, possesses none of the five, and thus is not a person.

25 See, for example, David Boonin, *A Defense of Abortion* (New York: Cambridge University Press, 2002), 115–32. For a response, see Francis J. Beckwith, "Defending Abortion Philosophically: A Review-Essay of David Boonin's *A Defense of Abortion*," *Journal of Medicine & Philosophy* 31 (2006): 177–203.

26 See, for example, Alberto Giubilini and Francesca Minerva, "After-Birth Abortion: Why Should the Baby Live?," *Journal of Medical Ethics* 39, no. 5 (2013): 261–63. For a response, see Francis J. Beckwith, "Potentials and Burdens: A Reply to Giubilini and Minerva," *Journal of Medical Ethics* 39 (2013): 341–44.

27 *Catechism of the Catholic Church*, 2270–75.

28 See, for example, "On the Sanctity of Human Life," resolution, Southern Baptist Convention, 2015, http://www.sbc.net/resolutions/2256/on-the-sanctity-of-human-life.

29 *Catechism of the Catholic Church*, 1957.

30 See, for example, J. Daryl Charles, *Retrieving Natural Law: A Return to Moral First Things* (Grand Rapids: Eerdmans, 2008); Jesse Covington, Bryan T. McGraw, and Micah Watson, eds., *Natural Law and Evangelical Political Thought* (Lanham, Md.: Lexington Books, 2012); Stephen J. Grabill, *Rediscovering the Natural Law in Reformed Theological Ethics* (Grand Rapids: Eerdmans, 2006); Robert C. Baker and Roland Cap Ehlke, eds., *Natural Law: A Lutheran Reappraisal* (St. Louis: Concordia, 2011); and Alan Johnson, "Is There a Biblical Warrant for Natural Law Theories?," *Journal of the Evangelical Theological Society* 25, no. 2 (1982): 185–99.

31 For a brief critique of the belief that that Protestant Reformers rejected the natural law, see chapter 7, "Debunking a Myth," in J. Budziszewski, *Natural Law for Lawyers* (Nashville: ACW Press, 2006).

32 Alan Jacobs, "More on Natural Law Arguments," *American Conservative* (blog), February 20, 2013, http://www.theamericanconservative.com/jacobs/more-on-natural-law-arguments/.

33 David Bentley Hart, "Is, Ought, and Nature's Laws," *First Things*, March 2013, https://www.firstthings.com/article/2013/03/is-ought-and-natures-laws. For a response to Hart, see Edward Feser's online article, "A Christian Hart, a Humean Head," *First Things*, March 2013, https://www.firstthings.com/web-exclusives/2013/03/a-christian-hart-a-humean-head.

34 Jacobs, "More on Natural Law Arguments."

35 Jacobs, "More on Natural Law Arguments."

36 *ST* I–II.Q94, art. 6.

37 *ST* I–II.Q94, art. 6.

38 C. S. Lewis, *The Abolition of Man* (New York: HarperOne, 1947), 44.

39 Obergefell v. Hodges, 576 U.S. ____ (2015) (slip opinion), 6.

40 *Obergefell*, 576 U.S. at 3.

41 *Obergefell*, 576 U.S. at 4. It is worth pointing out that this understanding of marriage would also include what is known as polygamy, since technically, in a polygamous marriage, each wife is married to one man, even though the husband in each union happens to be the same man. This is why when the husband dies all the unions are dissolved and the wives do not remain married to each other, since each was married to the same one man but not to each other.

42 Aquinas writes, "Matrimony is instituted both as an office of nature and as a sacrament of the Church. As an office of nature it is directed by two things, like every other virtuous act. One of these is required on the part of the agent and is the intention of the due end, and thus the 'offspring' is accounted a good of matrimony; the other is required on the part of the act, which is good generically through being about a due matter; and thus we have 'faith,' whereby a man has intercourse with his wife and with no other woman. Besides this it has a certain goodness as a sacrament, and this is signified by the very word 'sacrament.'" *ST* Supp.Q49, art. 2, *resp.*

43 *Catechism of the Catholic Church*, 1601–66.

44 Aside from conjugality, the other two have been slowly dissipating since the proliferation and ascendancy of no-fault divorce, serial monogamy, open marriage, nonmarital procreation, and the birth control pill. So, what I am suggesting is that the legal recognition of same-sex marriage is not a cause but a *consequence* of changes in marriage law, marriage culture, and sexual mores that are decades old. In fact, given this historical trajectory, it makes sense why so many people see it as prima facie unjust for the government not to legally recognize same-sex unions.

45 See, for example, Sherif Girgis, Ryan T. Anderson, and Robert P. George, *What Is Marriage? Man and Woman: A Defense* (New York: Encounter Books, 2012).

46 "No union is more profound than marriage, for it embodies the highest ideals of love, fidelity, devotion, sacrifice, and family. In forming a marital union, two people become something greater than once they were. As some of the petitioners in these cases demonstrate, marriage embodies a love that may endure even past death. It would misunderstand these men and women to say they disrespect the idea of marriage. Their plea is that they do respect it, respect it so deeply that they seek to find its fulfillment for themselves. Their hope is not to be condemned to live in loneliness, excluded from one of civilization's oldest institutions. They ask for equal dignity in the eyes of the law. The Constitution grants them that right." *Obergefell*, 576 U.S. at 33.

47 "In 2009, DeBoer and Rowse fostered and then adopted a baby boy. Later that same year, they welcomed another son into their family. The new baby, born prematurely and abandoned by his biological mother, required around-the-clock care. The next year, a baby girl with special needs joined their family. Michigan, however, permits only opposite-sex married couples or single individuals to adopt, so each child can have only one woman as his or her legal parent. If an emergency were to arise, schools and hospitals may treat the three children as if they had only one parent. And, were tragedy to befall either DeBoer or Rowse, the other would have no legal rights over the children she had not been permitted to adopt. This couple seeks relief from the continuing uncertainty their unmarried status creates in their lives." *Obergefell*, 576 U.S. at 10.

48 "Petitioner James Obergefell, a plaintiff in the Ohio case, met John Arthur over two decades ago. They fell in love and started a life together, establishing a lasting, committed relation." *Obergefell*, 576 U.S. at 9.

49 "Just as a couple vows to support each other, so does society pledge to support the couple, offering symbolic recognition and material benefits to protect and nourish the union. Indeed, while the States are in general free to vary the benefits they confer on all married couples, they have throughout our history made marriage the basis for an expanding list of governmental rights, benefits, and responsibilities. These aspects of marital status include: taxation; inheritance and property rights; rules of intestate

succession; spousal privilege in the law of evidence; hospital access; medical decision making authority; adoption rights; the rights and benefits of survivors; birth and death certificates; professional ethics rules; campaign finance restrictions; workers' compensation benefits; health insurance; and child custody, support, and visitation rules." *Obergefell*, 576 U.S. at 21–22 (citations omitted).

50 According to traditional natural law reasoning, a "proper accident" refers to any of those attributes that flow from the nature of a thing. For example, because human beings are rational animals they are ordered toward the ability to reason, laugh, communicate, and so on. But when a human being, because of disability or immaturity, does not exercise any or all of these abilities, he does not cease to be a "rational animal." In the same way, under the natural law, the conjugality condition of marriage may be fulfilled even if the perfection that flows from the nature of the act, the begetting of and caring for children, is never actualized due to disability or artificial contraception.

51 *Obergefell*, 576 U.S. at 44.

52 *Catechism of the Catholic Church*, 1958.

53 The previous three paragraphs were loosely adapted from portions of Francis J. Beckwith, "Is *The Abolition of Man* Conservative?," *Contemporary Perspectives on C. S. Lewis' "The Abolition of Man*," ed. Timothy M. Mosteller and Gayne John Anacker (London: Bloomsbury, 2017), 86–90.

54 See, for example, John Rawls, *Political Liberalism*, 2nd ed. (New York: Columbia University Press, 1996); and Ronald Dworkin, *Is Democracy Possible Here? Principles for a New Political Debate* (Princeton, N.J.: Princeton University Press, 2006).

55 A "public reason," in most accounts of liberalism, is a reason that it would be unreasonable for any citizen to reject.

56 This is not a quote from anyone in particular. It is just a shorthand way to describe what the Frustrated Fellow Traveler sometimes thinks he hears the natural law theorist saying.

57 Here is what two of the most prominent natural law advocates actually say about natural law's relationship to liberalism's public reason requirement: "On the one hand, if 'public reason' is interpreted broadly (perhaps we can even say literally), then natural law theorists believe that natural law theory is nothing more or less than the philosophy of public reason. Acting according to right reason—for good reasons—is, after all, precisely what natural law is all about. . . . On the other hand, if 'public reason' is interpreted in the narrower sense in which Rawls uses the phrase—a sense in which public reason generally excludes reliance on 'comprehensive' moral, philosophical, and religious doctrines—then natural law theorists reject the idea, precisely because it attempts to put the grounds, and often the substance, of people's deepest moral convictions off-limits in the most important public discourse." Robert P. George and Christopher Wolfe, introduction to *Natural Law and Public Reason*, ed. Robert P. George and

Christopher Wolfe (Washington, D.C.: Georgetown University Press, 2000), 2.

58 Johnny Lee, vocalist, "Lookin' for Love," by Wanda Mallette, Bob Morrison, and Patti Ryan, *Urban Cowboy* soundtrack, Full Moon, 1980.

59 Keith A. Mathison, *The Shape of* Sola Scriptura (Moscow, Idaho: Canon Press, 2001). See also Keith A. Mathison, "Solo Scriptura: The Difference a Vowel Makes," *Modern Reformation* 16, no. 2 (2007): 25–29. Mathison is arguing that the *sola scriptura* of the magisterial reformers such as Martin Luther and John Calvin is not the *sola scriptura* of the radical reformers such as Thomas Müntzer, Menno Simons, and large swaths of contemporary evangelicalism. He dubs the latter position *solo scriptura*, since unlike the *sola scriptura* of the magisterial reformers, it excludes from its reading of Scripture any interpretative traditions as authoritative. I am, of course, not implying that Mathison would agree with my conscripting of the term for my purposes here. I have no idea of what he thinks about natural law.

60 My friend the late Tristram H. Englehardt Jr. (1941–2018), held a position on natural law that sounds similar to the Solo Scripturist approach, though he was hardly a Protestant. A devout Orthodox Christian, he maintained that "a secular philosophical account of proper human deportment, including natural law approaches to morality and bioethics, will crucially misstate the focus and content of right action. They cannot recognize that human behavior must be guided by covenantal requirements that direct man towards God. Humans are under the New Covenant with God, which cannot be fully derived from or reduced to what natural law reflections can disclose." Tristram H. Englehardt Jr., "What Is Christian about Christian Bioethics? Metaphysical, Epistemological, and Moral Differences," *Christian Bioethics* 11, no. 3 (2005): 241. Nevertheless, Englehardt, unlike scholars like Henry, recognized that some natural law thinkers in fact conceded the limits of natural law reasoning (pp. 252n1). Oddly, Englehardt's claim that the "New Covenant . . . cannot be fully derived from or reduced to what natural law reflections can disclose" is not that far from Aquinas' claim that the natural law requires the divine law, as we shall see in the text.

61 Carl F. H. Henry, "Natural Law and Nihilistic Culture," *First Things*, January 1995, https://www.firstthings.com/article/1995/01/natural-law-and-a-nihilistic-culture.

62 *ST* II–I.Q93.a1, *resp.*

63 *ST* II–I.Q93, art. 1, *resp.*

64 *ST* II–I.Q93. art. 1, *resp.*

65 See, for example, David Van Drunen, *A Biblical Case for Natural Law* (Grand Rapids: Acton Institute, 2012).

66 Henry writes, "John Murray in his volume on Paul's epistle to the Romans in The New International Commentary series argues that the term 'law of nature' is a Christian concept rooted in Scripture, not a secular concept to be grasped independently of a revelatory epistemology. To interpret

Romans 1 and 2 in deistic terms of natural religion is unjustifiable" (Henry, "Natural Law"). This is a strange claim, since the defender of the Thomistic and Catholic view of natural law does not think of it as a "secular concept," nor does he read Romans 1 and 2 in "deistic terms of natural religion." This is why I say in the text that Henry "seemingly rejects" the reading held by Aquinas and Calvin.

67 Aquinas writes:

> [St. Paul] commends their observance of law, when he says, *they do by nature what the law requires,* i.e., the moral precepts, which flow from a dictate of natural reason. Thus Job (1:1) was blameless and upright, fearing God and turning away from evil. Hence he himself says: "My foot has held fast to his steps; I have kept his ways" (J[o]b 23:11).
>
> But the expression, *by nature,* causes some difficulty.
>
> For it seems to favor the Pelagians, who taught that man could observe all the precepts of the Law by his own natural powers.
>
> Hence, *by nature* should mean nature reformed by grace. For he is speaking of Gentiles converted to the faith, who began to obey the moral precepts of the Law by the help of Christ's grace. Or *by nature* can mean by the natural law showing them what should be done, as in Psalm 4 (v.6): "There are many who say, 'Who shows us good things!' The light of thy countenance, O Lord, is signed upon us," i.e., the light of natural reason, in which is God's image. All this does not rule out the need of grace to move the affections any more than the knowledge of sin through the Law (Rom 3:20) exempts from the need of grace to move the affections. (St. Thomas Aquinas, *Lectures on the Letter to the Romans,* trans. Fabian Larcher, ed. Jeremy Holmes with the support of the Aquinas Center for Theological Renew [Naples, Fla.: n.p., n.d.], 215–16)

68 Calvin writes:

> *For when the Gentiles, etc.* He now states what proves the former clause; for he did not think it enough to condemn us by mere assertion, and only to pronounce on us the just judgment of God; but he proceeds to prove this by reasons, in order to excite us to a greater desire for Christ, and to a greater love towards him. He indeed shows that ignorance is in vain pretended as an excuse by the Gentiles, since they prove by their own deeds that they have some rule of righteousness: for there is no nation so lost to every thing human, that it does not keep within the limits of some laws. Since then all nations, of themselves and without a monitor, are disposed to make laws for themselves, it is beyond all question evident that they have some notions of justice and rectitude, which the Greeks call preconceptions

προλήψεις, and which are implanted by nature in the hearts of men. They have then a law, though they are without law: for though they have not a written law, they are yet by no means wholly destitute of the knowledge of what is right and just; as they could not otherwise distinguish between vice and virtue; the first of which they restrain by punishment, and the latter they commend, and manifest their approbation of it by honoring it with rewards. He sets nature in opposition to a written law, meaning that the Gentiles had the natural light of righteousness, which supplied the place of that law by which the Jews were instructed, so that they were a law to themselves.

Who show the work of the law written, etc.; that is, they prove that there is imprinted on their hearts a discrimination and judgment by which they distinguish between what is just and unjust, between what is honest and dishonest. He means not that it was so engraven on their will, that they sought and diligently pursued it, but that they were so mastered by the power of truth, that they could not disapprove of it. For why did they institute religious rites, except that they were convinced that God ought to be worshipped? Why were they ashamed of adultery and theft, except that they deemed them evils? (John Calvin, *Commentaries on the Epistle of the Apostle Paul to the Romans* [1539], trans. and ed. the Rev. John Owen [Edinburgh: Calvin Translation Society, 1849], 14–15 [notes omitted])

69 *ST* I–II.Q94, art. 6, *resp.*

70 This section owes much to the trailblazing work of Vos, *Aquinas, Calvin, and Contemporary Protestant Thought.* Some of the references and citations in this section I originally gleaned from Vos' important book.

71 Vatican Council I, "Dogmatic Constitution concerning the Catholic Faith," in Denzinger, *The Sources of Catholic Dogma,* 443, quoting Rom 1:20.

72 *Catechism of the Catholic Church,* 34.

73 *ST* II–II.Q2, art. 4, *resp.*

74 *Catechism of the Catholic Church,* 27.

75 See Russell Re Manning, "Protestant Perspectives on Natural Theology," in *The Oxford Handbook of Natural Theology,* ed. John Hedley Brooke, Russell Re Manning, and Fraser Watts (New York: Oxford University Press, 2013), http://www.oxfordhandbooks.com/view/10.1093/oxfordhb/9780199556939 .001.0001/oxfordhb-9780199556939-e-13.

76 See the essays by Craig, Moreland, Collins, and Taliaferro in *The Blackwell Companion to Natural Theology,* ed. William Lane Craig and J. P. Moreland (Oxford: Blackwell, 2012).

77 See James F. Sennett and Douglas Groothius, eds., *In Defense of Natural Theology: A Post-Humean Assessment* (Downers Grove, Ill.: InterVarsity, 2005).

78   Swinburne, who converted to Eastern Orthodoxy in 1995, published the bulk of his work on natural theology while he was a member of the Anglican Church. See, for example, Richard Swinburne, *The Existence of God* (Oxford: Clarendon, 1979), and Richard Swinburne, *Faith & Reason* (Oxford: Clarendon, 1981). These books, it should be noted, were revised in 2004 and 2005, respectively.

79   Stephen T. Davis, *God, Reason, and Theistic Proofs* (Grands Rapids: Eerdmans, 1997).

80   See C. Stephen Evans, *Natural Signs and Knowledge of God: A New Look at Theistic Arguments* (New York: Oxford University Press, 2009).

81   See, for example, Alvin Plantinga, "Appendix: Two Dozen (or So) Theistic Arguments," in *Alvin Plantinga*, ed. Deane-Peter Baker (New York: Cambridge University Press, 2007), 203–28; Kelly James Clark, *Return to Reason: A Critique of Enlightenment Evidentialism and a Defense of Reason and Belief in God* (Grand Rapids: Eerdmans, 1990).

82   Karl Barth, "No!," in *Natural Theology: Comprising "Nature and Grace" by Professor Dr Emil Brunner and the Reply "No!" by Dr Karl Barth*, trans. Peter Frankel (London: Geoffrey Bles, 1946), 75.

83   On the first objection, see Edward Feser, *Five Proofs of the Existence of God* (San Francisco: Ignatius Press, 2017), 305–7. For a response to Barth, see James Barr, *Biblical Faith and Natural Theology* (Oxford: Clarendon, 1994), chapter 1; Thomas Joseph White, O.P., "Classical Christology after Schleiermacher and Barth: A Thomist Perspective," *Pro Ecclesia* 20, no. 3 (2011): 229–63.

84   Carl F. H. Henry, *God, Revelation, and Authority*, 6 vols. (Wheaton, Ill.: Crossway Books, 1999; originally published in 1976), 2:105, 1:184, quoting from St. Thomas Aquinas, *Boethii de Trinitate*, Q2, art. 3.

85   Colin Brown, *Philosophy and the Christian Faith: A Historical Sketch from the Middle Ages to the Present Day* (Downers Grove, Ill.: InterVarsity, 1968), 33.

86   Brown, *Philosophy and the Christian Faith,* 28.

87   Norman L. Geisler, *Philosophy of Religion* (Grand Rapids: Zondervan, 1974), 102.

88   Vatican Council I, "Dogmatic Constitution concerning the Catholic Faith," in Denzinger, *The Sources of Catholic Dogma*, 443.

89   *Catechism of the Catholic Church*, 156.

90   *ST* I.Q2, art. 2, ad. 2 (emphasis added).

91   *ST* I–II.Q1, art. 5, ad. 3.

92   Aquinas, *Questiones disputatae de veritate* (Disputed questions on truth), trans. James V. McGlynn, S.J., Q14, a9, https://dhspriory.org/thomas/QDdeVer14.htm#9.

93   I am not suggesting that St. Paul provided a demonstration of God's existence in his Athens sermon, for that is not what he did. He simply proclaimed the existence of the one true God.

94 "Sacred doctrine is a science. We must bear in mind that there are two kinds of sciences. There are some which proceed from a principle known by the natural light of intelligence, such as arithmetic and geometry and the like. There are some which proceed from principles known by the light of a higher science: thus the science of perspective proceeds from principles established by geometry, and music from principles established by arithmetic. So it is that sacred doctrine is a science because it proceeds from principles established by the light of a higher science, namely, the science of God and the blessed. Hence, just as the musician accepts on authority the principles taught him by the mathematician, so sacred science is established on principles revealed by God." *ST* I.Q1, art. 2, *resp.*

95 "Although arguments from human reason cannot avail to prove what must be received on faith, nevertheless, this doctrine argues from articles of faith to other truths." *ST* I.Q1, art. 8, ad. 1.

96 "If our opponent believes nothing of divine revelation, there is no longer any means of proving the articles of faith by reasoning, but only of answering his objections—if he has any—against faith. Since faith rests upon infallible truth, and since the contrary of a truth can never be demonstrated, it is clear that the arguments brought against faith cannot be demonstrations, but are difficulties that can be answered. . . . But sacred doctrine makes use even of human reason, not, indeed, to prove faith (for thereby the merit of faith would come to an end), but to make clear other things that are put forward in this doctrine." *ST* I.Q1, art. 8, *resp.,* and ad. 2.

97 "As other sciences do not argue in proof of their principles, but argue from their principles to demonstrate other truths in these sciences: so this doctrine does not argue in proof of its principles, which are the articles of faith, but from them it goes on to prove something else; as the Apostle from the resurrection of Christ argues in proof of the general resurrection (1 Cor 15). . . . Sacred Scripture, since it has no science above itself, can dispute with one who denies its principles only if the opponent admits some at least of the truths obtained through divine revelation; thus we can argue with heretics from texts in Holy Writ, and against those who deny one article of faith, we can argue from another." *ST* I.Q1, art. 8, *resp.*

98 St. Thomas Aquinas, *Super Boethium De Trinitate,* trans. Rose E. Brennan, S.H.N. (1946), Q2.a1, *resp.,* https://isidore.co/misc/Res%20pro%20Deo/ Aquinas/Bilingual/english/BoethiusDeTr.htm#21.

99 Norman L. Geisler, *Thomas Aquinas: An Evangelical Appraisal* (Grand Rapids: Baker Book House, 1991), 21.

100 See Alvin Plantinga, "Is Belief in God Properly Basic?," *Noûs* 15, no. 1 (1981): 41–51; Alvin Plantinga, "Reason and Belief in God," in *Faith and Rationality,* ed. Alvin Plantinga and Nicholas Wolterstorff (Notre Dame, Ind.: University of Notre Dame Press, 1983), 16–93; Plantinga, *Warranted Christian Belief*; Alvin Plantinga, *Knowledge and Christian Belief* (Grand Rapids: Eerdmans, 2015).

101 To say that a belief is "self-referentially incoherent" is just a fancy way of saying that a belief refutes itself. For example, if I tell you "don't believe anything I say," "I cannot say a word in English," "my brother is an only child," or "there are no absolute truths," what I am saying in each case is self-referentially incoherent. Plantinga is arguing that classical foundationalism, like each of these statements, refutes itself.

102 This may sound like an odd claim to nonphilosophers, since it seems that we do in fact believe in other minds based on evidence. But given the way that Plantinga thinks of evidence—something we point to in order to justify another belief—we actually don't believe in other minds based on evidence. When, for example, I enter the classroom to teach my students, I don't say to myself when the first one raises her hand and asks a question, "I believe there is a mind talking to me based on certain bodily movements, sounds, etc." Rather, I believe it immediately without pointing to evidence to try to justify my belief. See Alvin Plantinga, *God and Other Minds: A Study of the Rational Justification of Belief in God* (Ithaca, N.Y.: Cornell University Press, 1967).

103 Plantinga, "Is Belief in God Properly Basic?," 46.

104 It should be noted that just because a belief is properly basic does not mean that it is not defeasible. Plantinga himself argues that the problem of evil is a possible defeater to belief in God, though he believes that the theist can defeat that defeater. See Alvin Plantinga, *God, Freedom, and Evil* (New York: Harper & Row, 1974).

105 Writes Plantinga, "The principal answer is that faith is a work—the main work, according to Calvin—of the Holy Spirit; it is produced in us by the Holy Spirit. The suggestion that belief in the 'great things of the gospel' (Jonathan Edwards' phrase) is a result of some special work of the Holy Spirit is often thought of as especially the teaching of such Calvinist thinkers as Edwards and John Calvin himself." Plantinga, *Warranted Christian Belief,* 249.

106 Writes Aquinas, "Man, by assenting to matters of faith, is raised above his nature, this must needs accrue to him from some supernatural principle moving him inwardly; and this is God. Therefore faith, as regards the assent which is the chief act of faith, is from God moving man inwardly by grace." *ST* II–II.Q6, art. 1, *resp.*

107 *ST* I.Q1, art. 6, ad. 2.

108 Aquinas writes:

> There are two kinds of human reasoning. One is demonstrative, compelling the mind's assent. There can be no place in matters of faith for this kind of reasoning, but there can be in disproving claims that faith is impossible. For although matters of faith cannot be demonstratively proved, neither can they be demonstratively disproved. If this sort of reasoning were brought forward to prove what is held on faith, the merit of faith would be destroyed, because the assent to it would

not be voluntary but necessary. But persuasive reasoning, drawn from analogies to the truths of faith, does not take away the nature of faith because it does not render them evident, for there is no reduction to first principles intuited by the mind. Neither does it deprive faith of its merit, because it does not compel the mind's assent but leaves the assent voluntary. (St. Thomas Aquinas, "Commentary of Boethius's *De Trinitate*," in *Aquinas on Faith and Reason*, ed. Stephen Brown [Indianapolis: Hackett, 1993], QII. art. 1 ad. 5)

109 On how we should think of the "proof" of the miracle of Christ's resurrection, Aquinas writes:

> The word "proof" is susceptible of a twofold meaning: sometimes it is employed to designate any sort "of reason in confirmation of what is a matter of doubt" [Tully, *Topic.* ii]: and sometimes it means a sensible sign employed to manifest the truth; thus also Aristotle occasionally uses the term in his works [Cf. *Prior. Anal.* ii; *Rhetor.* i]. Taking "proof" in the first sense, Christ did not demonstrate His Resurrection to the disciples by proofs, because such argumentative proof would have to be grounded on some principles: and if these were not known to the disciples, nothing would thereby be demonstrated to them, because nothing can be known from the unknown. And if such principles were known to them, they would not go beyond human reason, and consequently would not be efficacious for establishing faith in the Resurrection, which is beyond human reason, since principles must be assumed which are of the same order, according to 1 Poster. But it was from the authority of the Sacred Scriptures that He proved to them the truth of His Resurrection, which authority is the basis of faith, when He said: "All things must needs be fulfilled which are written in the Law, and in the prophets, and in the Psalms, concerning Me," as is set forth Luke 24:44. But if the term "proof" be taken in the second sense, then Christ is said to have demonstrated His Resurrection by proofs, inasmuch as by most evident signs He showed that He was truly risen. Hence where our version has "by many proofs," the Greek text, instead of proof has *tekmerion*, i.e. "an evident sign affording positive proof." [Cf. *Prior. Anal.* ii] (*ST* III.Q55, art. 5, *resp.*)

110 John Jenkins, *Knowledge and Faith in Thomas Aquinas* (New York: Cambridge University Press, 1998), 185–86.

111 It should be noted that by the time Plantinga publishes *Warranted Christian Belief* in 2000 he is fully aware that the view of Aquinas' natural theology embraced by writers like Henry and Brown, and the early Plantinga ("Is Belief in God Properly Basic?" and "Reason and Belief in God"), is mistaken: "In 'Reason and Belief in God,' I suggested that Aquinas was also an evidentialist in this sense; various people (Alfred Freddoso, Norman Kretzmann, Eleonore Stump, Linda Zagzebski, and John Zeis in "Natural

Theology: Reformed?" in *Rational Faith: Catholic Responses to Reformed Epistemology*, ed. Linda Zagzebski [Notre Dame: University of Notre Dame Press, 1993], 72) remonstrated with me, pointing out that things were much more complicated than I thought. The fact is that Aquinas is an evidentialist with respect to *scientia*, scientific knowledge. But it doesn't follow that he thought a person could properly accept belief in God, say, only if he had (or there are) good theistic arguments. On the contrary, Aquinas thought it perfectly sensible and reasonable to accept this belief on faith." Plantinga, *Warranted Christian Belief*, 82n17.

3: Aquinas as Pluralist

1 *ST* I.Q13, art. 8.

2 Bob Dylan, "Ring Them Bells," *Oh Mercy,* Columbia, 1989.

3 Francis J. Beckwith, "Do Muslims and Christians Worship the Same God?," *Catholic Thing,* December 17, 2015, https://www.thecatholicthing.org/2015/12/17/do-muslims-and-christians-worship-the-same-god/; and Francis J. Beckwith, "Why Muslims and Christians Worship the Same God," *Catholic Thing,* January 7, 2016, https://www.thecatholicthing.org/2016/01/07/why-muslims-and-christians-worship-the-same-god/.

4 See Ruth Graham, "The Professor Wore a Hijab in Solidarity—Then Lost Her Job," *New York Times Magazine*, October 13, 2016.

5 Hawkins eventually resigned her tenured professorship in February 2016. According to a February 6, 2016, statement issued by both Hawkins and the college, "Wheaton College and Associate Professor of Political Science Dr. Larycia Hawkins announce they have come together and found a mutual place of resolution and reconciliation. The College and Dr. Hawkins have reached a confidential agreement under which they will part ways." "Joint Statement by Wheaton College and Dr. Larycia Hawkins Announcing a Resolution," https://web.archive.org/web/20160212025321/, https://www.wheaton.edu/Media-Center/Media-Relations/Statements/Joint-Statement-by-Wheaton-College-and-Dr-Larycia-Hawkins-Announcing-a-Resolution.

6 I tried to track down in my own writings when I first began to think that Christians, Muslims, and Jews worship the same God, since I am not sure I held that view in the 1990s. I had done some work on the Baha'i faith, which does claim that the founders of the great world religions—Buddha, Moses, Jesus, Muhammed—are manifestations of the same God. In my critique, I pointed out, among other things, that these founders (and their followers) held contrary views about the nature of God, but that's not the same thing as denying that Christians, Muslims, and Jews worship the same God, since, as I argue in this present chapter, two (or more) contrary views about God could still be about the same God, just as two contrary views of the solar system (e.g., Copernican and Ptolemaic) can still be about the same solar system. In the last piece I published on the Baha'i faith, in a

2005 anthology ("The Baha'i World Faith," in *Guide to New Religious Movements*, 2nd ed., ed. Ronald Enroth [Downers Grove, Ill.: InterVarsity, 2005], 155–68, 207–11), there is little indication of how I stood on the same God question. Nevertheless, I am not particularly proud of that chapter, for I was too polemical and not as charitable to the Baha'is as I should have been. This was partly because I had not adequately considered the Muslim roots of Baha'ism in interpreting what Baha'is mean by God. If I had, I would have concluded that Christians, Muslims, Jews, *and Baha'is* worship the same God, even though they hold contrary ideas about God due to what each tradition believes God has specially revealed.

7   Beckwith, "Do Muslims and Christians Worship the Same God?"

8   Beckwith, "Why Muslims and Christians Worship the Same God."

9   Vatican Council II, *Nostra Aetate: Declaration on the Relation of the Church to Non-Christian Religions*, October 28, 1965, 3 (citation omitted), http://www.vatican.va/archive/hist_councils/ii_vatican_council/documents/vat-ii_decl_19651028_nostra-aetate_en.html.

10 Quoted in John Paul II, "Message to the Faithful of Islam at the End of the Month of Ramadan," April 3, 1991, Vatican Council and Papal Statements on Islam.

11 C. F. Aiken, "Monotheism," in *The Catholic Encyclopedia* (New York: Robert Appleton, 1911), http://www.newadvent.org/cathen/10499a.htm. Spelling of "Qur'an" updated from original "Koran."

12 G. Oussani, "Mohammed and Mohammedanism," in *The Catholic Encyclopedia* (New York: Robert Appleton, 1911), http://www.newadvent.org/cathen/10424a.htm.

13 "Though [Muslims] do not acknowledge Jesus as God, they revere Him as a prophet. . . . As Holy Scripture testifies, Jerusalem did not recognize the time of [the Church's] visitation, nor did the Jews in large number, accept the Gospel; indeed not a few opposed its spreading." Vatican Council II, *Nostra Aetate*, 3, 4 (citations omitted).

14 See, for example, Craig, "Do Muslims and Christians Worship the Same God?"; Lydia McGrew, "The 'Same God' Debate Is Too Important to Leave to Philosophers," Gospel Coalition (website), January 16, 2016, https://www.thegospelcoalition.org/article/the-same-god-debate-is-too-important-to-leave-to-philosophers/; R. C. Sproul, "A Rose Is a Rose," April 1, 1998, Ligonier Ministries (website), https://www.ligonier.org/learn/articles/a-rose-is-a-rose/; Jerry Walls, "Wheaton, Allah, and the Trinity: Do Muslims Really Worship the Same God as C. S. Lewis?," Seedbed (website), January 13, 2016, https://www.seedbed.com/jerry-walls-wheaton-allah-the-trinity-do-muslims-really-worship-the-same-god-as-c-s-lewis/.

15 For example, according to David Novak, the Jewish philosopher Moses Maimonides held differing opinions about Christianity and Islam and its relation to Judaism.

Concerning Christianity, with which he probably had no real contact, Maimonides' views underwent a decided change over time. In his aversion to what he considered to be Christian dilutions of pure monotheism, especially in its doctrine of the Trinity, much of Maimonides' philosophical critique of Christian theology is similar to Islamic arguments against it. In his earlier work, Maimonides translated his theoretical disdain of Christianity into practice. He deemed Christians to be idolaters and bemoaned the fact that political necessity forced many European Jews to live in Christian societies.

Nevertheless, this is not the whole picture. At the end of his great code, *Mishneh Torah*, in his discussion of the political-legal role of the Messiah-to-come, Maimonides makes a predictable concession to Islam, but a surprising concession to Christianity. He argues that despite the errors of Jesus and Muhammad, the religions that emerged from their respective teachings are instruments of divine providence for bringing all of humankind to the worship of the one true God. Now it is obvious from this concession to Christianity that he no longer regarded it to be a form of idolatry, the worship of a "strange" god. Surely no form of radical idolatry could possibly be the means for the universal spread of monotheism. (Ironically enough, the Christian censors of the printed editions of *Mishneh Torah* forced the publishers to remove that passage). (David Novak, "The Mind of Maimonides," *First Things*, February 1999, https://www.firstthings.com/article/1999/02/the-mind-of-maimonides)

See also Reza Shah-Kazemi, "Do Muslims and Christians Believe in the Same God?" (paper presented at the Yale Center for Faith and Culture consultation "The Same God?," 2009), https://faith.yale.edu/sites/default/files/shah-kazemi_final_paper_0.pdf.

16   *ST* I.Q2, art. 1, ad. 1.

17   "The College of New Jersey, founded in 1746, changed its name to Princeton University during the culmination of the institution's sesquicentennial celebration in 1896. Historically, the university was often referred to as 'Nassau,' 'Nassau Hall,' 'Princeton College,' or 'Old North.'" April C. Armstrong, "When Did the College of New Jersey Change to Princeton University?," Mudd Manuscript Library (blog), Princeton University, July 8, 2015, https://blogs.princeton.edu/mudd/2015/07/when-did-the-college-of-new-jersey-change-to-princeton-university/.

18   I take this judgment from the review of *The God Delusion* by theist philosopher Alvin Plantinga: "You might say that some of his forays into philosophy are at best sophomoric, but that would be unfair to sophomores; the fact is (grade inflation aside), many of his arguments would receive a failing grade in a sophomore philosophy class." Alvin Plantinga, "The Dawkins

Confusion," *Books & Culture* (2007), http://www.booksandculture.com/articles/2007/marapr/1.21.html.

19 Avicenna, *The Metaphysics of the Healing*, trans. and ann. Michael E. Marmura (Provo, Utah: Brigham Young University Press, 2005).

20 Moses Maimonides, *Guide for the Perplexed,* trans. Michael Friedländer, 2nd ed. (London: Routledge Kegan Paul, 1904).

21 St. Thomas Aquinas, *On Being and Essence*, trans. Armand Maurer, 2nd rev. ed. (Toronto: Pontifical Institute of Mediaeval Studies, 1968).

22 Abstract objects, such as numbers and geometric figures (e.g., triangles, squares), which have no potential for change, are an exception. (I owe this point to Alex Pruss.) That is, the numbers "1" and "2" are distinct members of the kind "number," though neither has the potential to change as do particular creatures, like dogs, cats, human beings, stones, or angels. This raises questions as to the "creaturely" status of abstract objects. If, for example, some form of Platonism is correct, then at least some abstract objects necessarily exist and do not depend on the physical universe for their existence. For example, 2 + 2 = 4 is necessarily true even if there are no more than three particular objects in the universe or no universe at all. But if some abstract objects necessarily exist, then it appears that something other than God is unchanging, uncaused, and self-subsistent. Although theists have given differing answers to this conundrum, it seems to me that abstract objects have to have their source in God, since to suggest otherwise makes God dependent on them for his knowledge of abstract objects. On the other hand, because necessary truths are necessary, they are not like particular concrete objects that do not exist in every possible world. But if necessary truths have their source in God *and* they exist necessarily, what is the answer? To me, the most compelling answer is that abstract objects are indeed eternal and unchanging, but only insofar as they eternally exist in the mind of God. Of course, what it means for abstract objects to "exist" in God's mind is the $64,000 question and is outside the scope of this chapter. See, for example, Edward Feser's argument for God's existence from abstract objects in his book *Five Proofs of the Existence of God*, 87–116.

23 *ST* I.Q3, art. 4, *resp.*

24 See David Novak, "When Jews Are Christians," *First Things*, February 1991, https://www.firstthings.com/article/1991/11/005-when-jews-are-christians.

25 "Hear, O Israel: the Lord our God, the Lord is one" (Deut 6:4; JPS); "I believe in one God, the Father almighty, maker of heaven and earth, of all things visible and invisible" (The Nicene Creed [AD 381], U.S. Conference of Catholic Bishops [website], http://www.usccb.org/beliefs-and-teachings/what-we-believe/); "He is God: there is no god other than Him. It is He who knows what is hidden as well as what is in the open, He is the Lord of Mercy, the Giver of Mercy. He is God: there is no god other than

Him, the Controller, the Holy One, Source of Peace, Granter of Security, Guardian over all, the Almighty, the Compeller, the Truly Great; God is far above anything they consider to be His partner. He is God: the Creator, the Originator, the Shaper. The best names belong to Him. Everything in the heavens and earth glorifies Him: He is the Almighty, the Wise" (Qur'an Al-Hashr 59:22–24; trans. M. A. S. Abdel Haleem).

26 *ST* I.Q2, art. 2, ad. 1.

27 Observant Muslims and Jews, of course, accept as part of their faith that God is one, creator, and the source of our sanctification, and Jews call God "Father" while Muslims believe in the resurrection of the dead and that Jesus was virgin born and suffered, died, and was buried. (Judaism is divided on the resurrection of the dead, and, as a purely historical nonreligious matter, its scholars generally hold that Jesus suffered, died, and was buried.) Do Muslims and Jews then authentically assent to some of the articles of the Christian faith under Aquinas' understanding? As I read him, it is not clear. Aquinas maintains that one cannot assent to the articles of faith without the assistance of God's grace: "If we understand those things alone to be in a man's power, which we can do without the help of grace, then we are bound to do many things which we cannot do without the aid of healing grace, such as to love God and our neighbor, and likewise to believe the articles of faith" (*ST* II–II.Q2, art. 5, ad. 1). Nevertheless, it is possible, according to Aquinas, for people to have implicit faith as a consequence of God's grace, even if they have not explicitly assented to all the articles of faith: "If, however, some were saved without receiving any revelation, they were not saved without faith in a Mediator, for, though they did not believe in Him explicitly, they did, nevertheless, have implicit faith through believing in Divine providence, since they believed that God would deliver mankind in whatever way was pleasing to Him, and according to the revelation of the Spirit to those who knew the truth, as stated in Job 35:11: 'Who teacheth us more than the beasts of the earth'" (*ST* II–II.Q2, art. 7, ad. 3). On the other hand, Aquinas says that Jews and pagans (which include Muslims) who are unwilling to assent to Christ have an evil will and thus are unbelievers (*ST,* II–II.Q11, art. 1, *resp.*). However, Aquinas claims that there is a certain type of unbeliever, "who though he intends to assent to Christ, . . . fails in his choice of those things wherein he assents to Christ, because he chooses not what Christ really taught, but the suggestions of his own mind" (*ST,* II–II.Q11, art. 1, *resp.*). The Catholic Church appropriates some of Aquinas' reasoning but softens it quite a bit: "Those also can attain to salvation who through no fault of their own do not know the Gospel of Christ or His Church, yet sincerely seek God and moved by grace strive by their deeds to do His will as it is known to them through the dictates of conscience. Nor does Divine Providence deny the helps necessary for salvation to those who, without blame on their part, have not yet arrived at an explicit knowledge of God and with His grace strive to live a good life. Whatever good or truth is found amongst them is looked upon by

the Church as a preparation for the Gospel." Vatican Council II, *Lumen Gentium: Dogmatic Constitution of the Church*, November 21, 1964, 16 (citation omitted), http://www.vatican.va/archive/hist_councils/ii_vatican_council/documents/vat-ii_const_19641121_lumen-gentium_en.html.

28 *ST* II–II.Q1, art. 8, *resp.*

29 You may have noticed that the articles of faith correspond to the different sections of the Apostles' Creed:

> I believe in God the Father almighty, creator of heaven and earth.
> I believe in Jesus Christ, his only Son, our Lord.
> He was conceived by the power of the Holy Spirit and born of the Virgin Mary
> Under Pontius Pilate He was crucified, died, and was buried.
> He descended to the dead.
> On the third day he rose again.
> He ascended into heaven and is seated at the right hand of the Father.
> He will come again to judge the living and the dead.
>
> I believe in the Holy Spirit,
> the holy catholic Church,
> the communion of saints,
> the forgiveness of sins,
> the resurrection of the body,
> and the life everlasting.
> Amen. (*Catechism of the Catholic Church*, credo)

30 *ST* I.Q2, art. 2, ad. 1.

31 For the Qur'an's account of Moses at the burning bush, see Qur'an Ta-Ha 20.

32 See Matthew Levering, *Scripture and Metaphysics: Aquinas and the Renewal of Trinitarian Theology* (Oxford: Blackwell, 2004), chapter 2; and Jaroslav Pelikan, *The Emergence of the Catholic Tradition (100–600)*, vol. 1 of *The Christian Tradition: A History of the Development of Doctrine* (Chicago: University of Chicago Press, 1971), 53–54.

33 Levering, *Scripture and Metaphysics*, 40–41, 63–64.

34 J. N. D. Kelly, *Early Christian Doctrines*, 5th ed. (San Francisco: HarperCollins, 1978), 226–31.

35 Athanasius, *De Synodis*, trans. John Henry Newman and Archibald Robertson, as found in *Nicene and Post-Nicene Fathers*, 2nd ser., vol. 4, ed. Philip Schaff and Henry Wace (Buffalo, N.Y.: Christian Literature, 1892), rev. and ed. for New Advent by Kevin Knight, http://www.newadvent.org/fathers/2817.htm.

36 The Nicene Creed.

37 McGrew, "The 'Same God' Debate Is Too Important to Leave to Philosophers."

38 "The Trinity of traditional Christianity is referred to as the Godhead by members of the Church of Jesus Christ of Latter-Day Saints (Mormon). Like

other Christians, Latter-Day Saints believe in the Father, the Son and the Holy Spirit (or Holy Ghost). Yet, Church teachings about the Godhead differ from those of traditional Christianity. For example, while some believe the three members of the Trinity are of one substance, Latter-Day Saints believe they are three physically separate beings, but fully one in love, purpose and will." "Godhead," Newsroom of the Church of Jesus Christ of Latter-Day Saints, https://www.mormonnewsroom.org/article/godhead.

39   "The incarnation is the foundational Christian teaching that Jesus Christ, who was God (Jehovah) in the premortal existence, 'was made flesh, and dwelt among us' (John 1:14). . . . The Great Jehovah, the Creator of all things (Mosiah 3:8; 5:15), the Eternal Father of heaven and earth (Mosiah 15:4), took upon himself the tabernacle of a mortal body." Andrew C. Skinner, "The Incarnation/Incarnate God," in *LDS Beliefs: A Doctrinal Reference,* by Robert L Millet, Camille Fronk Olson, Andrew C. Skinner, and Brent L. Top (Salt Lake City: Deseret Books, 2011), 319.

40   "The formula used by the Mormons might seem at first sight to be a Trinitarian formula. The text states: *Being commissioned by Jesus Christ, I baptize you in the name of the Father, and of the Son, and of the Holy Spirit.'* . . . The similarities with the formula used by the Catholic Church are at first sight obvious, but in reality they are only apparent. There is not in fact a fundamental doctrinal agreement. There is not a true invocation of the Trinity because the Father, the Son, and the Holy Spirit, according to the *Church of Jesus Christ of Latter-Day Saints,* are not the three persons in which subsists the one Godhead, but three gods who form one divinity. One is different from the other, even though they exist in perfect harmony. . . . The very word divinity has only a functional, not a substantial content, because the divinity originates when the three gods decided to unite and form the divinity to bring about human salvation. . . . This divinity and man share the same nature and they are substantially equal." Fr. Luis Ladaria, S.J., "The Question of the Validity of Baptism Conferred in the Church of Jesus Christ of Latter-Day Saints," *L'Osservatore Romano,* August 2001, 4, https://www.ewtn.com/library/theology/mormbap1.htm.

41   The Nicene Creed.

42   The Nicene Creed.

43   When the Nicene Creed affirms that the Son is eternally begotten of the Father and that the Spirit eternally proceeds from the Father and the Son, it is relying on what the Church believes has been revealed in Scripture. For example, we are told that the Word is both God and God's only Son (John 1:18, 3:16), and that the Spirit, who is also God (Acts 5:3–5), proceeds from both the Father and Son (John 15:26). Unlike created things that proceed from God, such as all the things that make up the universe, the Son and the Spirit are uncreated and share the Father's divine nature, not as separate beings (since that would be impossible), but as internal relations within the eternal and unchanging God. It is, of course, a deep mystery, one that I cannot explicate here.

44 Tomas Bogardus and Mallorie Urban, "How to Tell Whether Christians and Muslims Worship the Same God," *Faith and Philosophy* 34, no. 2 (2017): 176–200.

45 Bogardus and Urban, "How to Tell Whether Christians and Muslims Worship the Same God," 178.

46 Craig, "Do Muslims and Christians Worship the Same God?"

47 Mohammed Mostafa Ansari is the name of a Muslim Iranian cardiologist who my wife and I sat next to at Palm Sunday Mass in St. Peter's Square on March 29, 2015.

48 When I use the term "orthodox" here, I do not mean it in the sense of Eastern Orthodox or Orthodox Judaism. I mean it in the sense of those beliefs that each religion has held as fundamental in its creeds, confessions, authoritative writings, philosophical explications, and so on.

49 Brian Davies, *An Introduction to the Philosophy of Religion*, 3rd ed. (New York: Oxford University, 2004), 2

50 Bogardus and Urban, "How to Tell Whether Christians and Muslims Worship the Same God," 178.

51 For contemporary defenses of divine simplicity, see James Dolezal, *God without Parts: Divine Simplicity and the Metaphysics of God's Absoluteness* (Eugene, Ore.: Wipf & Stock, 2011); Hart, *The Experience of God*, 134–42; Feser, *Five Proofs of the Existence of God*, 189–96; and Hugh J. McCann, *Creation and the Sovereignty of God* (Bloomington, Ind.: Indiana University Press, 2012), 213–35.

52 See Lewis Ayers, *Nicaea and Its Legacy: An Approach to Fourth Century Trinitarian Theology* (New York: Oxford University Press, 2004).

53 Aquinas writes, "Therefore, as regards the primary points or articles of faith, man is bound to believe them, just as he is bound to have faith; but as to other points of faith, man is not bound to believe them explicitly, but only implicitly, or to be ready to believe them, in so far as he is prepared to believe whatever is contained in the Divine Scriptures. Then alone is he bound to believe such things explicitly, when it is clear to him that they are contained in the doctrine of faith." *ST* II–II.Q2, art. 5.

54 As Reformed historical theologian Richard Muller writes, "The doctrine of divine simplicity is among the normative assumptions of theology from the time of the church fathers, to the age of the great medieval scholastic systems, to the era of Reformation and post-Reformation theology, and indeed, on into the succeeding era of late orthodoxy and rationalism." Richard Muller, *The Divine Essence and Attributes*, vol. 3, *Post-Reformation Reformed Dogmatics*, 2nd ed. (Grand Rapids: Baker Book House, 2003), 39.

55 This is a point Ed Feser made to me in private email correspondence on Good Friday, March 30, 2018.

56 "Speech that demeans on the basis of race, ethnicity, gender, religion, age, disability, or any other similar ground is hateful; but the proudest boast of

our free speech jurisprudence is that we protect the freedom to express 'the thought that we hate.'" Matal v. Tam, 582 U.S. ___ (2017), slip op. at 25 (note omitted).

57 William Lane Craig and J. P. Moreland, *Philosophical Foundations of a Christian Worldview*, 2nd ed. (Downers Grove, Ill.: InterVarsity, 2017), 510–39.

58 Plantinga, *Does God Have a Nature?*

59 Richard Swinburne, *The Christian God* (New York: Oxford University Press, 1994).

60 The label "theist personalism," as far as I know, was coined by the philosopher Brian Davies. See Davies, *An Introduction to the Philosophy of Religion*, 9–15.

61 Plantinga, for example, writes, "Accordingly, Christians ordinarily take it for granted that it is possible to refer to God by such descriptions as 'the all-powerful, all-knowing creator of the universe,' and furthermore predicate properties (wisdom, goodness) of the being thus referred to. . . . For Christians believe that there is an infinite, transcendent, ultimate being about whom they hold beliefs." Plantinga, *Warranted Christian Belief*, 4.

62 The Eastern Orthodox theologian David Bentley Hart believes that the caveats are so misguided that he thinks the label "theistic personalism" is too mild: "I prefer to call it monopolytheism myself (or perhaps 'mono-poly-theism'), since it seems to me to involve a view of God not conspicuously different from the polytheistic picture of the gods as merely very powerful discrete entities who possess a variety of distinct attributes that lesser entities also possess, if in smaller measure; it differs from polytheism, as far I can tell, solely in that it posits the existence of only one such being. It is a way of thinking that suggests that God, since he is only a particular instantiation of various concepts and properties, is logically dependent on some more comprehensive reality embracing both him and other beings. For philosophers who think in this way, practically all the traditional metaphysical attempts to understand God as the source of all reality become impenetrable." Hart, *Experience of God*, 127–28.

63 Craig, for example, writes, "So on the traditional conception, God is what the philosopher Brian Leftow calls 'the sole ultimate reality,' the pinnacle of being, so to speak. For all other beings have been created by Him and therefore depend on Him for their existence, whereas God depends upon nothing else for His existence and is the source of existence of everything else." William Lane Craig, *God over All: Divine Aseity and the Challenge of Platonism* (New York: Oxford University Press, 2017), 2 (citation omitted). In chapter 2 of this book Craig defends this traditional conception as the biblical conception subsequently affirmed by the Church Fathers.

64 David B. Burrell, C.S.C., *Knowing the Unknowable God: Ibn-Sina, Maimonides, Aquinas* (Notre Dame, Ind.: University of Notre Dame Press, 1986), 111.

65 Special thanks to Alex Pruss for commenting on an earlier draft of this chapter.

4: Aquinas as Theologian

1 *ST* I.Q79, art. 9, *respondeo.*

2 Pope Benedict XVI, general audience in St. Peter's Square (February 3, 2013), https://w2.vatican.va/content/benedict-xvi/en/audiences/2013/documents/hf_ben-xvi_aud_20130206.html.

3 Francis J. Beckwith, "Dawson, Joseph Martin," *Encyclopedia of American Civil Liberties*, ed. Paul Finkelman (New York: Routledge, 2007), 397–98.

4 See, for example, Beckwith, *Law, Darwinism, and Public Education*; Beckwith, "A Liberty Not Fully Evolved?"; Beckwith, "Science and Religion 20 Years after *McLean v. Arkansas.*"

5 Beckwith, "Rethinking *Edwards v. Aguillard*?"

6 See Epperson v. Arkansas, 393 U.S. 97 (1968), McLean v. Arkansas Board of Education, 529 F.Supp. 1255 (1982); Edwards v. Aguillard, 482 U.S. 578 (1987).

7 Testimony of Francis J. Beckwith, July 9, 2003, State Board of Education, Austin, Texas.

8 The name of the center was the Center for the Renewal of Science & Culture. It has since changed its name to the Center for Science & Culture.

9 Dawson writes an astonishing passage that seems echoed today in the fear of some American Evangelicals who see Muslim immigration as the first step in a conspiracy to bring sharia law to the United States.

> The Catholics, who are now [1948] claiming a near majority over all Protestants in the United States, would abolish our public school system which is our greatest single factor in national unity and would substitute their old-world, medieval parochial schools, with their alien culture. Or else they make it plain that they wish to install facilities for teaching their religion in the public schools.... Perhaps the burning issue has arisen soon enough to enable the friends of the native American culture to arrest the progress of the long-range plan of those who would supplant it. There can be no doubt about the Catholic plan. Having lost enormous prestige in Europe, the Church now looks to the United States as a suitable stage for the recovery of its lost influence. Here it would seek new ground, consolidate and expand, as compensation for its weakened position in bankrupt Europe, with the hope of transforming this continent, a Protestant country, into a Catholic citadel from which to exert a powerful rule. If this seems exaggerated and fanciful, the reader has only to open his eyes to what the Catholics are doing to achieve this end. (J. M. Dawson, *Separate Church & State Now* [New York: R. R. Smith, 1948], 96)

10 Paul Blanshard, *American Freedom and Catholic Power* (Boston: Beacon
    Press, 1949).

11 This is largely the thesis defended by Columbia University law professor
    Philip Hamburger in his *Separation of Church and State* (Cambridge,
    Mass.: Harvard University Press, 2002). I published a very positive review
    of the book a few years after it was released: Francis J. Beckwith, "Gimme
    That Ol' Time Separation: A Review Essay of *Separation of Church and
    State* by Philip Hamburger," *Chapman Law Review* 8, no. 1 (2005): 109–27.

12 *Dignitatis Humanae: Vatican Declaration on Religious Freedom*, Decem-
    ber 7, 1965, http://www.vatican.va/archive/hist_councils/ii_vatican
    _council/documents/vat-ii_decl_19651207_dignitatis-humanae_en.html.

13 John Courtney Murray, S.J., *We Hold These Truths: Catholic Reflections
    on the American Proposition* (New York: Sheed & Ward, 1960); Robert P.
    George, "A Clash of Orthodoxies," *First Things,* August/September 1999,
    www.firstthings.com/article/1999/08/a-clash-of-orthodoxies; Richard John
    Neuhaus, *The Naked Public Square: Religion and Democracy in America*
    (Grand Rapids: Eerdmans, 1984); Richard John Neuhaus, *American Baby-
    lon: Notes of a Christian Exile* (New York: Basic Books, 2009). Fr. Neuhaus
    published *The Naked Public Square* while he was still a Lutheran minister.

14 Stephen V. Monsma, *Positive Neutrality: Letting Religious Freedom Ring*
    (Westport, Conn.: Greenwood Press, 1993); Daniel Driesbach, *Thomas
    Jefferson and the Wall of Separation between Church and State* (New York
    University Press, 2002); Stephen D. Smith, "Is a Coherent Theory of Reli-
    gious Freedom Possible?, *Constitutional Commentary* 15 (1998): 73–86;
    Michael W. McConnell, "The Origins and Historical Understanding of
    Free Exercise of Religion," *Harvard Law Review* 103, no. 7 (1990): 1409–517;
    Hamburger, *Separation of Church and State.*

15 Phillip E. Johnson, *Darwin on Trial* (Chicago: Regnery Gateway, 1991).

16 Dembski, *Design Inference*; Behe, *Darwin's Black Box.*

17 I make that very point in a 2003 article: "Unlike their creationist predeces-
    sors, ID proponents have developed highly sophisticated arguments, have
    had their works published by prestigious presses and in academic journals,
    have aired their views among critics in the corridors of major universities
    and institutions, and have been recognized by leading periodicals, both
    academic and non-academic. This is no small accomplishment. Given the
    negative image of 'creationists,' what the ID movement has accomplished
    in fewer than two decades is nothing short of astounding." Beckwith, "Sci-
    ence and Religion 20 Years after *McLean v. Arkansas*," 466–67.

18 I am referring to politically liberal views of religion in the public square
    often associated with thinkers like Ronald Dworkin, John Rawls, Bruce
    Ackerman, and Richard Rorty. See, for example, Ronald Dworkin, *Life's
    Dominion: An Argument about Abortion, Euthanasia, and Individual Free-
    dom* (New York, Knopf, 1993); Rawls, *Political Liberalism*; Bruce Ackerman,
    Social Justice in the Liberal State (New Haven, Conn.: Yale University Press,

1980); and Richard Rorty, "Religion as a Conversation Stopper," *Common Knowledge* 3 (1994): 106.

19 Take, for example, my comments in the introduction to *Law, Darwinism, and Public Education* (xxii): "My primary concern in this book is not with the soundness or persuasive power of the scientific and philosophical arguments of ID proponents, even though we will touch on those arguments and their strengths. Rather, my chief focus will be on answering a question of constitutional jurisprudence and political philosophy: given the Supreme Court's holding in *Edwards*, would a statute or government policy requiring or permitting the teaching of ID in public schools violate the Establishment Clause of the First Amendment?"

20 I eventually left the Dawson Institute in 2007 after the dean of Baylor's College of Arts & Science invited me to join the philosophy department. Because the university had decided to end its graduate programs in Church-State Studies, all of the institute's remaining faculty members were placed in other academic units.

21 Francis J. Beckwith and Douglas Laycock, "Is Teaching Intelligent Design Legal?," *Legal Affairs*, September 26, 2005, http://www.legalaffairs.org/webexclusive/debateclub_id0905.msp.

22 Beckwith in Beckwith and Laycock, "Is Teaching Intelligent Design Legal?"

23 When I use the term "orthodox Christian" I am not referring to Eastern Orthodoxy, but rather to Christians—whether Catholic, Protestant, or Orthodox—who can affirm the Nicene Creed (A.D. 381).

24 Dawkins writes:

> A universe in which we are alone except for other slowly evolved intelligences is a very different universe from one with an original guiding agent whose intelligent design is responsible for its very existence. I accept that it may not be so easy in practice to distinguish one kind of universe from the other. Nevertheless, there is something utterly special about the hypothesis of ultimate design, and equally special about the only known alternative: gradual evolution in the broad sense. They are close to being irreconcilably different. Like nothing else, evolution really does provide an explanation for the existence of entities whose improbability would otherwise, for practical purposes, rule them out. And the conclusion to the argument, as I shall show . . . is close to being terminally fatal to the God Hypothesis. (Richard Dawkins, *The God Hypothesis* [London: Bantam, 2006], 61)

25 Writes Dennett:

> Almost no one is indifferent to Darwin, and no one should be. The Darwinian theory is a scientific theory, and a great one, but that is not all it is. The creationists who oppose it so bitterly are right about one thing: Darwin's dangerous idea cuts much deeper into the fabric of

our most fundamental beliefs than many of its sophisticated apologists have yet admitted, even to themselves.

The sweet, simple vision of the song, taken literally, is one that most of us have outgrown, however fondly we may recall it. The kindly God who lovingly fashioned each and every one of us (all creatures great and small) and sprinkled the sky with shining stars for our delight—*that* God is, like Santa Claus, a myth of childhood, not anything a sane, undeluded adult could literally believe in. *That* God must either be turned into a symbol for something less concrete or abandoned altogether. (Daniel Dennett, *Darwin's Dangerous Idea: Evolutions and the Meanings of Life* [London: Penguin, 1995], 18)

26 Etienne Gilson, *From Aristotle to Darwin and Back Again: A Journey in Final Causality, Species, and Evolution*, trans. John Lyon (Notre Dame, Ind.: University of Notre Dame Press, 1994); William E. Carroll, "Creation, Evolution, and Thomas Aquinas," *Revue des Questions Scientifiques* 171 (2000): 319–47; William E. Carroll, "At the Mercy of Chance? Evolution and the Catholic Tradition," *Revue des Questions Scientifiques* 177 (2006): 179–204; Stephen Barr, "Defining Darwinisms," letters in response to Avery Cardinal Dulles' "God and Evolution," *First Things*, January 2008, https://www.firstthings.com/article/2008/01/january-letters-8; Edward Feser, *The Last Superstition* (South Bend, Ind.: St. Augustine's Press, 2008), 110–19; Feser, *Aquinas*, 110–20; Sr. Damien Marie Savino, F.S.E., "Atheistic Science: The Only Option?," *Logos: A Journal of Catholic Thought and Culture* 12, no. 4 (2009): 56–73; Ric Machuga, *In Defense of the Soul: What It Means to Be Human* (Grand Rapids: Baker Book House, 2002), especially 161–66; Brad S. Gregory, "Science v. Religion? The Insights and Oversights of the 'New Atheists,'" *Logos: A Journal of Catholic Thought and Culture* 12, no. 4 (2009): 17–55; Thomas W. Tkacz, "Thomas Aquinas vs. the Intelligent Designers: What Is God's Finger Doing in My Pre-biotic Soup?," in *Intelligent Design: Real Science or Religion in Disguise?*, ed. Robert Baird and Stuart Rosenbaum (Amherst, N.Y.: Prometheus Books, 2007), 275–82.

27 Walter Bradley, Charles Thaxton, and Roger L. Olsen, *The Mystery of Life's Origin: Reassessing Current Theories* (Dallas: Lewis & Stanley, 1984).

28 Another important work in this regard is the textbook *Of Pandas and People*, 2nd ed. (Dallas: Haughton, 1993), coauthored by Dean Percival Davis and Dean Kenyon (biologist at San Francisco State University), the latter of whom wrote the foreword to the Bradley, Thaxton, and Olsen book *The Mystery of Life's Origin. Of Pandas and People* was not only influenced by *The Mystery of Life's Origin* but also by the legal battles over the teaching of creationism in public schools in the 1980s. It is clear that Davis and Kenyon wrote it in such a way as to avoid the constitutional flaws that had plagued earlier legislative attempts to inject creationism into public education

science curricula. Thaxton, one of the coauthors of *The Mystery of Life's Origin*, also served as the academic editor for the second edition of *Of Pandas and People* (see Library of Congress, https://lccn.loc.gov/00711376).

29 See, for example, Bradley, Thaxton, and Olsen, *The Mystery of Life's Origin*, 130–31.

30 William A. Dembski, *No Free Lunch: Why Specified Complexity Cannot Be Purchased without Intelligence* (Lanham, Md.: Rowman & Littlefield); and William A. Dembski, *Intelligent Design: The Bridge between Science and Theology* (Downers Grove, Ill.: InterVarsity, 1999), 122–52.

31 See, for example, Behe, *Darwin's Black Box*, 38–45.

32 See, for example, Dembski, *Design Inference*, 26–31, 62; Dembski, *Intelligent Design*, 127–31; and Michael Behe, "Philosophical Objections to Intelligent Design: Response to Critics," The Discovery Institute, July 31, 2000, https://evolutionnews.org/2016/10/philosophical_o/.

33 See, for example, Meyer, *Signature in the Cell*, 215–24.

34 Beckwith, *Law, Darwinism, and Public Education*, xiii.

35 See Ronald H. Numbers, *The Creationists: From Scientific Creationism to Intelligent Design*, 2nd ed. (Cambridge, Mass.: Harvard University Press, 2006).

36 Not all Evangelicals and Fundamentalists took this approach to Darwinian evolution. Take, for example, the comments made by Scottish theologian James Orr, a contributor to the seven-volume *The Fundamentals* (1910–1915), which is the foundational document of American fundamentalism. Arguing that Darwinian evolution is not inconsistent with the providence of God, he wrote, "The conclusion from the whole is, that, up to the present hour, science and the Biblical views of God, man, and the world, do not stand in any real relation of conflict." James Orr, "Science and the Christian Faith," in *The Fundamentals*, vol. 4, ed. R. A. Torrey and A. C. Dixon (LaSalle, Ill.: Testimony, 1910–1915), 103.

37 See, generally, Numbers, *The Creationists*.

38 Statement of Biblical Worldview, Patrick Henry College, https://www.phc.edu/statement-of-biblical-worldview.

39 Doctrinal Statement, Cedarville University, https://www.cedarville.edu/Why-Cedarville/Doctrinal-Statement.aspx#believe.

40 Doctrinal Statement, Biola University, https://www.biola.edu/about/doctrinal-statement.

41 Doctrinal Statement, Biola University.

42 *The World's Most Famous Court Trial: State of Tennessee v. John Thomas Scopes,* complete stenographic report of trial, July 10–21, 1925, including speeches and arguments of attorneys (New York: Da Capo Press, 1971); Scopes v. State, 289 S.W. 363 (1927).

43 This was in fact the conclusion drawn in 1874 about Darwinism by the great American Presbyterian theologian Charles Hodge: "We have thus arrived at the answer to our question, What is Darwinism? It is Atheism. This does

not mean, as before said, that Mr. Darwin himself and all who adopt his views are atheists; but it means that his theory is atheistic; that the exclusion of design from nature is, as Dr. Gray says, tantamount to atheism." Charles Hodge, *What Is Darwinism?* (New York: Scribner, Armstrong, and Co., 1874), 177.

44 Chapter 27, Tenn. Acts 1925; Tenn.Code.Ann. § 49–1922 (1966 Repl. Vol); Initiated Act No. 1, Ark Acts 1929; Ark Stat Ann §§ 80–1627, 80–1628 (1960 Repl Vol).

45 *Epperson*, 393 U.S.

46 Ark. Stat. Ann. § 80–1663, *et seq.* (1981 Supp.); La. Rev. Stat. Ann. §§ 17:286.1–17:286.7 (West 1982).

47 *McLean*, 529 F.Supp.; *Edwards*, 482 U.S.

48 Beckwith, *Law, Darwinism, and Public Education*, 91–144.

49 Dembski, *Intelligent Design*, 133 (emphasis original).

50 Dembski, *Intelligent Design*, 129.

51 William A. Dembski, *The Design Revolution: Answering the Toughest Questions about Intelligent Design* (Downers Grove, Ill.: InterVarsity, 2004), 44.

52 Dembski, *The Design Revolution*.

53 Charles Darwin, *On the Origin of Species* (1876; repr., New York: New York University Press, 1988), 151, as quoted in Michael J. Behe, "Evidence for Design at the Foundation of Life," in *Science and Evidence for Design in the Universe*, by Michael J. Behe, William A. Dembski, and Stephen C. Meyer (San Francisco: Ignatius Press, 2000), 119.

54 Behe, "Evidence for Design at the Foundation of Life," 120.

55 Behe, *Darwin's Black Box*, 4.

56 Behe, *Darwin's Black Box*, 26–39, 65–73.

57 Behe, "Evidence for Design at the Foundation of Life," 123. In this quote Behe is referring to the cilium, though he draws the same conclusion about the bacterial flagellum as well.

58 Behe himself holds to common descent and rejects a Darwinian account only in these few seemingly exceptional cases.

> Many people think that questioning Darwinian evolution must be equivalent to espousing creationism. As commonly understood, creationism involves belief in an earth formed only about ten thousand years ago, an interpretation of the Bible that is still very popular. For the record, I have no reason to doubt that the universe is the billions of years old that physicists say it is. Further, I find the idea of common descent (that all organisms share a common ancestor) fairly convincing, and have no particular reason to doubt it. I greatly respect the work of my colleagues who study the development and behavior of organisms within an evolutionary framework, and I think that evolutionary biologists have contributed enormously to our understanding of the world. Although Darwin's mechanism—natural selection

working on variation—might explain many things, however, I do not believe it explains molecular life. I also do not think it surprising that the new science of the very small might change the way we view the less small. (Behe, *Darwin's Black Box*, 5–6)

59 Behe, *Darwin's Black Box*, 193 (emphasis original).

60 Behe, *Darwin's Black Box*, 194–96.

61 Behe, *Darwin's Black Box*, 196–97, 232–53.

62 Behe, *Darwin's Black Box*, 243–45.

63 Dembski, *Intelligent Design*, 119.

64 Phillip Johnson, *Reason in the Balance: The Case against Naturalism in Science, Law, and Education* (Downers Grove, Ill.: InterVarsity, 1996), 208.

65 See, for example, Branden Fitelson, Christopher Stephens, and Elliott Sober, "How Not to Detect Design," Philosophy of Science 66, no. 3 (1999): 472–88 (review of Dembski, *Design Inference*); Kenneth R. Miller, *Finding Darwin's God: A Scientist's Search for Common Ground between God and Evolution* (New York: Harper, 2000); Robert T. Pennock, ed., *Intelligent Design Creationism and Its Critics: Philosophical, Theological, and Scientific Perspectives* (Cambridge, Mass.: M.I.T. Press, 2001); Elliott Sober, "What Is Wrong with Intelligent Design," *Quarterly Review of Biology* 82, no. 1 (2007): 3–8; Matt Young and Taner Edis, eds., *Why Intelligent Design Fails: A Scientific Critique of the New Creationism* (Piscataway, N.J.: Rutgers University Press, 2004).

66 The Nicene Creed.

67 "But if in efficient causes it is possible to go on to infinity, there will be no first efficient cause, neither will there be an ultimate effect, nor any intermediate efficient causes; all of which is plainly false. Therefore it is necessary to admit a first efficient cause, to which everyone gives the name of God." *ST* I.Q2, art. 3, *resp.*

68 See, for example, St. Thomas Aquinas, *Summa Contra Gentiles*, book II: *Creation*, trans. James F. Anderson (Notre Dame, Ind.: University of Notre Dame Press, 1975), 38.13.

69 Aquinas writes, "Thus, it is accidental to Socrates' father that he is another man's son or not. But it is not accidental to the stick, in moving the stone, that it be moved by the hand; for the stick moves just so far as it is moved." Aquinas, *Summa contra gentiles*, II.38.13.

70 Quoted by John Haldane in *Atheism & Theism*, 2nd ed., by J. J. Smart and J. J. Haldane (London: Blackwell, 2003), 116. I first discovered this interesting example as it is employed by Caleb Cohoe in his article "There Must Be a First: Why Thomas Aquinas Rejects Infinite, Essentially Ordered, Causal Series," *British Journal for the History of Philosophy* 21, no. 5 (2013): 838–56.

71 Cohoe, "There Must Be a First," 840.

72 See William Lane Craig, *The Kalām Cosmological Argument* (London: Macmillan Press, 1979).

73   "To understand this we must consider that the efficient cause, which acts
     by motion, of necessity precedes its effect in time; because the effect is only
     in the end of the action, and every agent must be the principle of action.
     But if the action is instantaneous and not successive, it is not necessary for
     the maker to be prior to the thing made in duration as appears in the case
     of illumination. Hence they say that it does not follow necessarily if God is
     the active cause of the world, that He should be prior to the world in dura-
     tion; because creation, by which He produced the world, is not a successive
     change." *ST* I.Q46, art. 2, ad. 1.

74   "The articles of faith cannot be proved demonstratively, because faith is of
     things 'that appear not' (Hebrews 11:1). But that God is the Creator of the
     world: hence that the world began, is an article of faith; for we say, 'I believe
     in one God,' etc. And again, Gregory says (Hom. i in Ezech.), that Moses
     prophesied of the past, saying, 'In the beginning God created heaven and
     earth': in which words the newness of the world is stated. Therefore the
     newness of the world is known only by revelation; and therefore it cannot
     be proved demonstratively." *ST* I.Q46, art. 2, *sed contra*.

75   See, for example, Plantinga, *God, Freedom, and Evil*, 108–12.

76   See, for example, Richard Swinburne, *The Existence of God*, rev. ed.
     (Oxford: Oxford University Press, 2004), especially chapter 6.

77   To say that God is simple is to say that he has no composition. As I noted
     in chapter 3, since all created things by nature must be composed in some
     way—whole/parts, substance/accidents, essence/existence—and God is
     not a creature, God must be simple. This is why for the classical theist,
     God's attributes, though conceptually separable in our intellects, are
     not separable in God. According to Aquinas, divine simplicity follows
     from God as first cause. Included among his reasons are the following:
     (1) "Every composite is posterior to its component parts, and is depen-
     dent on them; but God is the first being," and thus could not be a com-
     posite being. (2) "Every composite has a cause, for things in themselves
     different cannot unite unless something causes them to unite. But God is
     uncaused [. . .], since He is the first efficient cause." *ST* I.Q3, art. 7, *resp.*

78   "We must say, however, that all things are subject to divine providence,
     not only in general, but even in their own individual selves. This is made
     evident thus. For since every agent acts for an end, the ordering of effects
     towards that end extends as far as the causality of the first agent extends."
     ST I.Q22, art. 2, *resp.*

79   "Two things belong to providence—namely, the type of the order of things
     foreordained towards an end; and the execution of this order, which
     is called government. As regards the first of these, God has immediate
     providence over everything, because He has in His intellect the types of
     everything, even the smallest; and whatsoever causes He assigns to certain
     effects, He gives them the power to produce those effects. Whence it must
     be that He has beforehand the type of those effects in His mind. As to the

second, there are certain intermediaries of God's providence; for He governs things inferior by superior, not on account of any defect in His power, but by reason of the abundance of His goodness; so that the dignity of causality is imparted even to creatures." *ST* I. Q22, art. 3, *resp.*

80 St. Thomas Aquinas, *Summa Contra Gentiles*, book III: *Providence*, trans. Vernon J. Bourke (Notre Dame, Ind.: University of Notre Dame Press, 1975), 70.8.

81 "A full-blown occasionalist, then, might be described as one who subscribes to the following two tenets: (1) the positive thesis that God is the only genuine cause; (2) the negative thesis that no creaturely cause is a genuine cause but at most an occasional cause." Sukjae Lee, "Occasionalism," *Stanford Encyclopedia of Philosophy,* October 20, 2008, https://plato .stanford.edu/entries/occasionalism/.

82 "Deism in the popular sense asserts that a supreme being created the world but then, like an absentee landlord, left it to run on its own." William L. Rowe, "The Meaning of Deism," in "Deism," *Routledge Encyclopedia of Philosophy* (New York: Taylor & Francis, 1998), https://www.rep.routledge .com/articles/thematic/deism/v-1/sections/the-meaning-of-deism.

83 "God is in all things; not, indeed, as part of their essence, nor as an accident, but as an agent is present to that upon which it works. For an agent must be joined to that wherein it acts immediately and touch it by its power. . . . Now since God is very being by His own essence, created being must be His proper effect; as to ignite is the proper effect of fire. Now God causes this effect in things not only when they first begin to be, but as long as they are preserved in being; as light is caused in the air by the sun as long as the air remains illuminated. Therefore as long as a thing has being, God must be present to it, according to its mode of being. But being is innermost in each thing and most fundamentally inherent in all things since it is formal in respect of everything found in a thing, as was shown above. . . . Hence it must be that God is in all things, and innermostly." *ST* I.Q8, art. 1, *resp.*

84 Gregory, "Science v. Religion?," 41.

85 As three of ID advocates claim, "Design theory, unlike neo-Darwinism, attributes this appearance to a designing intelligence, but it does not address the characteristics or identity of the designing intelligence." David K. DeWolf, Stephen C. Meyer, and Mark Edward DeForrest, "Teaching the Origins Controversy: Science, or Religion, or Speech?," *Utah Law Review* (2000): 85.

86 Dembski, *No Free Lunch*, 334–35.

87 *ST* I.Q105, art. 7, ad. 1.

88 *ST* I.Q105, art. 7, ad. 1.

89 *ST* I.Q105, art. 8, *resp.*

90 "The rational soul can be made only by creation; which, however, is not true of other forms." *ST* I.Q90, art. 2, *resp.*

91 Koons and Gage, "St. Thomas Aquinas on Intelligent Design," 82–85.

92 Jonathan Wells, "Unseating Naturalism: Recent Insights in Developmental Biology," in *Mere Creation: Science, Faith, and Intelligent Design*, ed. William A. Dembski (Downers Grove, Ill.: InterVarsity, 1998), 51–70.

93 Center for Renewal of Science and Culture, the Discovery Institute, "The Wedge" (1998), 2, https://ncse.com/creationism/general/wedge-document.

94 So says the Discovery Institute:

> The social consequences of materialism have been devastating. As symptoms, those consequences are certainly worth treating. However, we are convinced that in order to defeat materialism, we must cut it off at its source. That source is scientific materialism. This is precisely our strategy. If we view the predominant materialistic science as a giant tree, our strategy is intended to function as a "wedge" that, while relatively small, can split the trunk when applied at its weakest points. The very beginning of this strategy, the "thin edge of the wedge," was Phillip Johnson's critique of Darwinism begun in 1991 in *Darwinism on Trial*, and continued in *Reason in the Balance* and *Defeating Darwinism by Opening Minds*. Michael Behe's highly successful *Darwin's Black Box* followed Johnson's work. We are building on this momentum, broadening the wedge with a positive scientific alternative to materialistic scientific theories, which has come to be called the theory of intelligent design (ID). Design theory promises to reverse the stifling dominance of the materialist worldview, and to replace it with a science consonant with Christian and theistic convictions. ("The Wedge," 5)

95 Dembski, *Intelligent Design*, 120.

96 Lynn Sagan, "On the Origin of Mitosing Cells," *Journal of Theoretical Biology* 14, no. 3 (1967): 255–74.

97 Simon Conway Morris, *Life's Solution: Inevitable Humans in a Lonely Universe* (Cambridge: Cambridge University Press, 2003).

98 This, by the way, is the view embraced by the great Catholic and Thomist philosopher, Etienne Gilson.

> Finalists . . . are constrained by the evidence of facts, which in the tradition and through the example of Aristotle they desire to make intelligible. As far as I know, they do not claim anymore that "scientific" evidence is on their side; the scientific description of ontogenesis and phylogenesis remains identically what it is without the need of going back to the first, transscientific principles of mechanism or finalism. Natural science neither destroys final causality nor establishes it. These two principles belong to the philosophy of the science of nature, to that which we have called its "wisdom." What scientists, as scientists, can do to help clarify the problem of natural teleology is not to busy themselves with it. They are the most qualified of all to keep philosophizing about it, if they so desire; but it is then necessary

that they agree to philosophize. . . . *Finalist philosophies are respon-sible to themselves; they do not involve themselves with science at all, and science, as such, has no cause to concern itself with them.* (Gilson, *From Aristotle to Darwin and Back Again*, 15–16, 133) (emphasis added)

99   Meyer, for example, in 2000 claimed that thanks to advances in ID theory "we may find that we have also restored some of the intellectual underpinning of traditional Western metaphysics and theistic belief." Stephen C. Meyer, "DNA and Other Designs," *First Things*, April 2000, https://www .firstthings.com/article/2000/04/dna-and-other-designs.

100   Beckwith, *Taking Rites Seriously*, 158.

101   Edward Feser, *Scholastic Metaphysics: A Contemporary Introduction* (Neunkirchen-Seelscheid, Ger.: Editiones Scholasticae, 2014), 91.

102   Having already established the impossibility of an infinite regress of here and now causes in the first three ways, Aquinas leaves out that premise in the fifth way.

103   *ST* I.Q2, art. 3, *resp.*

104   Dawkins, *The God Delusion*, 61.

105   Dawkins, *The God Delusion*, 285. According to Dawkins, these quotes from Wise are taken from his contribution to the book *In Six Days: Why 50 Scientists Choose to Believe in Creation*, ed. John F. Ashton (Green Forrest, Ark.: Master Books, 2000).

106   Dawkins, *The God Delusion*, 284, 285.

107   Dawkins, *The God Delusion*, 79.

108   William Paley, *Natural Theology; Or, Evidences of the Existence and Attributes of the Deity, Collected from the Appearances of Nature*, 6th ed. (New York: Cambridge University Press, 2009; originally published 1803), 1–18.

109   Writes Dawkins, "The young Darwin was impressed by it when, as a Cambridge undergraduate, he read it in William Paley's *Natural Theology*. Unfortunately for Paley, the mature Darwin blew it out of the water. There has probably never been a more devastating rout of popular belief by clever reasoning than Charles Darwin's destruction of the argument from design. It was so unexpected. Thanks to Darwin, it is no longer true to say that nothing that we know looks designed unless it is designed. Evolution by natural selection produces an excellent simulacrum of design, mounting prodigious heights of complexity and elegance. And among these eminences of pseudo-design are nervous systems which—among their more modest accomplishments—manifest goal-seeking behaviour that, even in a tiny insect, resembles a sophisticated heatseeking missile more than a simple arrow on target" (Dawkins, *The God Delusion*, 79).

110   *ST* I.Q16, art. 2, *resp.*

111   *ST* I–II.Q1, art. 8, *sed contra.*

112   *ST* I–II.Q5, art. 5, *resp.*

113   See *ST* I–II.Q4.

114   See Koons and Gage, "St. Thomas Aquinas on Intelligent Design"; J. P. Moreland, *Scientism and Secularism* (Wheaton, Ill.: Crossway, 2018); Jay W. Richards, ed., *God and Evolution* (Seattle: Discovery Institute Press, 2010); and C. John Collins, "How to Think about God's Action in the World," in *Theistic Evolution: A Scientific, Philosophical, and Theological Critique*, ed. J. P. Moreland et al. (Wheaton, Ill.: Crossway, 2017), 659–81.

115   I should note that Logan was my teaching assistant for two classes while he was studying for his Ph.D. at Baylor University (2009–2014). Also, I served on the committee for his dissertation, "Objectivity and Subjectivity in Epistemology: A Defense of the Phenomenal Conception of Evidence" (Ph.D. diss., Baylor University, 2014).

116   *ST* I.Q44, art. 3, *resp.*

117   *ST* I.Q44, art. 3, ad. 1.

118   It is my understanding that this is likely, though no one knows for sure. However, assuming that Darwinian evolution is true, we know that *Homo sapiens* had some predecessor species. So, if you are not comfortable with *Homo heidelbergensis*, just imagine it is another.

119   In defense of this interpretation of Aquinas, they cite this passage from the *Summa theologica*: "But in the first production of corporeal creatures no transmutation from potentiality to act can have taken place, and accordingly, the corporeal forms that bodies had when first produced came immediately from God, whose bidding alone matter obeys, as its own proper cause. To signify this, Moses prefaces each work with the words, 'God said, Let this thing be,' or 'that'" (*ST* I.Q65, art. 4, *resp.*). But all this passage is saying is that when God first creates, he is not actualizing some potential in matter, since he is the absolute creator of both form and matter. As we shall see in the text, Aquinas does hold that living creatures of one species can be progenitors of another species and thus produce new forms.

      Another passage, brought to my attention by a friend in private correspondence, states: "It is impossible for any creature to create, either by its own power or instrumentally—that is, ministerially" (*ST* I.Q45, art. 5, *resp.*). However, it is clear from the context that Aquinas is not referring to God working through secondary causes but, rather, is addressing the question as to whether God can impart to other beings the power to create ex nihilo, which Aquinas argues is a power unique to the divine nature.

120   Koons and Gage, "St. Thomas Aquinas on Intelligent Design," 85.

121   Koons and Gage, "St. Thomas Aquinas on Intelligent Design," 85.

122   "In government there are two things to be considered; the design of government, which is providence itself; and the execution of the design. As to the design of government, God governs all things immediately; whereas in its execution, He governs some things by means of others." *ST* I.Q103, art. 6, *resp.*

123 Koons and Gage point out that Aquinas argued that "it therefore follows of necessity that the form of the universe is intended and willed by God, and for that reason is not the result of chance" ("St. Thomas Aquinas on Intelligent Design," 88, quoting Aquinas, *Summa contra gentiles*, II.39.6. They mistakenly cite it as II.40). The implication here is that the randomness component in Darwinian theory is ruled out by Aquinas. But that's not the type of "chance" that Aquinas is discussing. He is addressing the question of whether the distinctions between creatures in creation *ultimately* derive from chance. The answer is clearly "no," since, as Brian Davies puts it, Aquinas "takes all creatures to spring from God's eternal will, which he certainly does not believe to be a random process or something coming about by chance" (Brian Davies, *Thomas Aquinas' "Summa Contra Gentiles"* [New York: Oxford University Press, 2016], 161). If this were not the case, it would mean that the winnings of my late uncle, Jimmy "Fiore" Casella (1924–1976), in the World Series of Poker in 1971 and 1974 were outside the scope of God's providence.

124 "[In God is] . . . the most perfect wisdom for ordering and the most perfect power for operating. So, He Himself through His wisdom must arrange the orders for all things, even the least; on the other hand, He may execute the small details by means of other lower powers, through which He Himself works, as does a universal and higher power through a lower and particular power. It is appropriate, then, that there be inferior agents as executors of divine providence." Aquinas, *Summa contra gentiles*, III.77.1.

125 "It is certain however, that God has willed from eternity the existence of whatever He now wills to exist, for no new movement of will can possibly accrue to Him. Nor could any defect or obstacle stand in the way of His power, nor could anything else be looked for as cause of the universal production of creatures, since nothing besides Him is uncreated, as we have proved above. Therefore, it seems necessary to conclude that God brought creatures into being from all eternity." Aquinas, *Summa contra gentiles*, II.32.6.

126 "The preservation of things by God is a continuation of that action by which He gives existence, which action is without either motion or time; so also the light in the air is by the continual influence of the sun." *ST* I.Q104, art 1, ad. 1.

127 *ST* I.Q90, art. 2, *resp.*

128 *ST* I.Q73, art. 1, ad. 3.

129 Aquinas, *Summa contra gentiles*, III.70.6.

130 *ST* I.Q90, art. 2, *resp.* What Aquinas means here by "create" is creation ex nihilo, or to directly create, rather than producing an effect through secondary causes as in the case of animal generation.

5: Aquinas as Evangelical

1 Carl F. H. Henry, *Remaking the Modern Mind* (Grand Rapids: Eerdmans, 1946), 283.

2 "The Thomistic empiricism throws both and religion into turmoil." Edward John Carnell, *An Introduction to Christian Apologetics: A Philosophical Defense of the Trinitarian-Theistic Faith* (Grand Rapids: Eerdmans, 1948), 150.

3 "Following in the footsteps of the medieval synthesis and particularly that of Thomas [Aquinas], the church of Luther's day expressed its loyalty to Christ with vehemence. At the same time, it was also loyal to the growing ethical consciousness of man speaking through the infallible authoritative pronouncements of the church. The Christ of the Bible was permitted to teach only what the living church said it could teach. This meant that Christ was allowed to teach nothing that was out of accord with the Socratic-Plotinian vision. The synthesis of nature and grace, involved at every major point of doctrine, is in great measure a reduction of the biblical teaching to that of the self-sufficient moral man." Cornelius Van Til, "Confessing Jesus Christ," in *Scripture and Confession: A Book about Confessions Old and New*, ed. John H. Skilton (Princeton, N.J.: Presbyterian and Reformed, 1973), http://www.the-highway.com/articleMar09.html.

4 "Aquinas held that man had revolted against God and thus was fallen. But Aquinas had an incomplete view of the Fall. He thought that the Fall did not affect man as a whole but only in part. In his view the will was fallen or corrupted, but the intellect was affected. Thus people could rely on their own human wisdom, and this meant that people were free to mix the teachings of the Bible with the teachings of the non-Christian philosophers." Francis A. Schaeffer, *How Should We Then Live? The Rise and Decline of Western Thought and Culture* (Old Tappan, N.J.: Fleming H. Revell, 1976), 51–52.

5 "Just as faith apprehends salvation truth, so reason apprehends creation truth. Although Thomas [Aquinas] held to the reality of general revelation, one wishes that he had made more explicit revelations informing of nature in order that his rather stark antithesis between nature and grace might have been softened." Bruce Demarest, *General Revelation* (Grand Rapids: Zondervan, 1982), 40.

6 "The first [side-effect of Aquinas' thought] is that, where a theology is based partly upon Christian revelation and partly upon alien philosophical ideas, the result is often a misguided hotchpotch. At best the end-product is a mixture containing ideas that cancel each other out." Brown, *Philosophy and the Christian Faith*, 38.

7 J. P. Moreland, for example, defends a view of the soul that he calls "Thomistic." See, for example, J. P. Moreland and Scott B. Rae, *Body & Soul: Human Nature & the Crisis in Ethics* (Downers Grove, Ill.: InterVarsity, 2000). See also Moreland, *The Recalcitrant* Imago Dei. For a critique, see Christine Van Dyke, "Not Properly a Person: The Rational Soul and 'Thomistic Substance Dualism,'" *Faith and Philosophy* 26, no. 2 (2009): 186–204.

8 Ken Collins and Jerry Walls, *Roman but Not Catholic: What Remains at Stake 500 Years after the Reformation* (Grand Rapids: Baker Book House, 2017).

9   For more detailed presentations of Aquinas' view on salvation (including justification), see Romanus Cessario, "Aquinas on Christian Salvation"; and Daniel A. Keating, "Justification, Sanctification, and Divinization in Thomas Aquinas," both in *Aquinas on Doctrine: A Critical Introduction*, ed. Thomas G. Weinday, O.F.M., Daniel A. Keating, and John P. Yocum (New York: T&T Clark, 2004), 117–58; and Davies, *The Thought of Thomas Aquinas*, 260–73, 320–39.

10 See Beckwith, *Return to Rome*; Beckwith, "A Journey to Catholicism"; and Beckwith, "Catholicism Rejoinder," in *Journeys of Faith: Evangelicalism, Eastern Orthodoxy, Catholicism, and Anglicanism*, ed. Robert L. Plummer (Grand Rapids: Zondervan, 2012), 129–36.

11 Norman L. Geisler and Ralph McKenzie, *Roman Catholics and Evangelicals: Agreements and Differences* (Grand Rapids: Baker, 1995), 93.

12 Geisler and McKenzie, *Roman Catholics and Evangelicals*, 93.

13 Geisler and McKenzie, *Roman Catholics and Evangelicals*, 93n51.

14 John Gerstner, "Aquinas Was a Protestant," *Tabletalk Magazine*, May 1994, 14. For a strong and compelling critique of Gerstner's article from a Reformed perspective, see Robert L. Reymond, "Dr. John H. Gerstner on Thomas Aquinas as a Protestant," *Westminster Journal of Theology* 59 (1997): 113–21.

15 Norman L. Geisler, *Systematic Theology*, vol. 3, *Sin, Salvation* (Grand Rapids: Baker, 2004), 288.

16 John Gerstner, "History of the Doctrine of Justification," http://www .apuritansmind.com/justification/gerstnerjohnjustificationhistory.htm; and R. C. Sproul, *Faith Alone: The Evangelical Doctrine of Justification* (Grand Rapids: Baker, 1995), 135–39.

17 See, for example, Geisler, *Systematic Theology*, 3:277–98.

18 Geisler, *Systematic Theology*, 3:259.

19 Geisler, *Systematic Theology*, 3:261–67.

20 See also Geisler and MacKenzie, *Roman Catholics and Evangelicals*, 221–28.

21 "In recent years the Roman communion has published a new Catholic catechism, which unequivocally reaffirms the doctrines of the Council of Trent, including Trent's definition of the doctrine of justification." R. C. Sproul, "Is the Reformation Over?," *Tabletalk Magazine*, September 1, 2009, http://www.ligonier.org/learn/articles/reformation-over/.

22 Sproul, "Is the Reformation Over?"

23 Writes Sproul:

> I was surprised to learn (when I was in seminary) that his strange-sounding teaching (i.e., regeneration precedes faith) was not novel. Augustine, Martin Luther, John Calvin, Jonathan Edwards, George Whitefield—even the great medieval theologian Thomas Aquinas taught this doctrine. Thomas Aquinas is the Doctor Angelicus of the Roman Catholic Church. For centuries his theological teaching

was accepted as official dogma by most Catholics. So he was the last
person I expected to hold such a view of regeneration. Yet Aquinas
insisted that regenerating grace is operative grace, not cooperative
grace. Aquinas spoke of prevenient grace, but he spoke of a grace that
comes before faith, which is regeneration. (R. C. Sproul, "Regeneration
Precedes Faith" [1990], http://www.monergism.com/thethreshold/
articles/onsite/sproul01.html)

24   Sproul, "Regeneration Precedes Faith."

25   Gerstner, "Aquinas Was a Protestant," 13–14.

26   As we have seen, Gerstner maintains that Thomas Aquinas' view is practically indistinguishable from views embraced by the Protestant Reformers,
whereas Geisler takes the more modest view that Thomas' position, though
not fully Protestant, did not fall prey to the semi-Pelagianism of late medieval Catholicism, the Council of Trent, and contemporary Catholicism.

27   For example, Geisler, Sproul, and Gerstner each connect Aquinas' view
with St. Augustine's account of justification. (See Geisler, *Systematic Theology,* 3:291–93; Sproul, *Faith Alone,* 135–39; Gerstner, "Aquinas Was a
Protestant," 14.) Geisler places Aquinas in continuity with not only Augustine but with John Chrysostom, Cyril of Jerusalem, and Irenaeus of Lyons
(Geisler, *Systematic Theology,* 3:289–91). (I address in the text Geisler's use
of these four church fathers.) Gerstner mentions St. Anselm of Canterbury
(1033–1109) as a "solafideian," quoting A. H. Strong's citation of Anselm
(Gerstner, "History of the Doctrine of Justification").

28   For example, in the *Summa theologica,* Thomas employs two of St. Augustine's distinctions on the nature of grace in his account of grace and justification. The first is the distinction between operating and cooperating grace
(*ST* II–I.Q111, art. 2). The second is the distinction between prevenient and
subsequent grace. Writes Aquinas, "And hence grace, inasmuch as it causes
the first effect in us, is called prevenient with respect to the second, and
inasmuch as it causes the second, it is called subsequent with respect to
the first effect. And as one effect is posterior to this effect, and prior to that,
so may grace be called prevenient and subsequent on account of the same
effect viewed relatively to diverse others. And this is what Augustine says
(De Natura et Gratia xxxi): 'It is prevenient, inasmuch as it heals, and subsequent, inasmuch as, being healed, we are strengthened; it is prevenient,
inasmuch as we are called, and subsequent, inasmuch as we are glorified.'"
ST II–I.Q111, art. 3.

29   The following quotes are employed by Geisler, *Systematic Theology,*
3:289–91. However, because I contrast them with another set of quotes
from the same church fathers, I am using the translations published on
the New Advent Catholic website (http://www.newadvent.org/fathers/).
I chose Geisler's book because my endorsement of it appears on its back

cover. It is an endorsement I penned while I was still identified as an Evangelical Protestant.

30   St. Irenaeus of Lyons, *Against Heresies* 4.8.1, trans. Alexander Roberts and William Rambaut, in *Ante-Nicene Fathers*, vol. 1, ed. Alexander Roberts, James Donaldson, and A. Cleveland Coxe (Buffalo, N.Y.: Christian Literature, 1885), rev. and ed. for New Advent by Kevin Knight, http://www .newadvent.org/fathers/0103408.htm.

31   Cyril of Jerusalem, *Catechetical Lecture 1*, trans. Edwin Hamilton Gifford, in *Nicene and Post-Nicene Fathers*, 2nd ser., vol. 7, ed. Philip Schaff and Henry Wace (Buffalo, N.Y.: Christian Literature, 1894), rev. and ed. for New Advent by Kevin Knight, http://www.newadvent.org/fathers/310101.htm.

32   St. John Chrysostom, *Homily 4 on Ephesians*, trans. Gross Alexander, in *Nicene and Post-Nicene Fathers*, 1st ser., vol. 13, ed. Philip Schaff (Buffalo, N.Y.: Christian Literature, 1889), rev. and ed. for New Advent by Kevin Knight, http://www.newadvent.org/fathers/230104.htm; St. John Chrysostom, *Homily 11 on 2 Corinthians*, trans. Talbot W. Chambers, in *Nicene and Post-Nicene Fathers*, 1st ser., vol. 12, ed. Philip Schaff (Buffalo, N.Y.: Christian Literature, 1889), rev. and ed. for New Advent by Kevin Knight, http://www.newadvent.org/fathers/220211.htm.

33   St. Augustine, *On the Spirit and the Letter*, trans. Peter Holmes and Robert Ernest Wallis, rev. Benjamin B. Warfield, in *Nicene and Post-Nicene Fathers*, 1st ser., vol. 5, ed. Philip Schaff (Buffalo, N.Y.: Christian Literature, 1887), rev. and ed. for New Advent by Kevin Knight, http://www.newadvent .org/fathers/1502.htm.

34   See Hilaire Belloc, *How the Reformation Happened* (Rockford, Ill.: TAN Books, 1928), 1–37; and Louis Bouyer, *The Spirit and Forms of Protestantism* (London: Harvill Press, 1956).

35   For example, Geisler and MacKenzie critique and reject the Catholic views on sacramentalism, ecclesiology, and purgatory, even though, as we shall see, the early church fathers that Geisler procures to demonstrate the historical continuity of a non-Catholic view of justification seem to accept the Catholic views on sacramentalism, ecclesiology, and purgatory that the Catholic view on justification requires. See Geisler and MacKenzie, *Roman Catholics and Evangelicals*, 249–97, 331–55.

36   Writes Sproul, "All the benefits of sacramental grace, as powerful and effective as they are claimed to be, do not gain us the holiness required by absolute justice. We need a greater righteousness than whatever inheres in us, by whatever means of grace it so inheres, in order to stand before God's judgment." Sproul, *Faith Alone*, 106–7.

37   St. Irenaeus, *Against Heresies* 4.37.7.

38   Cyril of Jerusalem, *Catechetical Lectures* 1.3.4. Italicized words are St. Cyril's as noted in the first set of quotes.

39   Cyril of Jerusalem, *Catechetical Lectures* 23.9–10p33, 1116–17, as quoted in the *Catechism of the Catholic Church*, 1371.

40 St. John Chrysostom, *Homily 41 on 1 Corinthians*, trans. Talbot W. Cham-
    bers, in *Nicene and Post-Nicene Fathers*, 1st ser., vol. 12, ed. Philip Schaff
    (Buffalo, N.Y.: Christian Literature, 1889), rev. and ed. for New Advent by
    Kevin Knight, http://www.newadvent.org/fathers/220141.htm.

41 St. John Chrysostom, *Homily 3 on Philippians*, trans. John A. Broadus, in
    Nicene and Post-Nicene Fathers, 1st ser., vol. 13, ed. Philip Schaff (Buffalo,
    N.Y.: Christian Literature, 1889), rev. and ed. for New Advent by Kevin
    Knight, http://www.newadvent.org/fathers/230203.htm.

42 St. Augustine, *On Man's Perfection in Righteousness*, 20 [43] (A.D. 415),
    trans. Peter Holmes and Robert Ernest Wallis, rev. Benjamin B. Warfield,
    in *Nicene and Post-Nicene Fathers*, 1st ser., vol. 5, ed. Philip Schaff (Buf-
    falo, N.Y.: Christian Literature, 1887), rev. and ed. for New Advent by Kevin
    Knight, http://www.newadvent.org/fathers/1504.htm.

43 The *Catechism* reads:

> All who die in God's grace and friendship, but still imperfectly puri-
> fied, are indeed assured of their eternal salvation; but after death they
> undergo purification, so as to achieve the holiness necessary to enter
> the joy of heaven.

> The Church gives the name Purgatory to this final purification of the
> elect, which is entirely different from the punishment of the damned.
> The Church formulated her doctrine of faith on Purgatory especially
> at the Councils of Florence and Trent The tradition of the Church,
> by reference to certain texts of Scripture, speaks of a cleansing fire
> [Cf. 1 Cor 3:15; 1 Pet 1:7]. . . .

> This teaching is also based on the practice of prayer for the dead,
> already mentioned in Sacred Scripture: "Therefore [Judas Maccabeus]
> made atonement for the dead, that they might be delivered from their
> sin" [2 Macc 12:46]. From the beginning the Church has honored the
> memory of the dead and offered prayers in suffrage for them, above
> all the Eucharistic sacrifice, so that, thus purified, they may attain
> the beatific vision of God. . . .

> The Church also commends almsgiving, indulgences, and works of
> penance undertaken on behalf of the dead. (*Catechism of the Catholic
> Church*, 1030–32; bracketed scripture citations taken from footnotes)

44 One finds prayers for the dead inscribed in the catacombs (first through
    fourth centuries), in the earliest liturgies, and in the works of many early
    Christian writers dating back to the mid-second century (P. J. Toner,
    "Prayers for the Dead," transcr. Michael T. Barrett, *The Catholic Encyclo-
    pedia*, vol. 4 [New York: Robert Appleton, 1908], http://www.newadvent
    .org/cathen/04653a.htm). According to Robert Louis Wilken, "Early in
    the church's history Christians gathered at the tombs of martyrs to pray
    and celebrate the Eucharist. The faithful of one generation were united to

the faithful of former times, not by a set of ideas or teachings (though this was assumed), but by the community that remembered their names. . . . The communion of the saints was a living presence in every celebration of the Eucharist." Robert Louis Wilken, *The Spirit of Early Christian Thought: Seeking the Face of God* (New Haven, Conn.: Yale University Press, 2003), 46.

45 Wilken, *Spirit of Early Christian Thought*, 45, 47. From *The Catholic Encyclopedia*:

> The testimony of the early liturgies is in harmony with that of the monuments. Without touching the subject of the various liturgies we possess, without even enumerating and citing them singly, it is enough to say here that all without exception—Nestorian and Monophysite as well as Catholic, those in Syriac, Armenian, and Coptic as well as those in Greek and Latin—contain the commemoration of the faithful departed in the Mass, with a prayer for peace, light, refreshment and the like, and in many cases expressly for the remission of sins and the effacement of sinful stains. The following, from the Syriac Liturgy of St James, may be quoted as a typical example: "we commemorate all the faithful dead who have died in the true faith. . . . We ask, we entreat, we pray Christ our God, who took their souls and spirits to Himself, that by His many compassions He will make them worthy of the pardon of their faults and the remission of their sins." (citations omitted) (Toner, "Prayers for the Dead")

46 Geisler, for example, writes that "Catholicism's overreaction to Luther obfuscated the purity and clarity of the gospel and conflicted with their own earlier Council of Orange (529), which denied semi-Pelagianism." Geisler, *Systematic Theology*, 3:267.

47 Sproul writes, "The views of Cassian were condemned at the Council of Orange in 529, which further established the views of Augustine as expressions of Christian and biblical orthodoxy. However, with the conclusion of the Council of Orange in the sixth century (529), the doctrines of semi-Pelagianism did not disappear. They were fully operative through the Middle Ages and were set in concrete at the Council of Trent in the sixteenth century. They continue to be a majority view in the Roman Catholic Church, even to the twenty-first century (R. C. Sproul, "The Battle for Grace Alone," *Tabletalk Magazine,* August 1, 2006, http://www.ligonier.org/learn/articles/battle-grace-alone/). See also R. C. Sproul, "The Pelagian Captivity of the Church," *Modern Reformation* 10, no. 3 (2001): 22–23, 26–29.

48 From the canons of the Council of Orange:

> CANON 1. If anyone denies that it is the whole man, that is, both body and soul, that was "changed for the worse" through the offense of Adam's sin, but believes that the freedom of the soul remains unimpaired and that only the body is subject to corruption, he is deceived

by the error of Pelagius and contradicts the scripture. (*The Canons of the Council of Orange* [AD 529], http://www.ewtn.com/library/COUNCILS/ORANGE.htm; all subsequent quotations of the Canons are from this translation)

49 From the canons of the Council of Orange:

> CANON 4. If anyone maintains that God awaits our will to be cleansed from sin, but does not confess that even *our will to be cleansed comes to us through the infusion and working of the Holy Spirit*, he resists the Holy Spirit himself who says through Solomon, "The will is prepared by the Lord" (Prov 8:35, LXX), and the salutary word of the Apostle, "For God is at work in you, both to will and to work for his good pleasure" (Phil 2:13).
>
> CANON 5. If anyone says that not only the increase of faith but also its beginning and the very desire for faith, by which we believe in Him who justifies the ungodly and comes to the *regeneration of holy Baptism—if anyone says that this belongs to us by nature and not by a gift of grace, that is, by the inspiration of the Holy Spirit amending our will and turning it from unbelief to faith and from godlessness to godliness, it is proof that he is opposed to the teaching of the Apostles.* (emphasis added)

50 In the words of the council: "We also believe and confess to our benefit that in every good work it is not we who take the initiative and are then assisted through the mercy of God." *Canons of the Council of Orange*, conclusion.

51 *Canons of the Council of Orange* (found in the conclusion).

52 From the canons of the Council of Orange:

> CANON 24. Concerning the branches of the vine. *The branches on the vine do not give life to the vine, but receive life from it; thus the vine is related to its branches in such a way that it supplies them with what they need to live, and does not take this from them. Thus it is to the advantage of the disciples, not Christ, both to have Christ abiding in them and to abide in Christ. For if the vine is cut down another can shoot up from the live root; but one who is cut off from the vine cannot live without the root* (John 15:5ff).
>
> CONCLUSION. . . . According to the catholic faith *we also believe that after grace has been received through Baptism, all baptized persons have the ability and responsibility, if they desire to labor faithfully, to perform with the aid and cooperation of Christ what is of essential importance in regard to the salvation of their soul.* We not only do not believe that any are foreordained to evil by the power of God, but even state with utter abhorrence that if there are those who want to believe so evil a thing, they are anathema. We also believe and confess to our

benefit that in every good work it is not we who take the initiative and are then assisted through the mercy of God, but God himself first inspires in us both faith in him and love for him without any previous good works of our own that deserve reward, so that we may both faithfully seek the sacrament of Baptism, and after Baptism be able by his help to do what is pleasing to him. We must therefore most evidently believe that the praiseworthy faith of the thief whom the Lord called to his home in paradise, and of Cornelius the centurion, to whom the angel of the Lord was sent, and of Zacchaeus, who was worthy to receive the Lord himself, was not a natural endowment but a gift of God's kindness. (emphasis added)

53 *Canons of the Council of Orange*, canon 20.

54 *ST* II–I.Q81, art. 1.

55 *ST* III.Q69, art. 1

56 Aquinas writes, "We must needs say that in some way the sacraments of the New Law cause grace. For it is evident that through the sacraments of the New Law man is incorporated with Christ: thus the Apostle says of Baptism (Gal 3:27): 'As many of you as have been baptized in Christ have put on Christ.' And man is made a member of Christ through grace alone." *ST* III.Q62, art. 1.

57 *ST* II–I.Q111, art. 2.

58 *ST* II–I.Q111, art. 2.

59 Writes Aquinas:

> Augustine says (De Natura et Gratia xxvi) that "as the eye of the body though most healthy cannot see unless it is helped by the brightness of light, so, neither can a man, even if he is most righteous, live righteously unless he be helped by the eternal light of justice." But justification is by grace, according to Romans 3:24: "Being justified freely by His grace." Hence even a man who already possesses grace needs a further assistance of grace in order to live righteously.
>
> … In order to live righteously a man needs a twofold help of God—first, a habitual gift whereby corrupted human nature is healed, and after being healed is lifted up so as to work deeds meritoriously of everlasting life, which exceed the capability of nature. Secondly, man needs the help of grace in order to be moved by God to act.
>
> Now with regard to the first kind of help, man does not need a further help of grace, e.g. a further infused habit. Yet he needs the help of grace in another way, i.e. in order to be moved by God to act righteously, and this for two reasons: first, for the general reason that no created thing can put forth any act, unless by virtue of the Divine motion. Secondly, for this special reason—the condition of the state of human nature. For although healed by grace as to the mind, yet it

Notes to Page 98

remains corrupted and poisoned in the flesh, whereby it serves "the law of sin," Romans 7:25. In the intellect, too, there seems the darkness of ignorance, whereby, as is written (Romans 8:26): "We know not what we should pray for as we ought"; since on account of the various turns of circumstances, and because we do not know ourselves perfectly, we cannot fully know what is for our good, according to Wisdom 9:14: "For the thoughts of mortal men are fearful and our counsels uncertain." Hence we must be guided and guarded by God, Who knows and can do all things. For which reason also it is becoming in those who have been born again as sons of God, to say: "Lead us not into temptation," and "Thy Will be done on earth as it is in heaven," and whatever else is contained in the Lord's Prayer pertaining to this. (ST II–I.Q109, art. 9)

60 Writes Aquinas:

Nothing can act beyond its species, since the cause must always be more powerful than its effect. Now the gift of grace surpasses every capability of created nature, since it is nothing short of a partaking of the Divine Nature, which exceeds every other nature. And thus it is impossible that any creature should cause grace. For it is as necessary that God alone should deify, bestowing a partaking of the Divine Nature by a participated likeness, as it is impossible that anything save fire should enkindle.

. . . Christ's humanity is an "organ of His Godhead," as Damascene says (De Fide Orth. iii, 19). Now an instrument does not bring forth the action of the principal agent by its own power, but in virtue of the principal agent. Hence Christ's humanity does not cause grace by its own power, but by virtue of the Divine Nature joined to it, whereby the actions of Christ's humanity are saving actions. (ST II–I.Q112, art. 1)

61 See Alister McGrath, *Iustitia Dei: A History of the Christian Doctrine of Justification*, 3rd ed. (New York: Cambridge University Press, 2005), 208–92.

62 Writes Aquinas:

If, however, we speak of a meritorious work, inasmuch as it proceeds from the grace of the Holy Ghost moving us to life everlasting, it is meritorious of life everlasting condignly. For thus the value of its merit depends upon the power of the Holy Ghost moving us to life everlasting according to John 4:14: "Shall become in him a fount of water springing up into life everlasting." *And the worth of the work depends on the dignity of grace, whereby a man, being made a partaker of the Divine Nature, is adopted as a son of God, to whom the inheritance is due by right of adoption, according to Romans 8:17: "If sons, heirs also."* (emphasis added) (ST II–I.Q114, art. 3)

63 *ST* II–I.Q111, art. 2.

64 Peter J. Kreeft offers a similar phrasing in his presentation of the Catholic view of faith and works: "We do not do good works to get to heaven, but we do good works because heaven has gotten to us." Peter J. Kreeft, *Catholic Christianity: A Complete Catechism of Catholic Beliefs Based on the* Catechism of the Catholic Church (San Francisco: Ignatius, 2001), 126.

65 "Further, Augustine says (De Cure pro Mort. i): 'Of no small weight is the authority of the Church whereby she clearly approves of the custom whereby a commendation of the dead has a place in the prayers which the priests pour forth to the Lord God at His altar.' This custom was established by the apostles themselves according to the Damascene in a sermon on suffrages for the dead [De his qui in fide dormierunt, 3], where he expresses himself thus: 'Realizing the nature of the Mysteries the disciples of the Saviour and His holy apostles sanctioned a commemoration of those who had died in the faith, being made in the awe-inspiring and life-giving Mysteries.'" *ST* Supp.Q71, art. 2.

66 *ST* III.Q60–Q90.

67 *ST* III.Q73–Q83.

68 John Gerstner, "Aquinas Was a Protestant," *Tabletalk Magazine*, May 1994, 14.

69 Sproul, *Faith Alone*, 140.

70 Sproul, *Faith Alone*, 140. Sproul quotes *The Canons and Decrees of the Council of Trent*, trans. and intro. Rev. H. J. Schroeder, O.P. (Rockford, Ill.: TAN, 1978), 31–32. In quoting this passage, Sproul leaves out the two Scripture quotes the council cites as part of its conclusion in this chapter: "Hence, when it is said in the sacred writings: *Turn ye to me, and I will turn to you*, [Zachariah 1:3] we are reminded of our liberty; and when we reply: *Convert us, O Lord, to thee, and we shall be converted*, [Lamentations 5:21] we confess that we need the grace of God." *The Canons and Decrees of the Council of Trent*, 32.

71 Sproul, *Faith Alone*, 140.

72 Sproul, *Faith Alone*, 140.

73 *Catechism of the Catholic Church*, 2002.

74 Sproul, *Faith Alone*, 140.

75 See n. 47.

76 *Canons of the Council of Orange*, conclusion.

77 *Canons of the Council of Orange*, canon 13.

78 "The instrumental cause is the sacrament of Baptism, which is the sacrament of faith, without which no man was ever justified finally." *Canons and Decrees of the Council of Trent*, 33 (note omitted).

79 "The grace of the Holy Spirit has the power to justify us, that is, to cleanse us from our sins and to communicate to us 'the righteousness of God through faith in Jesus Christ' and through Baptism." *Catechism of the Catholic Church*, 1987 (note omitted).

80 *Canons of the Council of Orange*, canon 9.

81 From chapter 5 of Trent's sixth session, as quoted by Sproul in his book, *Faith Alone* (140): "His quickening and helping grace to convert themselves to their own justification *by freely assenting to and cooperating with that grace . . .*" (*Canons and Decrees of the Council of Trent,* 31–32 [emphasis added])

82 See notes 49 and 52.

83 *Canons of the Council of Orange,* canon 24 and conclusion.

84 *The Canons and Decrees of the Council of Trent,* 41 (notes omitted).

85 *Catechism of the Catholic Church,* 1989.

86 *Catechism of the Catholic Church,* 2008 (emphasis in original).

87 Geisler and MacKenzie, *Roman Catholics and Evangelicals,* 231.

88 "Through the power of the Holy Spirit we take part in Christ's Passion by dying to sin, and in his Resurrection by being born to a new life; we are members of his Body which is the Church, branches grafted onto the vine which is himself: '[God] gave himself to us through his Spirit. By the participation of the Spirit, we become communicants in the divine nature. . . . For this reason, those in whom the Spirit dwells are divinized.'" *Catechism of the Catholic Church,* 1988 (citations omitted).

89 *Catechism of the Catholic Church,* 2009.

90 "Man is made a member of Christ through grace alone." *ST* III.Q62, art. 1. "Now in both these ways grace is fittingly divided into operating and cooperating. For the operation of an effect is not attributed to the thing moved but to the mover. Hence in that effect in which our mind is moved and does not move, but in which God is the sole mover, the operation is attributed to God, and it is with reference to this that we speak of "operating grace." *ST* II.I, Q111, art. 2.

91 "It is furthermore declared that in adults the beginning of that justification must proceed from the predisposing grace of God through Jesus Christ, that is, from His vocation, whereby, without any merits on their part, they are called." *Canons and Decrees of the Council of Trent,* 31.

92 "The first work of the grace of the Holy Spirit is *conversion,* effecting justification in accordance with Jesus' proclamation at the beginning of the Gospel: 'Repent, for the kingdom of heaven is at hand.' Moved by grace, man turns toward God and away from sin, thus accepting forgiveness and righteousness from on high." *Catechism of the Catholic Church,* 1989 (citation omitted).

93 Writes Aquinas:

> Nothing can act beyond its species, since the cause must always be more powerful than its effect. Now the gift of grace surpasses every capability of created nature, since it is nothing short of a partaking of the Divine Nature, which exceeds every other nature. And thus it is impossible that any creature should cause grace. For it is as necessary that God alone should deify, bestowing a partaking of the Divine Nature by a participated likeness, as it is impossible that anything save fire should enkindle. (*ST,* II–I.Q112, art. 1)

94   *ST* II–I.Q111, art. 2. Aquinas writes elsewhere:

> There are four things which are accounted to be necessary for the justi-
> fication of the ungodly, viz. the infusion of grace, the movement of the
> free-will towards God by faith, the movement of the free-will towards
> sin, and the remission of sins. The reason for this is that . . . the justifi-
> cation of the ungodly is a movement whereby the soul is moved by God
> from a state of sin to a state of justice. Now in the movement whereby
> one thing is moved by another, three things are required: first, the
> motion of the mover; secondly, the movement of the moved; thirdly,
> the consummation of the movement, or the attainment of the end.
> On the part of the Divine motion, there is the infusion of grace; on
> the part of the free-will which is moved, there are two movements—of
> departure from the term "whence," and of approach to the term
> "whereto"; but the consummation of the movement or the attainment
> of the end of the movement is implied in the remission of sins; for in
> this is the justification of the ungodly completed. (*ST* II–I.Q113, art. 6)

95   Sproul, *Faith Alone*, 140.
96   "Augustine says (De Gratia et Lib. Arbit. xvii): 'God by cooperating with
      us, perfects what He began by operating in us, since He who perfects by
      cooperation with such as are willing, beings by operating that they may
      will.' But the operations of God whereby He moves us to good pertain to
      grace. Therefore grace is fittingly divided into operating and cooperating."
      ST II–I.Q111, art. 2. "But God made thee without thyself. For thou didst
      not give any consent, that God might make thee. How didst thou consent,
      who wast not? He then Who made thee without thine own self, doth not
      justify thee without thyself. He made thee then without thy knowledge, He
      justified thee with thy will." St. Augustine, "Sermon 169, 13" in *Sermons on
      Selected Lessons of the New Testament*, vol. 2, trans. English Church (Lon-
      don: Oxford, John Henry Parker, 1845), 865–66.
97   Sproul, *Faith Alone*, 140.
98   "Now what shall I say of love? Without it, faith profits nothing; and in its
      absence, hope cannot exist. The Apostle James says, *'The devils also believe,
      and tremble'*—that is, they, having neither hope nor love, but believing
      that what we love and hope for is about to come, are in terror. And so the
      Apostle Paul approves and commends the *'faith that works by love;'* and
      this certainly cannot exist without hope. Wherefore there is no love with-
      out hope, no hope without love, and neither love nor hope without faith."
      St. Augustine, *Handbook on Faith, Hope, and Love*, trans. J. F. Shaw, from
      Nicene and Post-Nicene Fathers, 1st ser., vol. 3, ed. Philip Schaff, rev. and ed.
      Kevin Knight (Buffalo, N.Y.: Christian Literature, 1887), chapter 8, http://
      www.newadvent.org/fathers/1302.htm.
99   *Catechism of the Catholic Church*, 1991.
100 *Canons and Decrees of the Council of Trent*, 34 (note omitted).

101 *ST* II–II.Q24, art. 12.

102 *ST* II–I.Q110, art. 3.

103 St. Thomas Aquinas, *Lectures on the Letter to the Romans*, trans. Fr. Fabian Larcher, O.P., ed. Jeremy Holmes with the support of the Aquinas Center for Theological Renewal, 106, 108, www.aquinas.avemaria.edu/Aquinas _on_Romans.pdf.

104 Aquinas, *Lectures on the Letter to the Romans*, 108.

105 "God touches the heart of man through the illumination of the Holy Ghost, man himself neither does absolutely nothing while receiving that inspiration, since he can also reject it, nor yet is he able by his own free will and without the grace of God to move himself to justice in His sight." *Canons and Decrees of the Council of Trent*, 32.

106 "Mortal sin destroys charity in the heart of man by a grave violation of God's law; it turns man away from God, who is his ultimate end and his beatitude, by preferring an inferior good to him." *Catechism of the Catholic Church*, 1855.

107 *ST* III.Q89, art. 4.

108 *Catechism of the Catholic Church*, 1030.

109 Bishop Kallistos Ware writes:

> So the Orthodox Church prays for the faithful departed; and again: "O God of spirits and of all flesh, who hast trampled down death and overthrown the Devil, and given life unto Thy world: Do thou, the same Lord, give rest to the souls of Thy departed servants, in a place of light, refreshment, and repose, whence all pain, sorrow, and sighing have fled away. Pardon every transgression which they have committed, whether by word or deed or thought."
>
> Orthodox are convinced that Christians here on earth have a duty to pray for the departed, and they are confident that the dead are helped by such prayers. But precisely in what way do our prayers help the dead? What exactly is the condition of souls in the period between death and the Resurrection of the Body at the Last Day? Here Orthodox teaching is not entirely clear, and has varied somewhat at different times. (Timothy Ware [Bishop Kallistos Ware], *The Orthodox Church*, rev. ed. [New York: Penguin, 1997], 255)

110 Jerry Walls, *Purgatory: The Logic of Total Transformation* (New York: Oxford University Press, 2012).

111 "I offer my defense of purgatory not as a dogma, but as a theological proposal that resolves issues and questions that no developed system of theology can ignore." Walls, *Purgatory*, 177.

112 "I offer [my defense of Purgatory] . . . as a Protestant with a distinctive concern to articulate the doctrine in an ecumenical fashion that may appeal to Christians on both sides of the Reformation divide. The prospects for such an ecumenical version of the doctrine are raised not only by the fact that a

number of Protestant spokesmen have shown a willingness to reconsider it lately, but also by the fact that contemporary Catholic accounts of purgatory are much more amenable to Protestant theology than previously." Walls, *Purgatory*, 178.

113   M. F. Egan, "The Two Theories of Purgatory," *Irish Theological Journal* 17 (1922): 26–27, as quoted in Walls, *Purgatory*, 65.

114   "It follows from all this, that the principal—one might even say the unique—reason for the existence of Purgatory, is the temporal punishment due to sins committed after Baptism, since neither venial sin nor vicious inclination survives the first instant that follows death. Immediately on its entering Purgatory, the soul is perfectly holy, perfectly turned towards God, filled with the purest love. It has no means of bettering itself nor of progressing in virtue. That would be an impossibility after death, and it must suffer for love the just punishment which its sins have merited." Fr. Martin Jugie, *Purgatory and the Means to Avoid It,* trans. Malachy Gerard Carroll (Cork: Mercier Press, 1950), 5, as quoted in Walls, *Purgatory*, 67.

115   Egan, "The Two Theories of Purgatory," 27, as quoted in Walls, *Purgatory*, 65.

116   Council of Lyons II (1274), in Denzinger, *The Sources of Catholic Dogma*, 464.

117   Clement VI, "Purgatory," from the letter "Super Quibusdam," to the Consolator, the Catholicon of the Armenians, September 20, 1351, in Denzinger, *The Sources of Catholic Dogma*, 570s.

118   Council of Florence (1439), in Denzinger, *The Sources of Catholic Dogma*, 693.

119   *Catechism of the Council of Trent*, trans. Rev. J. Donovan (Baltimore: Lucas Brothers, 1829), 51, quoting Rev 22:27.

120   *Catechism of Christian Doctrine*, no. 3 (New York: Benziger Brothers, 1885).

121   *Catechism of the Catholic Church,* 1030.

122   See, for example, Margaret Farley, *Just Love: A Framework for Christian Sexual Ethics* (London: Continuum, 2008).

123   Walls, *Purgatory*, 71.

124   "Some venial sins cling more persistently than others, according as the affections are more inclined to them, and more firmly fixed in them. And since that which clings more persistently is more slowly cleansed, it follows that some are tormented in Purgatory longer than others, for as much as their affections were steeped in venial sins." *ST* appendix I.Q2, art. 6.

125   "Whosoever is another's debtor, is freed from his indebtedness by paying the debt. And, since the obligation incurred by guilt is nothing else than the debt of punishment, a person is freed from that obligation by undergoing the punishment which he owed. Accordingly the punishment of Purgatory cleanses from the debt of punishment." *ST* appendix I.Q2, art. 5.

126   The one criticism I am not addressing is what I call "the pain objection." The reason for this is that it is not so much a criticism of the Catholic Church's satisfaction/sanctification model as much as it is a criticism of a particular account of the sanctification half of that model. Walls is critical

Notes to Pages 108–110

of the quality and quantity of the pains of purgatory as described by some
Catholic theologians, including St. Augustine and Aquinas. Writes Walls:
"I am thinking here particularly of Augustine's claim, endorsed by Aquinas and many others, that any pain of purgatory is worse than any pain
or suffering in this life. Now the question is whether such intense pain
would not be so overwhelming as to rule out any meaningful sense of a
free response to it that could be morally significant." Walls, *Purgatory*, 81.
It's an interesting question but one that I think can be easily answered: if it
is logically possible for God to protect the will's integrity in a disembodied
afterlife that cannot be replicated in our premortem existence because of
its bodily nature, then it is possible for the pain and suffering in the afterlife
to be worse than anything experienced in this life without it undermining
the soul's freedom to respond.

127 Walls, *Purgatory*, 80.
128 *ST* appendix I.Q2, art. 4.
129 *ST* III.Q86, art. 4.
130 Joseph Ratzinger, *Eschatology: Death and Eternal Life* (Washington, D.C.:
     Catholic University of America Press, 1988), 231, as quoted in Walls, *Purga-
     tory*, 179.
131 Walls, *Purgatory*, 80.
132 *ST* II–I.Q113, art. 1.
133 "It might be suggested that the answer to the previous question lies in the
     willing embracing of punishment, and that is the essential correlation
     between the demands of justice and spiritual transformation. This sug-
     gestion, however, raises the question of whether embracing punishment as
     just is merely a necessary condition for sanctification, or a fully sufficient
     one." Walls, *Purgatory*, 80.
134 Walls, *Purgatory*, 81.
135 Aquinas writes:

> Grace, as a quality, is said to act upon the soul, not after the manner of
> an efficient cause, but after the manner of a formal cause, as whiteness
> makes a thing white, and justice, just.
>
> . . . Every substance is either the nature of the thing whereof it is the
> substance or is a part of the nature, even as matter and form are called
> substance. And because grace is above human nature, it cannot be a
> substance or a substantial form, but is an accidental form of the soul.
> Now what is substantially in God, becomes accidental in the soul par-
> ticipating the Divine goodness, as is clear in the case of knowledge.
> And thus because the soul participates in the Divine goodness imper-
> fectly, the participation of the Divine goodness, which is grace, has its
> being in the soul in a less perfect way than the soul subsists in itself.
> Nevertheless, inasmuch as it is the expression or participation of the

Divine goodness, it is nobler than the nature of the soul, though not in its mode of being. (*ST* II–I.Q110, art. 2)

136 *Canons of the Council of Orange*, canon 24 and conclusion.

137 *Canons and Decrees of the Council of Trent*, 41.

138 Pope John Paul II, general audience, Wednesday, August 4, 1999, §6, available at http://www.vatican.va/holy_father/john_paul_ii/audiences/1999/documents/hf_jp-ii_aud_04081999_en.html.

139 It should be noted that "what is known as 'the power of the keys' [Matt 16:18-19; 18:18] does not extend to the souls in purgatory. . . . So, while the Church can, with Christ's authority, apply the merits of Christ to her members living on earth with certainty as to their effect, it can present those same share in Christ's merits known as indulgences to the souls in purgatory not 'by way of jurisdiction,' but only by way of prayer or request, or technically, 'suffrage.' To be sure, the prayers by which indulgences are offered on behalf of the poor souls are the prayers of Christ's Church, and they represent the efforts to share the love of God with our departed brothers and sisters; as such, one can be confident that such indulgences are received by God and applied in the most beneficial way according to his wisdom. It is not for us to have specific certainty about the precise result of those indulgences, but only to have the confidence that we are doing what God wants us to do as best we know how to do it." Edward Peters, *A Modern Guide to Indulgences* (Chicago: Hildebrand Books, 2008), 49 (notes omitted). Thus, Walls is mistaken when he claims that a plenary indulgence applied to a soul in purgatory would completely and instantaneously remit the punishment necessary for that soul's sanctification. (He made this claim to me as part of a panel discussion on his book that took place in Milwaukee, Wisconsin, on November 16, 2012, at the annual meeting of the Evangelical Philosophical Society).

6: *The Aquinas Option*

1 Quoted by Pope Benedict XVI, general audience in St. Peter's Square, June 16, 2010, http://w2.vatican.va/content/benedict-xvi/en/audiences/2010/documents/hf_ben-xvi_aud_20100616.html.

2 See *ST* II.II.Q2, art. 1, *sed contra and respondeo.*

3 See *ST* I.Q2–43; and St. Thomas Aquinas, *Summa contra gentiles* I.

4 Aquinas writes:

To proceed against individual errors, however, is a difficult business, and this for two reasons. In the first place, it is difficult because the sacrilegious remarks of individual men who have erred are not so well known to us so that we may use what they say as the basis of proceeding to a refutation of their errors. This is, indeed, the method that the ancient Doctors of the Church used in the refutation of the errors of the Gentiles. For they could know the positions taken by the Gentiles since they themselves had been Gentiles, or at least had lived among the Gentiles and had been instructed in their teaching.

In the second place, it is difficult because some of them, such as the Mohammedans and the pagans, do not agree with us in accepting the authority of any Scripture, by which they may be convinced of their error. Thus, against the Jews we are able to argue by means of the Old Testament, while against heretics we are able to argue by means of the New Testament. But the Muslims and the pagans accept neither the one nor the other. We must, therefore, have recourse to the natural reason, to which all men are forced to give their assent. However, it is true, in divine matters the natural reason has its failings. (Aquinas, *Summa contra gentiles* I.2.3)

5　Aquinas interacts with Maimonides and Avicenna when discussing God as if all three were referring to the same God. See, for example *ST* I.Q22 and Q45.

6　See, for example, Abraham Kuyper, *Common Grace*, vol. 1, *God's Gifts for a Fallen World*, Abraham Kuyper Collected Works in Public Theology, trans. Nelson D. Kloosterman and Ed M. van der Maas, ed. Jordan J. Ballor and Stephen J. Grabill (Grand Rapids: Action Institute for the Study of Religion and Liberty, 2015)

7　Christopher Hitchens, *God Is Not Great: How Religion Poisons Everything* (New York: Twelve, 2007)

8　*ST* I.Q48, art. 3, *respondeo.*

9　"Finals Prayers—St. Thomas Aquinas," *Baylor Catholic Blog*, December 9, 2011, https://baylorcatholic.wordpress.com/2011/12/09/finals-prayers-st -thomas-aquinas/.

Bibliography

Ackerman, Bruce. *Social Justice in the Liberal State*. New Haven, Conn.: Yale University Press, 1980.

Aiken, C. F. "Monotheism." In *The Catholic Encyclopedia*. New York: Robert Appleton, 1911. http://www.newadvent.org/cathen/10499a.htm.

Aquinas, Thomas. "Commentary of Boethius's *De Trinitate*." In *Aquinas On Faith and Reason*, edited by Stephen Brown. Indianapolis: Hackett Publishing, 1993.

———. *Lectures on the Letter to the Romans*. Translated by Fabian Larcher. Edited by Jeremy Holmes with the support of the Aquinas Center for Theological Renewal. Naples, Fla.: n.p., n.d. www.aquinas.avemaria.edu/ Aquinas_on_Romans.pdf.

———. *On Being and Essence*. Translated, introduction, and notes by Armand Maurer, 2nd rev. ed. Toronto: Pontifical Institute of Mediaeval Studies, 1968.

———. *Questiones Disputatae de Veritate* (Disputed questions on truth). Translated by James V. McGlynn, S.J. https://dhspriory.org/atica/Qdde Ver14.htm.

———. *Summa Contra Gentiles*. Book 1, *God*. Translated by Anton C. Pegis. Notre Dame, Ind.: University of Notre Dame Press, 1975.

———. *Summa Contra Gentiles*. Book 2, *Creation*. Translated by James F. Anderson. Notre Dame, Ind.: University of Notre Dame Press, 1975.

———. *Summa Contra Gentiles*. Book 3, *Providence*. Translated by Vernon J. Bourke. Notre Dame, Ind.: University of Notre Dame Press, 1975.

———. *Summa Theologica*, 2nd rev. ed., literally translated by Fathers of the English Dominican Province. 1920. http://www.newadvent.org/summa/ index.html.

Armstrong, April C. "When Did the College of New Jersey Change to Princeton University?" Mudd Manuscript Library (blog). Princeton University. July 8, 2015. https://blogs.princeton.edu/mudd/2015/07/when-did-the-college-of-new-jersey-change-to-princeton-university/.

Athanasius. *De Synodis*. Translated by John Henry Newman and Archibald Robertson. In *Nicene and Post-Nicene Fathers*, 2nd ser., vol. 4, edited by Philip Schaff and Henry Wace. Buffalo, N.Y.: Christian Literature, 1892. Revised and edited for New Advent by Kevin Knight. http://www.newadvent.org/fathers/2817.htm.

Augustine. *Handbook on Faith, Hope, and Love*. Translated by J. F. Shaw. In *Nicene and Post-Nicene Fathers*, 1st ser., vol. 3, edited by Philip Schaff. Buffalo, N.Y.: Christian Literature, 1887. Revised and edited for New Advent by Kevin Knight. http://www.newadvent.org/fathers/1302.htm.

———. *On the Spirit and the Letter*. Translated by Peter Holmes and Robert Ernest Wallis. Revised by Benjamin B. Warfield. In *Nicene and Post-Nicene Fathers*, 1st ser., vol. 5, edited by Philip Schaff. Buffalo, N.Y.: Christian Literature, 1887. Revised and edited for New Advent by Kevin Knight. http://www.newadvent.org/fathers/1502.htm.

———. "Sermon 169, 13." In *Sermons on Selected Lessons of the New Testament*, translated by members of the English Church, vol. 2. London: Oxford, John Henry Parker, 1845.

Avicenna. *The Metaphysics of the Healing*. Translated, introduction, and annotation by Michael E. Marmura. Provo, Utah: Brigham Young University Press, 2005.

Ayers, Lewis. *Nicaea and Its Legacy: An Approach to Fourth Century Trinitarian Theology*. New York: Oxford University Press, 2004.

Baker, Robert C., and Roland Cap Ehlke, eds. *Natural Law: A Lutheran Reappraisal*. St. Louis: Concordia, 2011.

Barr, James. *Biblical Faith and Natural Theology*. Oxford: Clarendon Press, 1994.

Barr, Stephen. "Defining Darwinisms," letters in response to Avery Cardinal Dulles' "God and Evolution." *First Things*. January 2008. https://www.firstthings.com/article/2008/01/january-letters-8.

Barth, Karl. "No!" In *Natural Theology: Comprising "Nature and Grace" by Professor Dr Emil Brunner and the Reply "No!" by Dr Karl Barth*, translated by Peter Frankel, introduction by John Baillie. London: Geoffrey Bles, 1946.

Beauchamp, Tom, and James Childress. *Principles of Biomedical Ethics*. 7th ed. New York: Oxford University Press, 2013.

Beckwith, Francis J. "The Baha'i World Faith." In *Guide to New Religious Movements*, 2nd ed., edited by Ronald Enroth, 155–68, 207–11. Downers Grove, Ill.: InterVarsity, 2005.

———. "Catholicism Rejoinder." In *Journeys of Faith: Evangelicalism, Eastern Orthodoxy, Catholicism, and Anglicanism*, edited by Robert L. Plummer, 129–36. Grand Rapids: Zondervan, 2012.

———. "David Hume's Argument against Miracles: Contemporary Attempts to Rehabilitate It and a Response." Ph.D. diss., Department of Philosophy, Fordham University, 1988.

———. "Dawson, Joseph Martin." In *Encyclopedia of American Civil Liberties*, ed. Paul Finkelman, 397–98. New York: Routledge, 2007.

———. "Defending Abortion Philosophically: A Review-Essay of David Boonin's *A Defense of Abortion*." *Journal of Medicine & Philosophy* 31 (2006): 177–203.

———. *Defending Life: A Moral and Legal Case against Abortion Choice*. New York: Cambridge University Press, 2007.

———. "Do Muslims and Christians Worship the Same God?" *The Catholic Thing*. December 17, 2015. https://www.thecatholicthing.org/2015/12/17/do-muslims-and-christians-worship-the-same-god/.

———. "Gimme That Ol' Time Separation: A Review Essay of *Separation of Church and State* by Philip Hamburger." *Chapman Law Review* 8, no.1 (2005): 109–27.

———. "Is *The Abolition of Man* Conservative?" In *Contemporary Perspectives on C. S. Lewis' "The Abolition of Man*,*"* edited by Timothy M. Mosteller and Gayne John Anacker, 86–90. London: Bloomsbury, 2017.

———. "A Journey to Catholicism." In *Journeys of Faith: Evangelicalism, Eastern Orthodoxy, Catholicism, and Anglicanism*, edited by Robert L. Plummer, 81–114. Grand Rapids: Zondervan, 2012.

———. *Law, Darwinism, and Public Education: The Establishment Clause and the Challenge of Intelligent Design*. Lanham, Md.: Rowman & Littlefield, 2003.

———. "A Liberty Not Fully Evolved? The Case of Rodney LeVake and the Right of Public School Teachers to Criticize Darwinism." *San Diego Law Review* 39, no. 4 (2002): 1111–26.

———. "Mormon Theism, the Traditional Christian Concept of God, and Greek Philosophy: A Critical Analysis." *Journal of the Evangelical Theological Society* 44, no. 4 (2001): 671–95.

———. "Or We Can Be Philosophers: A Response to Barbara Forrest." *Synthese* 192, suppl. 1 (2015): 3–25.

———. "Potentials and Burdens: A Reply to Giubilini and Minerva." *Journal of Medical Ethics* 39 (2013): 341–44.

————. "Rethinking *Edwards v. Aguillard*? The Establishment Clause of the First Amendment and the Challenge of Intelligent Design." M.J.S. diss., Washington University School of Law, 2001.

————. *Return to Rome: Confessions of an Evangelical Catholic.* Grand Rapids: Brazos, 2009.

————. "Science and Religion 20 Years after *McLean v. Arkansas*: Evolution, Public Education, and the Challenge of Intelligent Design." *Harvard Journal of Law and Public Policy* 26, no. 2 (2003): 456–99.

————. *Taking Rites Seriously: Law, Politics, and the Reasonableness of Faith.* New York: Cambridge University Press, 2015.

————. "Why Muslims and Christians Worship the Same God." *Catholic Thing,* January 7, 2016. https://www.thecatholicthing.org/2016/01/07/why -muslims-and-christians-worship-the-same-god/.

Beckwith, Francis J., and Douglas Laycock. "Is Teaching Intelligent Design Legal?" *Legal Affairs,* September 26, 2005. http://www.legalaffairs.org/ webexclusive/debateclub_id0905.msp.

Behe, Michael. *Darwin's Black Box: The Biochemical Challenge to Evolution.* New York: The Free Press, 1996.

————. *The Edge of Evolution: The Search for the Limits of Darwinism.* New York: The Free Press, 2008.

————. "Evidence for Design at the Foundation of Life." In *Science and Evidence for Design in the Universe,* by Michael J. Behe, William A. Dembski, and Stephen C. Meyer. San Francisco: Ignatius Press, 2000.

————. "Philosophical Objections to Intelligent Design: Response to Critics." The Discovery Institute, July 31, 2000. https://evolutionnews.org/ 2016/10/philosophical_o/.

Belloc, Hilaire. *How the Reformation Happened.* Rockford, Ill.: TAN Books, 1928.

Benedict XVI (pope). General audience in St. Peter's Square. June 16, 2010. http://w2.vatican.va/content/benedict-xvi/en/audiences/2010/ documents/hf_ben-xvi_aud_20100616.html.

————. General audience in St. Peter's Square. February 3, 2013. https://w2 .vatican.va/content/benedict-xvi/en/audiences/2013/documents/hf_ben -xvi_aud_20130206.html.

Blanshard, Paul. *American Freedom and Catholic Power.* Boston: Beacon, 1949.

Bogardus, Tomas, and Mallorie Urban. "How to Tell Whether Christians and Muslims Worship the Same God." *Faith and Philosophy* 34, no. 2 (2017): 176–200.

Boonin, David. *A Defense of Abortion.* New York: Cambridge University Press, 2002.

Bouyer, Louis. *The Spirit and Forms of Protestantism*. London: Harvill Press, 1956.

Bradley, Walter, Charles Thaxton, and Roger L. Olsen. *The Mystery of Life's Origin: Reassessing Current Theories*. Dallas: Lewis and Stanley, 1984.

Brown, Colin. *Philosophy and the Christian Faith: A Historical Sketch from the Middle Ages to the Present Day*. Downers Grove, Ill.: InterVarsity, 1968.

Budziszewski, J. *Natural Law for Lawyers*. Nashville: ACW Press, 2006.

Burrell, David B., C.S.C. *Knowing the Unknowable God: Ibn-Sina, Maimonides, Aquinas*. Notre Dame, Ind.: University of Notre Dame Press, 1986.

Calvin, John. *Commentaries on the Epistle of the Apostle Paul to the Romans* (1539). Translated and edited by the Rev. John Owen. Edinburgh: Calvin Translation Society, 1849.

The Canons of the Council of Orange (AD 529). http://www.ewtn.com/library/COUNCILS/ORANGE.htm.

Carnell, Edward John. *An Introduction to Christian Apologetics: A Philosophical Defense of the Trinitarian-Theistic Faith*. Grand Rapids: Eerdmans, 1948.

Carroll, William E. "At the Mercy of Chance? Evolution and the Catholic Tradition." *Revue des Questions Scientifiques* 177 (2006): 179–204.

———. "Creation, Evolution, and Thomas Aquinas." *Revue des Questions Scientifiques* 171 (2000): 319–47.

Catechism of the Catholic Church: Revised in Accordance with the Official Latin Text Promulgated by Pope John Paul II. 2nd ed. Washington, D.C.: United States Conference of Catholic Bishops, 2000.

Catechism of Christian Doctrine, No. 3. New York: Benziger Brothers, 1885. http://www.gutenberg.org/cache/epub/14553/pg14553.html.

Center for Renewal of Science and Culture, the Discovery Institute. "The Wedge." 1998. https://ncse.com/creationism/general/wedge-document.

Cessario, Romanus. "Aquinas on Christian Salvation." In *Aquinas on Doctrine: A Critical Introduction*, edited by Thomas G. Weinday, O.F.M. Cap., Daniel A. Keating, and John P. Yocum, 117–58. New York: T&T Clark, 2004.

Charles, J. Daryl. *Retrieving Natural Law: A Return to Moral First Things*. Grand Rapids: Eerdmans, 2008.

Chrysostom, John. *Homily 4 on Ephesians*. Translated by Gross Alexander. In *Nicene and Post-Nicene Fathers*, 1st ser., vol. 13, edited by Philip Schaff. Buffalo, N.Y.: Christian Literature, 1889. Revised and edited for New Advent by Kevin Knight. http://www.newadvent.org/fathers/230104.htm.

Chrysostom, John. *Homily 11 on 2 Corinthians*. Translated by Talbot W. Chambers. In *Nicene and Post-Nicene Fathers*, 1st ser., vol. 12, edited by Philip Schaff. Buffalo, N.Y.: Christian Literature, 1889. Revised and edited for New Advent by Kevin Knight. http://www.newadvent.org/fathers/220211.htm.

Clark, Kelly James. *Return to Reason: A Critique of Enlightenment Evidentialism and a Defense of Reason and Belief in God.* Grand Rapids: Eerdmans, 1990.

Cohoe, Caleb. "There Must Be a First: Why Thomas Aquinas Rejects Infinite, Essentially Ordered, Causal Series." *British Journal for the History of Philosophy* 21, no. 5 (2013): 838–56.

Collins, C. John. "How to Think about God's Action in the World." In *Theistic Evolution: A Scientific, Philosophical, and Theological Critique*, edited by J. P. Moreland, Stephen C. Meyer, Christopher Shaw, Ann K. Gauger, and Wayne Grudem, 659–81. Wheaton, Ill.: Crossway, 2017.

Covington, Jesse, Bryan T. McGraw, and Micah Watson, eds. *Natural Law and Evangelical Political Thought.* Lanham, Md.: Lexington Books, 2012.

Craig, William Lane. "Do Muslims and Christians Worship the Same God?" Question of the Week (#459). Reasonable Faith (website), January 31, 2016. https://www.reasonablefaith.org/writings/question-answer/do-muslims-and-christians-worship-the-same-god#_ednref1.

————. *God over All: Divine Aseity and the Challenge of Platonism.* New York: Oxford University Press, 2017.

————. "*The Grand Design*—Truth or Fiction?" Reasonable Faith (website). https://www.reasonablefaith.org/writings/popular-writings/science-theology/the-grand-design-truth-or-fiction/.

————. *The Kalām Cosmological Argument.* London: Macmillan, 1979.

Craig, William Lane, and J. P. Moreland. *Philosophical Foundations of a Christian Worldview.* 2nd ed. Downers Grove, Ill.: InterVarsity, 2017.

————, eds. *The Blackwell Companion to Natural Theology.* Oxford: Blackwell, 2012.

Crookston, Paul. "Religious Freedom for Me but Not for Thee?" *National Review Online*, February 21, 2017. https://www.nationalreview.com/corner/russell-moore-muslim-mosques-religious-liberty-universal/.

Cyril of Jerusalem. *Catechetical Lectures.* Translated by Edwin Hamilton Gifford. In *Nicene and Post-Nicene Fathers*, 2nd ser., vol. 7, edited by Philip Schaff and Henry Wace. Buffalo, N.Y.: Christian Literature, 1894. Revised and edited for New Advent by Kevin Knight. http://www.newadvent.org/fathers/310101.htm.

Darwin, Charles. *On the Origin of Species.* 1876. Reprint, New York: New York University Press, 1988.

Davies, Brian. *An Introduction to the Philosophy of Religion*, 3rd ed. New York: Oxford University, 2004.

———. *Thomas Aquinas' Summa Contra Gentiles: A Guide and Commentary*. New York: Oxford University Press, 2016.

———. *The Thought of Thomas Aquinas*. New York: Oxford University Press, 1992.

Davis, Dean Percival, and Dean Kenyon. *Of Pandas and People*. 2nd ed. Dallas: Haughton, 1993.

Davis, Stephen T. *God, Reason, and Theistic Proofs*. Grand Rapids: Eerdmans, 1997.

Dawkins, Richard. *The God Delusion*. London: Bantam Press, 2006.

———. *The God Hypothesis*. London: Bantam, 2006.

Dawson, J. M. *Separate Church & State Now*. New York: R. R. Smith, 1948.

Demarest, Bruce. *General Revelation*. Grand Rapids: Zondervan, 1982.

Dembski, William A. *The Design Inference*. New York: Cambridge University Press, 1998.

———. *The Design Revolution: Answering the Toughest Questions about Intelligent Design*. Downers Grove, Ill.: InterVarsity, 2004.

———. *Intelligent Design: The Bridge between Science and Theology*. Downers Grove, Ill.: InterVarsity, 1999.

———. *No Free Lunch: Why Specified Complexity Cannot Be Purchased without Intelligence*. Lanham, Md.: Rowman & Littlefield, 2001.

Dembski, William A., and Michael Ruse, eds. *Debating Design: From Darwin to DNA*. New York: Cambridge University Press, 2004.

Dennett, Daniel. *Darwin's Dangerous Idea: Evolutions and the Meanings of Life*. London: Penguin, 1995.

Denzinger, Henry, ed. *The Sources of Catholic Dogma*. 13th ed. Revised by Karl Rahner (1954). Translated by Roy J. Deferrari. Boonville, N.Y.: Preserving Christian Publications, 2009.

DeWolf, David K., Stephen C. Meyer, and Mark Edward DeForrest. "Teaching the Origins Controversy: Science, or Religion, or Speech?" *Utah Law Review* (2000):39–110.

Dignitatis Humanae: Vatican Declaration on Religious Freedom. December 7, 1965. http://www.vatican.va/archive/hist_councils/ii_vatican_council/documents/vat-ii_decl_19651207_dignitatis-humanae_en.html.

Dolezal, James E. *All That Is in God: Evangelical Theology and the Challenge of Classical Christian Theism*. Grand Rapids: Reformation Heritage Books, 2017.

———. *God without Parts: Divine Simplicity and the Metaphysics of God's Absoluteness*. Eugene, Ore.: Wipf & Stock, 2011.

Driesbach, Daniel. *Thomas Jefferson and the Wall of Separation between Church and State.* New York University Press, 2002.

Dworkin, Ronald. *Is Democracy Possible Here? Principles for a New Political Debate.* Princeton, N.J.: Princeton University Press, 2006.

———. *Life's Dominion: An Argument about Abortion, Euthanasia, and Individual Freedom.* New York: Knopf, 1993.

Eberl, Jason T. *The Routledge Guidebook to Aquinas' "Summa Theologiae."* New York: Routledge, 2016.

Egan, M. F. "The Two Theories of Purgatory." *Irish Theological Journal* 17 (1922).

Englehardt, Tristram H., Jr. "What Is Christian about Christian Bioethics? Metaphysical, Epistemological, and Moral Differences." *Christian Bioethics* 11, no. 3 (2005).

Evans, C. Stephen. *Natural Signs and Knowledge of God: A New Look at Theistic Arguments.* New York: Oxford University Press, 2009.

Farley, Margaret. *Just Love: A Framework for Christian Sexual Ethics.* London: Continuum, 2008.

Feser, Edward. *Aquinas: A Beginner's Guide.* Oxford: Oneworld, 2009.

———. "A Christian Hart, a Humean Head." *First Things*, March 2013. https://www.firstthings.com/web-exclusives/2013/03/a-christian-hart-a -humean-head.

———. *Five Proofs of the Existence of God.* San Francisco: Ignatius Press, 2017.

———. *The Last Superstition.* South Bend, Ind.: St. Augustine's Press, 2008.

———. *Scholastic Metaphysics: A Contemporary Introduction.* Neunkirchen-Seelscheid, Germ.: Editiones Scholasticae, 2014.

Fitelson, Branden, Christopher Stephens, and Elliott Sober. "How Not to Detect Design." *Philosophy of Science* 66, no. 3 (1999): 472–88.

Francis (pope). *Amoris Laetitia.* Post-synodal apostolic exhortation. https://w2.vatican.va/content/dam/francesco/pdf/apost_exhortations/ documents/papa-francesco_esortazione-ap_20160319_amoris-laetitia _en.pdf.

Gage, Logan. "Can a Thomist Be a Darwinist?" In *God and Evolution*, edited by Jay W. Richards, 187–202. Seattle: Discovery Institute Press, 2010.

———. "Objectivity and Subjectivity in Epistemology: A Defense of the Phenomenal Conception of Evidence." Ph.D. diss., Baylor University, 2014.

Geisler, Norman L. *Philosophy of Religion.* Grand Rapids: Zondervan, 1974.

———. *Systematic Theology.* Vol. 3, *Sin, Salvation.* Grand Rapids: Baker, 2004.

———. *Thomas Aquinas: An Evangelical Appraisal.* Grand Rapids: Baker, 1991.

Geisler, Norman L., and Ralph McKenzie. *Roman Catholics and Evangelicals: Agreements and Differences.* Grand Rapids: Baker, 1995.

George, Robert P. "A Clash of Orthodoxies." *First Things.* August/September 1999. www.firstthings.com/article/1999/08/a-clash-of-orthodoxies.

George, Robert P., and Christopher Wolfe. Introduction to *Natural Law and Public Reason*, edited by Robert P. George and Christopher Wolfe. Washington, D.C.: Georgetown University Press, 2000.

Gerstner, John. "Aquinas Was a Protestant." *Tabletalk Magazine*, May 1994.

———. "History of the Doctrine of Justification." *A Puritan's Mind.* http://www.apuritansmind.com/justification/history-of-the-doctrine-of-justification-by-dr-john-gerstner/.

Gilson, Etienne. *From Aristotle to Darwin and Back Again: A Journey in Final Causality, Species, and Evolution.* Translated by John Lyon. Notre Dame, Ind.: University of Notre Dame Press, 1994.

Girgis, Sherif, Ryan T. Anderson, and Robert P. George. *What Is Marriage? Man and Woman: A Defense.* New York: Encounter Books, 2012.

Giubilini, Alberto, and Francesca Minerva. "After-Birth Abortion: Why Should the Baby Live?" *Journal of Medical Ethics* 39, no. 5 (2013): 261–63.

Grabill, Stephen J. *Rediscovering the Natural Law in Reformed Theological Ethics.* Grand Rapids: Eerdmans, 2006.

Graham, Ruth. "The Professor Wore a Hijab in Solidarity—Then Lost Her Job." *New York Times Magazine*, October 13, 2016.

Gregory, Brad S. "Science v. Religion? The Insights and Oversights of the 'New Atheists.'" *Logos: A Journal of Catholic Thought and Culture* 12, no. 4 (2009): 17–55.

Hamburger, Philip. *Separation of Church and State.* Cambridge, Mass.: Harvard University Press, 2002.

Hart, David Bentley. *The Experience of God: Being, Consciousness, and Bliss.* New Haven, Conn.: Yale University Press, 2013.

———. "Is, Ought, and Nature's Laws." *First Things*, March 2013. https://www.firstthings.com/article/2013/03/is-ought-and-natures-laws.

Hawking, Stephen, and Leonard Mlodinow. *The Grand Design.* New York: Bantam, 2010.

Henry, Carl F. H. *God Revelation, and Authority.* 6 vols. 1976. Reprint, Wheaton, Ill.: Crossway Books, 1999.

———. "Natural Law and Nihilistic Culture." *First Things*, January 1995. https://www.firstthings.com/article/1995/01/natural-law-and-a-nihilistic-culture.

———. *Remaking the Modern Mind.* Grand Rapids: Eerdmans, 1946.

Hitchens, Christopher. *God Is Not Great: How Religion Poisons Everything.* New York: Twelve, 2007.

Hodge, Charles. *What Is Darwinism?* New York: Scribner, Armstrong, and Co., 1874.

Irenaeus of Lyons. *Against Heresies*. Book 4.8.1, translated by Alexander Roberts and William Rambaut. In *Ante-Nicene Fathers*, vol. 1, edited by Alexander Roberts, James Donaldson, and A. Cleveland Coxe. Buffalo, N.Y.: Christian Literature, 1885. Revised and edited for New Advent by Kevin Knight. http://www.newadvent.org/fathers/0103408.htm.

Jacobs, Alan. "More on Natural Law Arguments." *American Conservative* (blog). February 20, 2013. http://www.theamericanconservative.com/atica/more-on-natural-law-arguments/.

John Paul II (pope). "Message to the Faithful of Islam at the End of the Month of Ramadan." Vatican Council and Papal Statements on Islam. April 3, 1991. http://www.usccb.org/beliefs-and-teachings/ecumenical-and-interreligious/interreligious/islam/vatican-council-and-papal-statements-on-islam.cfm.

Johnson, Alan. "Is There a Biblical Warrant for Natural Law Theories?" *Journal of the Evangelical Theological Society* 25, no.2 (1982): 185–99.

Johnson, Phillip E. *Darwin on Trial*. Chicago: Regnery Gateway, 1991.

———. *Reason in the Balance: The Case against Naturalism in Science, Law, and Education*. Downers Grove, Ill.: InterVarsity, 1996.

Jugie, Fr. Martin. *Purgatory and the Means to Avoid It*. Translated by Malachy Gerard Carroll. Cork, Ire.: Mercier Press, 1950.

Keating, Daniel A. "Justification, Sanctification, and Divinization in Thomas Aquinas." In *Aquinas on Doctrine: A Critical Introduction*, edited by Thomas G. Weinday, O.F.M. Cap., Daniel A. Keating, and John P. Yocum., 117–58. New York: T&T Clark, 2004.

Kelly, J. N. D. *Early Christian Doctrines*. 5th ed. San Francisco: HarperCollins, 1978.

King, Martin Luther, Jr. "Letter from a Birmingham Jail." April 16, 1963. https://www.africa.upenn.edu/Articles_Gen/Letter_Birmingham.html.

Koons, Robert C., and Logan Gage. "St. Thomas Aquinas on Intelligent Design." *Proceedings of the American Catholic Philosophical Association* 85 (2011): 82–85.

Kreeft, Peter J. *Catholic Christianity: A Complete Catechism of Catholic Beliefs Based on the "Catechism of the Catholic Church."* San Francisco: Ignatius, 2001.

Kretzmann, Norman. *The Metaphysics of Theism: Aquinas' Natural Theology in Summa Contra Gentiles I*. Oxford: Oxford University Press, 2002.

Kuyper, Abraham. *Common Grace*. Vol. 1, *God's Gifts for a Fallen World*. Abraham Kuyper Collected Works in Public Theology. Translated by Nelson D. Kloosterman and Ed M. van der Maas. Edited by Jordan J.

Ballor and Stephen J. Grabill. Grand Rapids: Action Institute for the Study of Religion and Liberty, 2015.

Ladaria, Fr. Luis, S.J. "The Question of the Validity of Baptism Conferred in the Church of Jesus Christ of Latter-Day Saints." *L'Osservatore Romano*, August 1, 2001, 4. https://www.ewtn.com/library/theology/mormbap1.htm.

Lee, Sukjae. "Occasionalism." *Stanford Encyclopedia of Philosophy*, October 20, 2008. https://plato.stanford.edu/entries/occasionalism/.

Levering, Matthew. *Scripture and Metaphysics: Aquinas and the Renewal of Trinitarian Theology*. Oxford: Blackwell, 2004.

Lewis, C. S. *The Abolition of Man*. New York: Harper One, 1947.

Machuga, Ric. *In Defense of the Soul: What It Means to Be Human*. Grand Rapids: Baker Book House, 2002.

Maimonides, Moses. *Guide for the Perplexed*. 2nd ed. Translated by Michael Friedländer. London: Routledge Kegan Paul, 1904.

Mascal, E. L. *He Who Is: A Study in Traditional Theism*. London: Longmans, Green, 1943.

Mathison, Keith A. *The Shape of* Sola Scriptura. Moscow, Idaho: Canon Press, 2001.

———. "Solo Scriptura: The Difference a Vowel Makes." *Modern Reformation* 16, no. 2 (2007): 25–29.

McCann, Hugh J. *Creation and the Sovereignty of God*. Bloomington: Indiana University Press, 2012.

McConnell, Michael W. "The Origins and Historical Understanding of Free Exercise of Religion." *Harvard Law Review* 103, no. 7 (1990): 1409–517.

McGrath, Alister. *Iustitia Dei: A History of the Christian Doctrine of Justification*. 3rd ed. New York: Cambridge University Press, 2005.

McInerny, Ralph. *A First Glance at St. Thomas Aquinas: A Handbook for Peeping Thomists*. Notre Dame, Ind.: University of Notre Dame Press, 1989.

Meyer, Stephen C. "DNA and Other Designs." *First Things*, April 2000. https://www.firstthings.com/article/2000/04/dna-and-other-designs.

———. *Signature in the Cell: DNA and the Evidence for Intelligent Design*. New York: HarperOne, 2009.

Milbank, John, and Catherine Pickstock. *Truth in Aquinas*. London: Routledge, 2001.

Miller, Kenneth R. *Finding Darwin's God: A Scientist's Search for Common Ground between God and Evolution*. New York: Harper, 2000.

Monsma, Stephen V. *Positive Neutrality: Letting Religious Freedom Ring*. Westport, Conn.: Greenwood Press, 1993.

Montgomery, John Warwick. *The Law above the Law.* Minneapolis: Bethany House, 1975.

Moreland, J. P., and Scott B. Rae. *Body & Soul: Human Nature & the Crisis in Ethics.* Downers Grove, Ill.: InterVarsity, 2000.

———. *The Recalcitrant* Imago Dei: *Human Persons and the Failure of Naturalism.* London: SCM Press, 2009.

———. *Scientism and Secularism.* Wheaton, Ill.: Crossway, 2018.

Morris, Simon Conway. *Life's Solution: Inevitable Humans in a Lonely Universe.* Cambridge: Cambridge University Press, 2003.

Muller, Richard. *Post-Reformation Reformed Dogmatics.* Vol. 3, *The Divine Essence and Attributes.* 2nd ed. Grand Rapids: Baker Book House, 2003.

Murray, John Courtney, S.J. *We Hold These Truths: Catholic Reflections on the American Proposition.* New York: Sheed & Ward, 1960.

Neuhaus, Richard John. *American Babylon: Notes of a Christian Exile.* New York: Basic Books, 2009.

———. *The Naked Public Square: Religion and Democracy in America.* Grand Rapids: Eerdmans, 1984.

Novak, David. "The Mind of Maimonides." *First Things,* February 1999. https://www.firstthings.com/article/1999/02/the-mind-of-maimonides.

———. "When Jews Are Christians." *First Things,* November 1991. https://www.firstthings.com/article/1991/11/005-when-jews-are-christians.

Numbers, Ronald H. *The Creationists: From Scientific Creationism to Intelligent Design.* 2nd ed. Cambridge, Mass.: Harvard University Press, 2006.

Orr, James. "Science and the Christian Faith." In *The Fundamentals,* edited by R. A. Torrey and A. C. Dixon, vol. 4. LaSalle, Ill.: Testimony, 1910–1915.

Oussani, G. "Mohammed and Mohammedanism." In *The Catholic Encyclopedia.* New York: Robert Appleton, 1911. http://www.newadvent.org/cathen/10424a.htm.

Paley, William. *Natural Theology; Or, Evidences of the Existence and Attributes of the Deity, Collected from the Appearances of Nature.* 6th ed. New York: Cambridge University Press, 2009. Originally published in 1803.

Pelikan, Jaroslav. *The Emergence of the Catholic Tradition (100–600).* Vol. 1 of *The Christian Tradition: A History of the Development of Doctrine.* Chicago: University of Chicago Press, 1971.

Pennock, Robert T., ed. *Intelligent Design Creationism and Its Critics: Philosophical, Theological, and Scientific Perspectives.* Cambridge, Mass.: M.I.T. Press, 2001.

Peters, Edward. *A Modern Guide to Indulgences.* Chicago: Hildebrand Books, 2008.

Plantinga, Alvin. "Appendix: Two Dozen (or So) Theistic Arguments." In *Alvin Plantinga*, edited by Deane-Peter Baker, 203–28. New York: Cambridge University Press, 2007.

———. "The Dawkins Confusion." *Books & Culture* (2007). http://www.booksandculture.com/articles/2007/marapr/1.21.html.

———. *Does God Have a Nature?* Milwaukee, Wisc.: Marquette University Press, 1980.

———. *God, Freedom, and Evil.* New York: Harper & Row, 1974. Reprint, Grand Rapids: Eerdmans, 1977.

———. "Is Belief in God Properly Basic?" *Noûs* 15, no. 1 (1981): 41–51.

———. *Knowledge and Christian Belief.* Grand Rapids: Eerdmans, 2015.

———. "Reason and Belief in God." In *Faith and Rationality*, edited by Alvin Plantinga and Nicholas Wolterstorff, 16–93. Notre Dame, Ind.: University of Notre Dame Press, 1983.

———. *Warranted Christian Belief.* New York: Oxford University Press, 2000.

Raith, Charles, II. *Aquinas and Calvin on Romans: God's Justification and Our Participation.* New York: Oxford University Press, 2014.

Ratzinger, Joseph. *Eschatology: Death and Eternal Life.* Washington, D.C.: Catholic University of America Press, 1988.

Rawls, John. *Political Liberalism.* 2nd ed. New York: Columbia University Press, 1996.

Re Manning, Russell. "Protestant Perspectives on Natural Theology." In *The Oxford Handbook of Natural Theology*, ed. John Hedley Brooke, Russell Re Manning, and Fraser Watts. New York: Oxford University Press, 2013.

Reymond, Robert L. "Dr. John H. Gerstner on Thomas Aquinas as a Protestant." *Westminster Journal of Theology* 59 (1997): 113–21.

Richards, Jay W., ed. *God and Evolution.* Seattle: Discovery Institute Press, 2010.

Roberts, Dewey. "Aquinas Is Not a Safe Guide for Protestants." *The Aquila Report.* October 16, 2016. https://www.theaquilareport.com/aquinas-is-no-safe-guide-for-protestants/.

Rorty, Richard. "Religion as a Conversation Stopper." *Common Knowledge* 3 (1994).

Rowe, William L. "The Meaning of Deism." In *Routledge Encyclopedia of Philosophy.* New York: Taylor & Francis, 1998.

Russell, Bertrand. *Why I Am Not a Christian (and Other Essays on Religion and Related Subjects).* New preface by Simon Blackburn. London: Routledge, 2004. First published in 1957.

Sagan, Lynn. "On the Origin of Mitosing Cells." *Journal of Theoretical Biology* 14, no. 3 (1967): 255–74.

Savino, Sr. Damien Marie, F.S.E. "Atheistic Science: The Only Option?" *Logos: A Journal of Catholic Thought and Culture* 12, no. 4 (2009): 56–73.

Schaeffer, Francis A. *How Should We Then Live? The Rise and Decline of Western Thought and Culture.* Old Tappan, N.J.: Fleming H. Revell, 1976.

Sennett, James F., and Douglas Groothius, eds. *In Defense of Natural Theology: A Post-Humean Assessment.* Downers Grove, Ill.: InterVarsity, 2005.

Shah-Kazemi, Reza. "Do Muslims and Christians Believe in the Same God?" Paper presented at the Yale Center for Faith and Culture consultation "The Same God?" New Haven, Conn., 2009. https://faith.yale.edu/sites/default/files/shah-kazemi_final_paper_0.pdf.

Shields, Christopher, and Robert Pasnau. *The Philosophy of Aquinas.* 2nd ed. New York: Oxford University Press, 2016.

Skinner, Andrew C. "The Incarnation/Incarnate God." In *LDS Beliefs: A Doctrinal Reference*, by Robert L Millet, Camille Fronk Olson, Andrew C. Skinner, and Brent L. Top. Salt Lake City, Utah: Deseret Books, 2011.

Smith, Stephen D. "Is a Coherent Theory of Religious Freedom Possible?" *Constitutional Commentary* 15 (1998): 73–86.

Sober, Elliott. "What Is Wrong with Intelligent Design." *Quarterly Review of Biology* 82, no. 1 (2007): 3–8.

Southern Baptist Convention. "On the Sanctity of Human Life" resolution. 2015. http://www.sbc.net/resolutions/2256/on-the-sanctity-of-human-life.

Sproul, R. C. "The Battle for Grace Alone." *Tabletalk Magazine*, August 1, 2006. http://www.ligonier.org/learn/articles/battle-grace-alone/.

———. *Faith Alone: The Evangelical Doctrine of Justification.* Grand Rapids: Baker, 1995.

———. "Is the Reformation Over?" *Tabletalk Magazine*, September 1, 2009. http://www.ligonier.org/learn/articles/reformation-over/.

———. *The Mystery of the Holy Spirit.* Carol Stream, Ill.: Tyndale House, 1990. Excerpt "Regeneration Precedes Faith" at http://www.monergism.com/thethreshold/articles/onsite/sproul01.html.

———. "The Pelagian Captivity of the Church." *Modern Reformation* 10, no. 3 (2001).

Sproul, R. C., John Gerstner, and Arthur Lindsley. *Classical Apologetics: A Rational Defense of the Christian Faith and a Critique of Presuppositional Apologetics.* Grand Rapids: Zondervan, 1984.

Svensson, Manfred, and David VanDrunen, eds. *Aquinas among the Protestants.* Oxford: Wiley Blackwell, 2018.

Swinburne, Richard. *The Christian God.* New York: Oxford University Press, 1994.

———. *The Existence of God.* 1979. Reprint, Oxford: Clarendon, 2004.

———. *Faith & Reason.* Oxford: Clarendon, 1981.

Thomson, Judith Jarvis. "A Defense of Abortion." *Philosophy & Public Affairs* 1, no. 1 (1971): 47–66.

Tkacz, Thomas W. "Thomas Aquinas vs. the Intelligent Designers: What Is God's Finger Doing in My Pre-biotic Soup?" In *Intelligent Design: Real Science or Religion in Disguise?*, edited by Robert Baird and Stuart Rosenbaum, 275–82. Amherst, N.Y.: Prometheus Books, 2007.

Toner, J. "Prayers for the Dead." Transcribed by Michael T. Barrett. In *The Catholic Encyclopedia*, vol. 4. New York: Robert Appleton, 1908. http://www.newadvent.org/cathen/04653a.htm.

Trueman, Carl. *Grace Alone—Salvation as a Gift of God: What the Reformers Taught and Why It Still Matters.* Grand Rapids: Zondervan, 2017.

Turner, Denys. *Thomas Aquinas: A Portrait.* New Haven, Conn.: Yale University Press, 2013.

Van Drunen, David. *A Biblical Case for Natural Law.* Grand Rapids: Acton Institute, 2012.

Van Dyke, Christine. "Not Properly a Person: The Rational Soul and 'Thomistic Substance Dualism.'" *Faith and Philosophy* 26, no. 2 (2009): 186–204.

Van Til, Cornelius. "Confessing Jesus Christ." In *Scripture and Confession: A Book about Confessions Old and New*, edited by John H. Skilton, 217–46. Princeton, N.J.: Presbyterian and Reformed, 1973.

Vatican Council I. "Dogmatic Constitution concerning the Catholic Faith." In *The Sources of Catholic Dogma*, by Henry Denzinger, 443. Fitzwilliam, N.H.: Loreto, 2002.

Vatican Council II. *Lumen Gentium: Dogmatic Constitution of the Church.* November 21, 1964. http://www.vatican.va/archive/hist_councils/ii _vatican_council/documents/vat-ii_const_19641121_lumen-gentium _en.html.

Vatican Council II. *Nostra Aetate: Declaration on the Relation of the Church to Non-Christian Religions.* October 28, 1965. http://www.vatican.va/archive/ hist_councils/ii_vatican_council/documents/vat-ii_decl_19651028_nostra -aetate_en.html.

Vos, Arvin. *Aquinas, Calvin, and Contemporary Protestant Thought.* Grand Rapids: Eerdmans, 1985.

Walls, Jerry. *Purgatory: The Logic of Total Transformation.* New York: Oxford University Press, 2012.

Ware, Timothy (Bishop Kallistos Ware). *The Orthodox Church.* Rev. ed. New York: Penguin, 1997.

Warren, Mary Anne. "On the Moral and Legal Status of Abortion Rights." *Monist* 57, no. 4 (1973): 43–61.

Wells, Jonathan. "Unseating Naturalism: Recent Insights in Developmental Biology." In *Mere Creation: Science, Faith, and Intelligent Design*, edited by William A. Dembski, 51–70. Downers Grove, Ill.: InterVarsity, 1998.

White, Thomas Joseph, O.P. "Classical Christology after Schleiermacher and Barth: A Thomist Perspective." *Pro Ecclesia* 20, no. 3 (2011): 229–63.

Wilken, Robert Louis. *The Spirit of Early Christian Thought: Seeking the Face of God*. New Haven, Conn.: Yale University Press, 2003.

The World's Most Famous Court Trial: State of Tennessee v. John Thomas Scopes. Complete stenographic report of trial, July 10–21, 1925, including speeches and arguments of attorneys. New York: Da Capo Press, 1971.

Young, Matt, and Taner Edis, eds. *Why Intelligent Design Fails: A Scientific Critique of the New Creationism*. Piscataway, N.J.: Rutgers University Press, 2004.

Index

uncaused, 42–45, 51–52, 54, 57,
139n22, 152n77; *see also* cause
Urban, Mallorie, 52, 55

Van Til, Cornelius, 87, 158n3
VanDrunen, David, 9
Vatican: First Council, 23–24, 26,
124n17; Second Council, 36–37, 61,
140n27–141n27
vice, 14, 18, 23, 111, 131n68
virtue, 14–15, 39–40, 110, 118n7,
131n68, 171n114
Vos, Arvin, 9, 131n70

Walls, Jerry, 88, 104–5, 108–9, 111–12,
170n111–171n112, 171n114, 172n126,
172n133, 173n139
Whitefield, George, 159n23
Wise, Kurt, 80–81
Wolterstorff, Nicholas, 3

Zimmerman, Robert: *see* Dylan,
Bob